Patina

Native American Copper Artifacts of the Western Great Lakes Region

Dedication

For my mother, who's unwavering support, devotion, and above all else, faith, has proven to be the cornerstone of our family.

ISBN: 9781932113839

Copyrighted 2022
Lauric Press
All rights reserved.

Table of Contents

Triangulates - 27
Common Ovates - 37
Barbed Ovates - 49
Long Rattails - 53
Short Rattails - 59
Barbed Tangs and Beavertails - 65
Sawtooth - 69
Straight Flat Tangs - 79
Swallow Tails - 89
Expanding Flat Tangs - 95
Socketed Develed Points and Northern - 101
Triangulate Conicals - 107
Ovate Conicals - 109
Harpoon Conicals - 119
Stick Harpoons - 127
Pine Trees - 133
Straight Back Knives - 141
Curved Back Knives - 155
Banana Knives - 161
Socketed Knives - 165
Footed Knives - 171
Stick Knives and Whiptails - 173
Tangless Curve Back Crescents - 182
Tangled Curved Back Crescents - 190
Back Tanged Crescents - 200
Twisted Tangs and Tangless Straight Back Crescents - 212
Tangled Straight Backs and Spatula Forms - 220
Round and Square Awls - 224
Punches Spikes and Drifts - 226
Needles and Pikes - 234
Traingulate Spuds - 242
Pinched - 244
Ovate Spuds - 260
Celts - 274
Adzes Wedges Chisels and Gouges - 290
Hooks Gorges Leisters and Gigs - 300
Decorate Items - 314
More Decorative - 320
Interesting Specimens - 332
References - 336

Special Thanks

Bob Hruska, I will miss our conversations, Doug Miller, I have no better friend in the artifact world, Jim Bussey, one of the field's all-time greats as far as I am concerned, Steve Livernash, for lighting the fire, Gary Weimer, for sharing your incredible Winnebago items with a noboby like me, Ryan Howell, for stepping over the fence and offering a hand along with some really solid advice, Lee Born, for all the visits and support, Scott Nelson and Noslen Photography, because the pictures you took for me were the best in the book, Don Spohn and Great Lakes Copper Research, because you truly have the patience of a saint to put up with me and for your wonderful copper journal work, Dave Johnson, for allowing me access to your incredible collection, Robin Hammer Mueller, for driving me through the big city traffic and being a fantastic friend, Dawn Thomae and the Milwaukee Public Museum staff, for opening the vault doors and giving the tour, Bill Green and Nicolette Meister from the Logan Museum of Anthropology, for your incredible hospitality, The staff of the Chicago Field Museum, for treating us like royalty, Jane Eden, for being much more than a business person, Jay Wegert, for all the miles we walked in the early years, Bill Phalin, for making me wonder, Nick Schanen, for sharing your fantastic copper collection, Devin Renner, for consistently providing the impetus for me to look further and harder, Matt Schanen, for your never-ending enthusiasm, Steve Miller, for providing the tools to do what we do, Larry Furo, for sharing your insight into the process that we debate, Tom Betka, Kevin Leszcynski, Bill Wasemiller, John Marz, Harold Alanen, Robert Zinkgraf, Mike Bradford, David "Buck" Peterson, Gary Ogren, The Marks Family, Bob Zellmer, Austin Martinez, Sara Pfannkuche and the Three Rivers Archaeological Society, Matt Rowe, Gary Thallacker, Gordon Morris, Sam Wasion, Bill Reardon, Roger and Bernadine Tallmadge, Melanie Sainz, Little Eagle Arts Foundation of Wisconsin Dells, Jon Schram, Linda Mathison, Jim Lang, John Ruth, Scott Strautmann, Ron Meyer, Gillware Data Recovery, Nate Miller, Frederick Schanen, Eugene and Cathy Schug, Dave Goeser, The Rathermel family, The Thunder Bay Museum of Ontario Canada, Ronald Ford, Jack Steinbring, John Moore, Ernie Tucker, Thomas Pleger, The Parr family, Emily and Allison Schanen, Jamie Lewis, Shawn and Janet Alonzo, Quade-Hudson family, Jamie Kelly, James R. Beer, Terry Wilson, Ashley Wilson, Larry, Matt, Gene, Bob, and to all the others that wanted to remain behind the scenes.

Contents

Introduction
Wittry, Steinbring, Schanen Groups
Typeological Changes
Line Drawings
Projectile Group
Knife Group
Crescent Group
Awls, Punches, Needles, Pikes, and Mandrels Group
Spud Group
Celts, Chisels, Wedges, Gouges, Axes, and Adzes Group
Hooks, Gorges, Leisters, and Gigs Group
Decorative Group
Interesting and exceptional Artifacts
Distributional Information
References

Introduction

The genesis of this guide is firmly rooted in research that was conducted while writing Native American Artifacts of Wisconsin (Schanen,Hunzicker 2013). In that earlier work a single chapter was written to give a brief overview of copper artifacts in general. It goes without saying that I quickly found one chapter to be grossly inadequate. I was also surprised to find that the most widely used and accepted classification system for copper had been written in 1950 (Wittry 1950, 1957) and remained largely unchanged in spite of a huge influx in the number of copper artifacts that have been found in recent decades. While viewing and photographing copper artifacts for Native American Artifacts of Wisconsin I started to compare them with Wittry's system and found that most artifacts did indeed fit quite nicely into their respective categories, but I also consistently found myself with nearly as many questions as answers. I shelved my questions and concerns about Wittry's system and moved on. After our book was published and I again found myself with extra free time I decided to go back and take a second look at copper.

I had inadvertently fell into the black hole of Great Lakes Archaeology that is copper research. I traded in my copy of Wittry's classification system, along with all the hand scribbled notes, drawings, and references, for a clean, freshly printed copy and attempted to clear my mind of bias. Keeping my distance from preconceived notions and biases turned out to be an ongoing challenge, and as others have pointed out, critical to the overall outcome of the work. (Trevelyan 2004) I sat down and examined Wittry's line drawings for the various groups and types. I read his descriptions, and then I did it again. I read, and re-read until I felt as though I was beginning to get a grip on the system. I also read Flaskard's 1940 attempt at copper classification, I read Griffin's important 1961 work, "Lake Superior Copper and the Indians: Miscellaneous Studies of Great Lakes Prehistory". I skimmed Drier and DuTemple's "Prehistoric Copper Mining in the Lake Superior Region" and read Susan Martin's "Wonderful Power". Mason, Quimby, Steinbring, Pleger, and countless issues of the Wisconsin Archaeologist rounded out my starting point. It became clear to me that while many individuals had made attempts at copper classification, only Wittry had any long lasting impact on how we reference the various types of copper artifacts in the Western Great Lakes. I started to compare actual copper artifacts to his system to see where they fit. At first I used nothing more than a random assortment of copper artifacts that were found using the internet. As time went on I started to reach out to both private and public collections for larger samples to compare to Wittry's system. Time and time again I found pieces which simply did not fit. I also remained vigilant for some types listed by Wittry which I never did find good examples of. After only a few short months I was convinced that while Wittry's system was still useful, it also was in dire need of reform. The fact that most copper artifacts still fit easily into his system speaks volumes about the quality of his work and the original system. He simply had too limited of a data set to work from, confining the design of his system to pieces which he examined in the Hamilton collection of the Wisconsin State Historical Society. I of course was far from being the first to recognize the need for revision to Wittry's system.

In 1975 the first thorough examination and revision of Wittry's system was completed. (Steinbring 1975). Steinbring solved many of the problems I had first observed when comparing collections by eliminating some categories and expanding others to include previously unrecorded varieties. In a few cases, he stopped just short of making further changes. He also cited Wittry's limited data base as the single largest factor contributing to the discrepancies found within. There was no way for Steinbring to know he was working on his revisions, with his larger data base, in the twilight of pre metal detecting days.

Metal detectors have been around for a long time but only became widespread at the end of WW2 when soldiers returning home picked up surplus metal detectors that had been used around the world for detecting mines, unexploded ordinance, and other wartime purposes. These detectors were large and heavy machines with comparatively little ability by today's standards. In the 1950's and 1960's a number of technological advances made lighter, and more sensitive metal detectors possible and as such, became a popular hobby. Sometime around the same time that Steinbring worked on and submitted his thesis paper (1975) some of the first individuals in the western Great Lakes region were realizing the treasure trove of copper artifacts beneath their feet.

The first individuals to start recovering copper artifacts in the 1970s and 1980's did so mostly in silence. Quietly, for better, and for worse, a handful of individuals recovered thousands upon thousands of copper artifacts, possibly more than all of those found prior. Trevelyan gives an estimate of 20,000 artifacts being made by the Late Archaic people of copper region (Trevelyan 2004) but after viewing many private collections that number can safely be multiplied by a factor of ten, twenty, or more. They were recovered from pristine sites on private land, from highly disturbed farm fields, gravel bars in rivers, lake shores, and essentially anywhere prehistoric man had called home. I have no desire to discuss the good, bad, or other moral aspects of this, but rather only wish to point out that the data base of copper artifacts has grown exponentially since Steinbring made his revisions to Wittry's system. Just as Steingbring pointed out a limited data base for Wittry's work, I too now see a need for a new look at Wittry and Steinbring's work. I also anticipate the need for further revisions as time goes on.

Before we can take an in-depth look at Steinbring's work, we must first briefly touch upon the original. Wittry's original classification system was actually produced in 1950, but the 1957 version which was published in The Wisconsin Archaeologist, Vol 38, no.4 remains the mostly widely referenced one. With only a few minor exceptions, both are the same. Wittry's original typology categorized copper into ten groups represented by Roman numerals I-X. Each group was further broken down into different types, in a few instances, time was taken to break the typology down still further into varieties. This system works well from a scientific stand point, but in reality, the complex diversity of copper types and varieties means that even at the surface we have common types being referred to as a III, G-1 or or a II, A-1 for instance. Depending upon how far one wished to break down the various varieties that have come to light since the 1950s, type "names" can become even more unwieldy. In other words, the system is not user friendly.

While Wittry is readily cited by today's archaeologists of the region and collectors are aware of him, very few people on either side of the fence are discussing the items with the same terms. (At least not without directly referring to Wittry's line drawings) A recent phone call to a friend in academia turned into the perfect example. I told him that I had an interesting III, G-2 I wanted him to look at. My request was met by an awkward pause before he asked me to "refresh his memory". I then re-worded my request and explained that I had a holed straight back crescent for him to take a look at. "Oh! ok!" came the instant reply. So, it was concluded that the common verbiage and Wittry's rigid alpha-numerical system needed some bridging so that people might be able to cross reference common and scientific names.

There is also the issue of the visual representation of the various groups and types by Wittry. Here again, Wittry can hardly be blamed, technology was not what it is now and simple line drawings were probably the most effective means of conveying a visual representation of his typological system. The real problem was that a single line drawing to represent an entire type (often times with one or more varieties) was woefully insufficient to show the real range often found in each type. It quickly became my goal then to not only marry the vernacular of the public with Wittry's system, but to also give it a more accurate visual representation.

While my initial goal was nothing more than a categorical and visual refinement of Wittry's system, other angles of prehistoric copper research quickly gathered steam as well. Distribution in particular is a word firmly nested in virtually all prehistoric copper discussions. Wittry's distributional maps have been cited for their bias (Martin 1999) and limited data base. The arguments for that bias are still relevant today, most of the copper plotted on his maps did indeed come from eastern or south eastern Wisconsin and were found because of that areas early settlement and cultivation. In similar fashion, certain bias' can be easily pointed out by much of the data gathered for this updated system having come from metal detectorist's finds. A bias also exists by researcher location, I have viewed and included numerous private collections for this work, both large and small, but most of them were from central Wisconsin. Now these same central Wisconsin collections were not all from this area, indeed many of them were found at considerable distance, but in the end there is still a bias because collections of a similar nature from northern Minnesota, southern Canada, and even the U.P. of Michigan, are nowhere near as well represented here. I am aware of large private collections from northern Minnesota, the U.P., and Ontario which I was unable to gain access to while working here and I am certain that if the true numbers of copper artiacts could be plotted from these areas our distributional maps would look different than they do now. In the grand scheme of things, an entire book could be written about distributional patterns and hypothesis, and in fact a lot has already been written about this topic (Griffin, Martin).

Copper gathering and mining techniques is another angle of copper research which could be discussed at great length, and like distribution, already has been (Holmes, Spohn, Griffin, Martin). Martin's "Wonderful Power" in particular does a wonderful job of summing up many of the earliest finds and excavations in places like Island Royale. There has been, relatively speaking, little excavating done in most copper mining sites, but what has been done has been well documented and thoroughly discussed. It is for that reason the subject is skipped here. Information about manufacturing techniques is relatively obscure by comparison but still available to the diligent researcher (Peterson, Cushing, Crook). To truly understand manufacturing techniques one should invest in a few small pieces of native copper, a few lake shore cobbles, and a good, hot fire. There is no substitute for this type of first-hand experience. After just a few weeks of "cold hammering" copper, one can very easily dispel some of the old persistent misinformation with ease as well as gain great insight into the mind of the ancient copper smith, very similar to the way that modern flintknappers might better understand stone tools by learning to knapp. I found out in just hours that median ridges can actually be created with relative ease on a perfectly flat rock by simply alternating the angle of the pounding from both sides. Pieces can be hammered hot or cold, but cold is certainly much easier to handle using primitive tools. No smelting was necessary to produce any of the old forms, only time and patience, as well as relatively problem free copper, something our region had no shortage of.

The chronological order of the various copper types, preserved organics and their associated carbon dates, discussion of well-known copper related burial sites, and several other angles of copper research have all been shelved in order to make room for the primary purpose of this book, the revision and visual expansion, of the Wittry style system of copper typology. Because this guide relies so heavily upon the visual aspect to portray the various copper types it's critical to point out that the sizes are not exact. Many artifacts photographed needed to be either shrunk or enlarged. Some artifacts were too big to fit on the pages of this book, conversely, some details were so fine, that the only way to show them was to enlarge them beyond actual size. In the end, effort was taken to keep artifacts to size, relatively speaking, but to properly compare the various artifacts, one should pay close attention to the listed measurements.

Wittry, Steinbring, Schanen Groups

The sorting out of the major copper groups is a farily straightforward and easy thing to do. The following is how Wittry(1950) broke down the various groups, then how Steinbring listed them (1975), and lastly, how I have reformed them into the system presented in the following pages.

Wittry's Groups
I - Projectile Points
II - Knives
III - Crescents
IV - Awls, Punches, Needles, Pikes, and Drills
V - Spuds
VI - Celts, Chisels, Wedges, Gouges, Axes, and Adzes
VII - Fishhooks, Gorges
VIII Spatulas
IX Bracelets
X Beads
XI Rings

Steinbring's Groups
I - Projectiles
II - Knives
III - Crescents
IV - Awls, Punches, Needles, Pikes, and Drills
V - Spuds
VI - Celts, Chisels, Wedges, Gouges, Axes, and Adzes
VII - Fishhooks, Gorges
VIII - Spatulas
IX - Bracelets
X - Beads
XI – Rings

Schanen's Groups
I - Projectiles
II - Knives
III - Crescents
IV, Awls, Punches, Needles, Pikes, Mandrels
V - Spuds
VI - Celts, Chisels, Wedges, Gouges, Axes, and Adzes
VII - Hooks, Gorges, Leisters/Gigs
VIII - Decorative Items

You will notice that the groups from Wittry to Steinbring do not change. While Steinbring did make extensive revisions to the Wittry's system, he did not reorganize anything at the group level. Comparing Schanen's groups then to Wittry and Steinbring's we see a number of changes. The first difference is in Group IV, this group is filled by both Wittry and Steinbring as consisting of Awls, Punches, Needles, Pikes, and Drills. In this version the group consists of

Awls, Punches, Needles, Pikes, and *Mandrels*. I have replaced Drills with mandrels, this is primarily because there is a distinct lack of anything that can be positively identified as a drill. I have examined thousands of copper artifacts recently and have not been able to find a single example of anything resembling a drill that could not also be called an awl, at least not in the traditional sense. That, combined with the fact that a number of sites have been located in recent years in the U.P. of Michigan as well as northern Wisconsin where a lot of copper tool production was taking place. Mandrels turn up at these sites over and over again. A mandrel is a tool used to aid in the forming of copper, helpful in maintaining socket shapes while finishing a piece in particular. Mandrels appear to have been made differently for different, but related, copper manufacturing tasks. They are frequently mistaken for bars or other preforms.

The next difference comes in Group VII. My predecessors have both defined this group as consisting of fishhooks and gorges. I have redefined it as hooks, gorges, leisters/gigs. My changing fishhooks to simply hooks is intentional and meant to point out that not all hook forms were for catching fish. The largest examples may have been used as gaffs, still others for suspension of items around the ancient households, and certainly many for fishing. In addition to dropping of fish from fishhook I have added leisters/gigs. There has been private discussion about these for years already and evidence strongly supports the idea that at least some of these angular hooks are actually leister or gig components. There is a strong possibility that organic components made from bone, antler, or wood, may have made up key portions of these ancient gigs as well. Aquatic resources were clearly an important part of ancient survival strategies in general, and perhaps even more so with people living in the western Great Lakes during the height of copper usage (Private conversation with Robert Hruska 2013). Copper leisters being used for fishing spears and frog gigs would not be a stretch of the imagination in any case.

You will note that Wittry's and Steinbring's Group VIII, Spatulas, is completely absent from this updated version. This is not because spatula forms don't exist, they most certainly do, but rather because I found all of them fit easily in either the crescent family of knives, or under the stick knife category. Even after reading Wittry's and Steinbring's works several times I can't be sure why these were deemed worthy of their own Group level status.

Last but not least, Wittry and Steinbring gave group status to Bracelets (IX), Beads, (X), and Rings, (XI). My problem here was two-fold. One, it omitted some of the most common decorative items like pendants and two, I felt one group that included all decorative items was a far more efficient way of capturing the diversity of this frequently neglected and over looked group. Part of this group's neglect may have been prompted by the idea that decorative items were not generally thought of as being "OCC" but rather the work of much later Woodland and Mississippian peoples. Decorative things do in fact seem to have become more prevalent in general as time went on but this should not be mistaken as meaning that copper using people of the Middle Archaic did not produce decorative items. Beads, bracelets, and pendants all show up at pre-ceramic copper related sites on a regular basis. The notion that Middle and Late Archaic people were focussed soley on the utilitarian aspect of copper can be safely dispelled. Yes, many of the Middle and Late Archaic copper use was built around making utilitarian items, wood working and aquatic resource harvesting tools in particular, but to think of decorative items as being Woodland and Mississippian is to error.

Unfortunately for the reader, these large group level changes are only the proverbial tip of the iceberg. Far more numerous, and arguably important, changes were made by Steinbring in 1975 to the type and variety level of organization. It has been said many times that a picture is worth a thousand words, and in that respect, it might be best for the casual student or reader to skip ahead to the pictures devoted to showing the various types. To understand why they have been grouped as they have however, a slower type by type discussion must first be had. It is a discussion made complicated by the relative obscurity of Steinbring's 1975 work.

Typological Changes

Wittry's original typology started with Group I, Projectiles. This was in turn lead off by the type I,A. The first version in 1950 listed the I,A as having two varieties, the I,A-1 and I,A-2. The two varieties were differentiated by examples having a step in the socket for shaft abutment and those examples which did not have the step. Examples lacking the step tend to be slightly more constricting at the front of the socket to prevent shaft slippage. By the time Wittry published his typology system in The Wisconsin Archaeologist in 1957 it no longer noted this distinction and instead the type was listed simply as I,A both the stepped and un-stepped variety apparently merged. When Steinbring revised Wittry's system he also noted this difference but chose to leave it as a single group citing a lack of evidence for differences in distribution for the two varieties as they were. I have made no attempt to study the distributional aspects of stepped and un-stepped I,As and assume that Steinbring's observations in this regard to be accurate. I would be remiss if I didn't mention my hesitation to leave these as a single group however. Even if we assume the distribution patterns are the same, it would certainly seem that the step and un-stepped varieties represent a change of technology, and even an advance in technology. With advancing technology one would assume some sort of chronological ordering as well, but in the end a self-imposed deadline has stopped the pursuit of this question any further. It's also worth noting that there appears to possibly be a correlation between shoulder formation and socket steps. While the overall traits of I,A are notoriously consistent, a close examination of the way the shoulders were created has lead to the observation that some have exceptionally sharp, clear, chisel-cut shoulders while others have softer shoulders that appear to have been formed more with the use of a mandrel and hammering than cutting. What, if any, correlation there is between these techniques and the steps, or lack there of, might be worth pursuit as well in some future revison.

As previously mentioned, some of Wittry's line drawings were adequate for some types with distinctive features and lacking numerous varieties, but in other cases, a single line drawing was woefully inadequate. This inadequacy is particularly apparent when looking at I,Bs. This is absolutely due in part to Wittry's narrow data base which consisted almost entirely of pieces collected in eastern and south eastern Wisconsin. We now know that I,Bs took other forms farther away from eastern and south eastern Wisconsin.

Wittry's I,B type of artifact, (Ovates) is represented by a single line drawing in the 1957 version published in the Wisconsin Archaeologist. The full 1950 version describes three varieties of I,Bs. The I,B-1 being the Common Ovate with a rivet hole, I,B-2 being the same except lacking a rivet hole, and finally the I,B-3 which is again the standard ovate but having the addition of a single barb along one edge, or Barbed Ovate. Steinbring makes significant revisions of the I,B type. He described the I,B-1 essentially the same as Wittry but also notes a sub-variety of the I,B-1 which has a median ridge. He points out that un-holed ovates are not deserving of a separate classification because they are virtually non-existent and where they are found, they may represent unfinished pieces. He therefor designates the I,B-2 as the barbed ovates. He then designates I,B-3 as being the bifacially beveled ovates and recognizes that Wittry has actually listed these as I,J. Because the I,Js are now designated I,B-3 the I,J type is vacated. Lastly he describes a northern style of ovate with a median ridge and discontinuous dorsal plain.

This latest edition of Wittry's system changes it further still. The sub-variety of I,B-1 that Steingbring describes as having a median ridge and the I,B-4 he describes as essentially the same thing but having a discontinuous dorsal plain, both are combined here as being Northern Ovates, albeit two different varieties of I,H. This edition lists only two types of I,B. I,B-1 Is the Common Ovate, I,B-2 encompasses the Barbed Ovates. The Bifacially Beveled Ovates are now placed with the flat tang family of points because their overall attributes much more closely relate to that family than the Ovates, and as mentioned, what was the Norther Ovate has been removed and placed into it's own type, the I-H. I will say that there is such variety of size, form, and quality in the I,B-1 Common Ovate type that there very well may prove to be additional varieties in time.

Some of the attributes used to define the next four types from I,C I,D, I,E and I,F (Long Rattail, Short Rattail, Barbed Tang, and Sawtooth Tang respectively) have changed, but their placement in the typology set have not. They remain for the most part, unchanged here. The only exception is that of the I,E or Barbed tang, which has now been divided into two types, the I,E-1 or Barbed Tang, and the I,E-2 or Beavertail.

I,G types are more complicated than most other types. They are recognized as being highly variable and sometimes overlapping with attributes. Wittry determined there were two varieties of I,Gs, the I,G-1 being the typical straight, rectangular shaped tang, triangular shaped blade, and beveling. He labels the I,G-2 as being the same except that the tang terminates in a split base, sometimes referred to as a "fishtail". Steinbring points out the close relationship between I,G-1, I,G-2 and I,I types and even questions if I,I needs it's own type or if it might be better suited somewhere under the I,G-1 but falls short of actually changing it. While all three of these types do in fact appear to be exceptionally closely related, they remain three distinct types. The type I,H described by Wittry is essentially the same as a I,G-1 but having a median ridge. Steinbring points out the rarity of the I,H but leaves it unmolested. In this updated version, this exceptionally rare variety is combined with the other flat tangs of I,G-1 type. The I,I becomes the I,G-3 and the

I,H is being used to describe the Northern Style points. I,H-1 Being the Shouldered Northern Point and I,H-2 being the Unshouldered Northern Point. The latter of the two has been drawn with a median ridge but this characteristic is not uniform to the type. Many examples have very weak or no median ridges.

I,I remained in place under Steinbring though, as mentioned, he did question if it was deserving of it's own name. In terms of size and sheer numbers the I,I does in fact seem to be worthy of it's own name. They are most commonly referred to as "Ace of Spades" types, but have been changed to the I,G-3 to better reflect it's close relationship stylistically with I,G-1 and I,G-2. Large examples of the I,G-3 (Probably knife forms) have been labeled as "Pommel Tangs" by Dr. Spohn, (The Prehistoric Copper Journal Vol. 9, No. 4 December 2013). Lastly, what Wittry and Steinbring both referred to as "Bifacially Beveled Ovates" has instead been placed here with the flat tang family because they share more attributes with the flat tangs than they do the ovates. In fact, the Socketed Beveled blades as I refer to them, appear to be identical to the flat tangs in every aspect except that the flat tang has been replaced with a socket instead. These Socketed Beveled blades are now I,G-5.

I,J was vacated and described under the I,B-3 "Bifacially Beveled" type Ovate but here are under the I,G-5 Socketed Beveled points.

I,K has remained unchanged from Wittry, to Steinbring, and to this version.

I,L is another type that can't be fully understood from a single line drawing. Steinbring briefly mentions the variety involved in this type but also states that "they could not be used to penetrate game" and goes on to suggest their use as ice probes. (Steinbring 1975, 118-119).

He leaves this group essentially the same as Wittry. This description appeared vastly understated however and the current system assigns no less than five different varieties of I,L (conicals) including the I,L-1 or Triangulate Conical, the I,L-2 or Ovate Conical, I,L-3a Holed Conicals, I,L-3b Pinch Points, and the I,L-3c Minnesota Style Toggle Harpoons. The reason for the expansion of the conicals is because they are without question one of the most numerous types of copper artifacts and they have clearly been made with different uses in mind. A small percentage of all conicals are made in identical fashion to I,As including median ridges, angular sockets, and tabs! I,L-2 are by far the most common however, these essentially share the same manufacturing style as I,Bs, these almost all have rounded or gently oval sockets. These points are so numerous in most collections that they simply could not be meant for testing ice as Steinbring suggests. An experiment carried out with an atl-atl and copper points made with traditional craft demonstrated it to be very effective at penetrating potential game. They may have indeed had other uses besides projectiles as well, the vast array of shapes and sizes makes most suggestions at least plausible. Hrouska suggested they could have been used on a pitchfork-like tool in the taking of fish from streams and lakes (personal coversation 2013). These Ovate conicals include what Wittry described as the I,O type, common referred to as the "skinny" conicals. Steinbring pointed out that there is such a variety of form and size in the conical family that the I,O was lacking any distinguishing characteristics that set it clearly apart from other conicals. Many collectors have since come to believe that Wittry's I,O were actually used like the metal tips on fish stringers today but this popular theory is lacking any significant proof thus far. For this reason Wittry's I,O is being included in the I,L-2, or ovate conical. Some future typology with stricter definitions within the conical family may wish to change this in the future. It should also be pointed out that these long skinny ovate-like conicals are fairly rare overall. The I,L-3a Holed conicals are not as well documented or understood. This type is differentiated by the presence of a hole roughly at the mid-point of the conical which I initially thought would have allowed it to turn side-ways on the opposite side of the fish, or possibly within the flesh of the fish if the forshaft remained attached to the point itself. Ron Mullins, a world renowned spear fishing expert, has assured me that the small examples of this type, which most of them are, would be all but useless as toggling haproon heads because the dynamics involved simply would not allow it to function as such. The holes may have been nothing more than a means to add a nail to keep the conical attached to the shaft in which case they would be nothing but an I,L-2 with the addition of a hole for attattchement. Future studies on this should be interesting and as is the case in other areas, future revisions may make changes here potentially.

     I,L-3b Pinch points are typically open faced conicals with a constriction in the middle. While some examples appear to be bi-pointed, most are in fact not truly bi-pointed but rather "tailed". These, function-wise, are the same as toggle heads in that they are meant to turn sideways in the prey, or on the opposite side of the penetration, once the shaft has been removed. I,L-3c do not in most cases appear to be conicals in the strictest sense, but their obvious use as small harpoons like many other conicals has bound them here. They normally consist of a socket and short diamond shaped blade, most examples are tailed and most are holed. Many of the classic forms of this type are found in Minnesota. This last type would have been the only toggling type copper point capable of consistently harvesting of the largest fish species like sturgeon (Personal correspondence with Ron Mullins).

     I,M is described by Wittry as a bi-pointed rod with a barb on one side. Steinbring points out that Wittry's type is based on only two samples and that he was only able to find one. This has remained here however because our current data base shows this to be far more common than Wittry or Steinbring ever anticipated.

I,N has been vacated and listed under I,L-3a Holed conicals.

I,O has been vacated and listed under I,L-2 Ovate Conicals.

I,P remains unchanged from Wittry to the current system. Steinbring seems to view it as a dumping ground for any copper point made that resembled stone counter parts. He goes on to say it's not even a type. (1975, 122) The current system keeps I,P as not just a place to put flat copper pieces resembling stone counterparts, but as a distinctive and fairly well known type. I,P is most commonly referred to as Pine Tree points. These typically large, very flat pieces come from almost exclusively upper and lower Michigan.

I,Q is a new type that has been added in light of recent finds, this new type, the Winged Sockets, are currently based upon three known examples.

Changes to Group II, Knives. Most of the knife forms remain the same. II,A-1 Straight Back knives and their close kin, the II,A-2 remained unchanged from Wittry to Steinbring and finally here. It's important to note that II,A-2 in their classic form are easy to identify, but on the other end of that spectrum there is considerable overlap between II,A-1 and II,A-2 making proper identification difficult at times. Given the amount of overlap and similar distributions the distinction between the two probably lacks importance.

II,B remains the same from Wittry to the present.

II,C was originally described as two types by Wittry, like the I,B-1 and I,B-2 above, he described these II,Cs as having two types, those with holed sockets, and those without. Steinbring didn't hesitate to combine these forms into a single type and Steinbring's adjustment continues to look reasonable even with many more examples to examine.

II,D Has remained unchanged. Steinbring has precious little to say about it other than it is quite rare. The rarity continues but there are enough examples in public and private collections to offer a good sampling. The typical large size and differences in tang structure seem to warrant it's own type.

Another change to the II Group is that two additional types were added here, the I,E type represents what is typically referred to as Stick Knives. In Wittry's original system these were designated Spatulas and assigned to a Group all their own! Group VIII was dedicated to these uncommon knives. Here they are added to the group containing the rest of the knives and thus eliminating the need for the distinct group. II,F Whiptails were also added because they have been found in sufficient numbers and have a unique form and hafting element.

Changes to Group III, Crescents. The changes made to Witttry's original system both here and by Steinbring are arguably some of most drastic and complicated. Steinbring changes Wittry's III,A and III,B to III,A-1 and III,A-2 respectively. He does this after pointing out that if you were to look at a large number of either of these types as defined by Wittry, many would be indistinguishable from one another. (Steinbring 1975 129-137) In other words, the only difference is the length of the tangs. They range from pseudo tang-like nubs to long spindly forms that are longer than the blade itself. Both have some degree of curvature to the back however.

For the III,C Steinbring says that he has never found an example and notes that Wittry had apparently based it off of one example. He (Steinbring) continues to list it as an individual type in his revision but does mention that it likely is better placed as a rare variation of the III,A-2. In similar fashion as the III,A-1 and 2 Steinbring combined the III,D and III,E making them instead III,D-1 and the III,D-2 based upon similarities and very low numbers of examples.

III,F is left alone as a type by Steinbring but it's obvious similarities to III,A- are also pointed out.

Steinbring combines Wittry's III,G-1 and III,G-2 into a single type, the III,G that includes both holed and unholed examples.

Lastly, type III,H remains unmolested from the original version to the current. It seems that crescents in general have a great deal of variation, particularly at a glance, but after long examination there are relatively few factors that differentiate between the various types. The defining attributes are most often the curvature of the back or lack thereof combined with the tang form. Does the crescent have tangs? Does it simply have up-curved ends? Does it have long spindly tangs? Are the tangs twisted together? In fact, to make an attempt at simplifying the system, it could be said that all crescents either have tangs or do not, and all crescents have either a straight or curved back. With that in mind the types in this version are listed as III,A-1 Tangless Curved Backs, III,A-2 Tanged Curved Backs, III,D-1 Back tanged, III,D-2 Box Tanged, III,D-3 Bridge Tanged, III,D-4 Twisted Tang, III,G-1 Tangless Straight Backs (both holed and un-holed), III,G-2 Tanged Straight Backs, and lastly, III,H which are the Spatula forms.

Changes to Group IV Awls, Punches, Needles, Pikes and Drills. The changes here are nominal. Steinbring made no changes to the group as a whole and only one has been made in this edition. IV,F called "drills" by Wittry, have been vacated here. Steinbring mentions that it is not included in any previous typologies and that he himself has not examined any. (Steingbring 1975 152). Subsequently, no new examples have shown themselves while working on the latest revisions and as such, the group is being replaced with a type that has become well-known in recent years, the mandrel.

Changes to Group V, Spuds. Wittry defines four major types, V,A being similar to the V,B but more narrow and having shorter socket walls. V,B is, as mentioned, similar to type V,A but typically being wider and longer socket walls. Wittry differentiates between stepped and unstepped V,As as he did with the I,A projectiles. He makes them V,A-1 and V,A-2 respectively. He also describes a V,C which is widely referred to as the Pinched type spud. Lastly he describes the V,D which is one of the most common of spud forms having a rolled socket and step. Steinbring's only change to the group is the combining of V,A-1 and V,A-2 into a single type just as had been done with the I,A projectiles.

This revision views spuds into four types, V,A Triangulate type, V,B Ovate type, V,C Pinched type, and lastly the V,D Pointed type. While one could easily argue that there is significant differences between Wittry's V,A and V,B to warrant different types they are viewed here as different varieties of the same type because both of them have most of the strong triangulate-like attributes including angular socket walls, a tab, and usually a median ridge. Similar arguments might be made for extra wide types of Ovate spuds vs their smaller more common forms as well. *The similarities outweigh their differences* and are thusly viewed as varieties of a common type. V,D, or Pointed spuds are a new addition to the system based upon several similar examples that have been found in recent years.

Changes to Group VI, Celts, Chisels, Wedges, Gouges, Axes, and Adzes. Wittry lists no less than ten types to the VI group. Steinbring however dismantles the group in quick fashion by pointing out the similarities between VI,B and VI,D. In a large sampling of these two types, the overlap between types is such that it would be practically impossible to differentiate between the them. It is for this reason that this latest revision lists all celts that are slightly constricting to the poll end to be one type. Likewise, Wittry's VI,D VI,E and VI,J all appear to represent similar adze forms, which because of identical use and similar form, are here put together as a single type. Wittry's VI,F has been vacated. His bell-shaped VI,F appears to be drawn in exaggerated form. I viewed several examples which were claimed by their curators to be VI,Fs but found the incurvate lines to be very shallow. Shallow enough in fact, that I have had no difficulty in including them in with the other VI,A Tapering celts type. Any truly bell shaped examples that might be out there must be considered more of an anomaly than anything. If examples with more pronounced curvature are found in the future the type could always be reinstated, but after looking at the numbers of celts that I have, I am comfortable with abandoning this type for now. VI,G for Wittry appears to represent only a wedge form artifact, but as Steinbring points out, there is no different between a similar sized straight lined celt (VI,C) or even chisel, the only distinguishing feature being the mushroomed poll end from use-wear. Because of this Wedges and Chisels have been combined here. We could suppose that smaller and more narrow pieces had a function similar to a chisel, while the larger and wider examples had a use more closely related to wedges as we know them today but both cases rely heavily upon our own cultural bias' as the main support for the idea. One could ask why not include the VI,A Tapering celt in the same category, but the VI,As are present in great enough numbers (without significant poll damage) to support the idea that most were in fact used as celts (axe-like function). VI,C has been designated the Straight Celts, the largest examples might be from the Mississippian Period.

    Changes to Group VII, Fishooks and Gorges. From Wittry to Steinbring there were no to major changes to this group. It has been changed now however to instead read, Hooks, Gorges, Leisters, and Giggs. Fish was dropped from "Fishhooks" to recognize the potential for hooks being used in other capacities in addition to fishing. Leisters and Gigs have also been added to this group because evidence seems to support it.

    Changes to Group VIII Spatulas This group has been vacated. Large classic spatula forms are now included with the crescent family of knives and the smaller spatula forms similar to Wittry's original representation have been included in the knife group under their own type heading, "Stick Knives".

    Changes to Group IX Bracelets This group has been vacated and added to the "Decorative" group of artifacts.

    Changes to Group X Beads This group has been vacated and added to the "Decorative" group of artifacts.

    Changes to Group XI Rings This group has been vacated and added to the "Decorative" group of artifacts.

Defining copper use...

    Unlike tradition, complex, and industry, there is no standard definition of Old Copper Culture. While it remains one of the most popular terms relating to prehistoric copper use it is also outdated. Copper culture would indicate a singular culture is responsible for the thousands of years of copper use. In truth, copper was used by a wide range of prehistoric cultures from the artic people of the far north to the Mississippians of the southeast. Additionally it was used for thousands of years from perhaps the Early Archaic all the way up to the time of contact. I don't have the time or gumption to try and persuade readers to adhere to one term or another, I can only point out, as others have (Martin, Pledger 1999) that Old Copper Culture should be a term relegated to the past.

Cold working and smelting…

    There is a persistent myth that copper was at least sometimes smelted in the prehistoric great lakes region. There is no evidence of this however, period. It's not for lack of trying, many have looked into the subject at length (Martin, pg 136) and all have come to the same conclusion, it just didn't happen. The bubbles sometimes seen on copper artifacts have been reproduced with cold hammering techniques many times over including by the author. Likewise, there's no great cover up regarding the removal of copper from the great lakes by European or Asian peoples. If there had been there would have been some shred of evidence now but none have ever been discovered. People like to also point to astronomical numbers in terms of pounds of copper removed from the ancient mines but in the end they are nothing but a guess. I must also add though that a lot of copper was removed from the ancient mines by nearly anybody's estimation, but the idea that some of it is somehow "missing" just isn't accurate. When a person goes and views the private collections of Mr. Johnson, Mr. Miller, Mr. Bussey, the Milwaukee Public Museum, the Logan Museum of Anthropology, the Chicago Field Museum, the Hamilton Collection in Madison, plus hundreds of smaller collections both public and private and realize that only a small fraction of all the copper tools ever produced have been found, then the massive amount of copper pulled from the mines makes perfect sense... none of it is missing. Lastly, thought there's no evidence of smelting in this area, it did happen in South America. The Moche Culture of Peru in particular took metal working to a level never dreamed of in the Midwest, the Moche made numerous alloys, mastered smelting, and mass produced many items.(Muro 1998)

Cultural bias and the shifting baseline...

Both cultural bias and the shifting or sliding baseline phenomanon are problematic to our understanding of the prehistoric copper tool assemblage. Their impact on our interpretation of the evidence can't be stressed enough. Even with a solid understanding of their influence on us the serious copper student might be easily lead astray by their own life experiences. We, the author included, have *assumed* a great deal about copper tools. If a piece looks like a modern knife in your kitchen drawer we don't hesitate to call it a knife. Taking it still further some examples might remind a person of a knife found in their tackle box and thus, by assumption, the type becomes a "fish knife". This same type of thought and deduction has lead to the naming of all copper tools as we know them in this book and elsewhere. While I'm certain that not all our assumptions are wrong, I am equally certain that some of our assumptions are. Our preconcieved notions of form versus use wreak havoc on these classification systems. I do not know when copper celt forms were first called as such, but I surmise they were called celts because there was already a group called axes. This labeling of copper celts versus copper axes likely carried over from their stone counterparts where stone axes are common and it was *assumed* they would be eventually found in similar numbers made from copper as well. In the end, they weren't. Traditonal looking copper axes are the epitome of rare and I very much wonder about their existence as a group in general. My own cultural bias has essentially forced me to leave the category here because it *should* work that way in spite of all the evidence to the contrary. Similarly, the group known as celts carries along through revision after revison because it must. In spite of having a function like a modern axe, it doesn't look like a modern axe and therefor is left unmolested. Cultural bias has prevented me (and most everybody) from being completely honest with themselves at some point. Of course to buck this trend would likely make any attempt at a Wittry style classification system revison so odd and foreign in the end that it would be rejected outright by nearly everyone (That's not an axe! That's a celt!). In the end I don't think it's too terribly important as long as we try to be concious of the idea that our cultural bias does play a role in what we call these ancient tools. And our cultural bias ties in neatly with the shifting baseline phenomenon.

A shifting baseline phenomenon is a change in how we measure things. For copper research in particular, it's plays its most critical role in how we measure our natural resources when compared to the resources of the ancient inhabitants. All too often we apply what we know about the resources of our environment today to the their ancient resources. We must understand however that there is quite literally no comparison to be made. Changing climates, weather patterns, human populations, and a multitude of other things mean that resources have flucuated more than we can scarcely imagine over time. We might picture the ancient inhabitants of the land spearing sturgeon not unlike we do today (though it's much more closely controlled and monitored for the sake of the species today) but in reality the sturgeon populations in the Archaic creeks of say eastern Wisconsin were likely filled with a number and size of sturgeon that by today's standards would be comepletely, and literally, unbelievable. The three hundred or so thousand white tailed deer harvested in Wisconsin in 2016 might be represative of a population that would've caused massive starvation to a dependant population five thousand years ago, or perhaps, it would've represented a population of deer that lead to such a boon of meat and supplies that it lead to a population hike in the area. So, we must keep in mind this shifting baseline and our own cultural bias when looking at the copper tool set of ancient man and know that we have far more to ask than to answer.

The role of recycling...

I think stone artifacts might be able to give us an unique insight into the prehistoric use of copper. When we examine the typical farm field collection of stone points picked up anywhere in the country we quickly see that the overwhelming majority of what is found is either artifacts that broke during use and were discarded, or were used and resharpened so much that they eventually wore down to an all but useless nub in it's final stage. People find more purposely discarded pieces that had become too small to work with than they do artifacts which were lost and represent an early stage artifact. This is important to think about. If the majority of stone artifacts that are found are pieces that were broken or discarded and only a very small percentage represent pieces that were lost before this final stage what can we make of the copper we find? Steinbring (1975 pg 35) briefly eludes to copper's unique ability to be resharpened or reworked almost indefinitely into new tools. The majority of the copper we find is *not* final stage broken and discarded material, but more often than not something that appears to have been lost during it's life cycle, not at the end. If we assume that the percentage of copper artifacts that were lost prior to being "used up" mirrors it's stone counterparts (remember with stone that what we find early or mid-life versus final stage represents only a very small percentage of the overall artifact population, perhaps one or two percent?) then we must ask ourselves where all the broken and used up copper has gone that should compose the majority of what we find. But copper is different of course, copper has unique properties which allow it to be recycled and re-used an almost infinite number of times and ways. There's absolutely no doubt that copper was reworked when it broke or wore down. Examples are scattered throughout the pages that follow, broken crescents turned into stick knives, spuds turned into celt forms, etc. When copper broke or approached final stage the ancient smith needed only to throw it back into the fire to give the piece a second life as a new tool. A well worn knife could be turned into a large awl, a well worn awl into a hook or a bead. The possibilities are endless. Perhaps recycling into other usable, albeit slightly smaller, tools is why we find such large numbers of awls? Perhaps it is why we find so few late stage copper artifacts in general? Perhaps these typically early and mid life copper pieces we find only represent, like their stone counterparts, one or two percentage of what was originally made?! This would also go a long ways in determining where some people's tons of "lost copper" went!

.

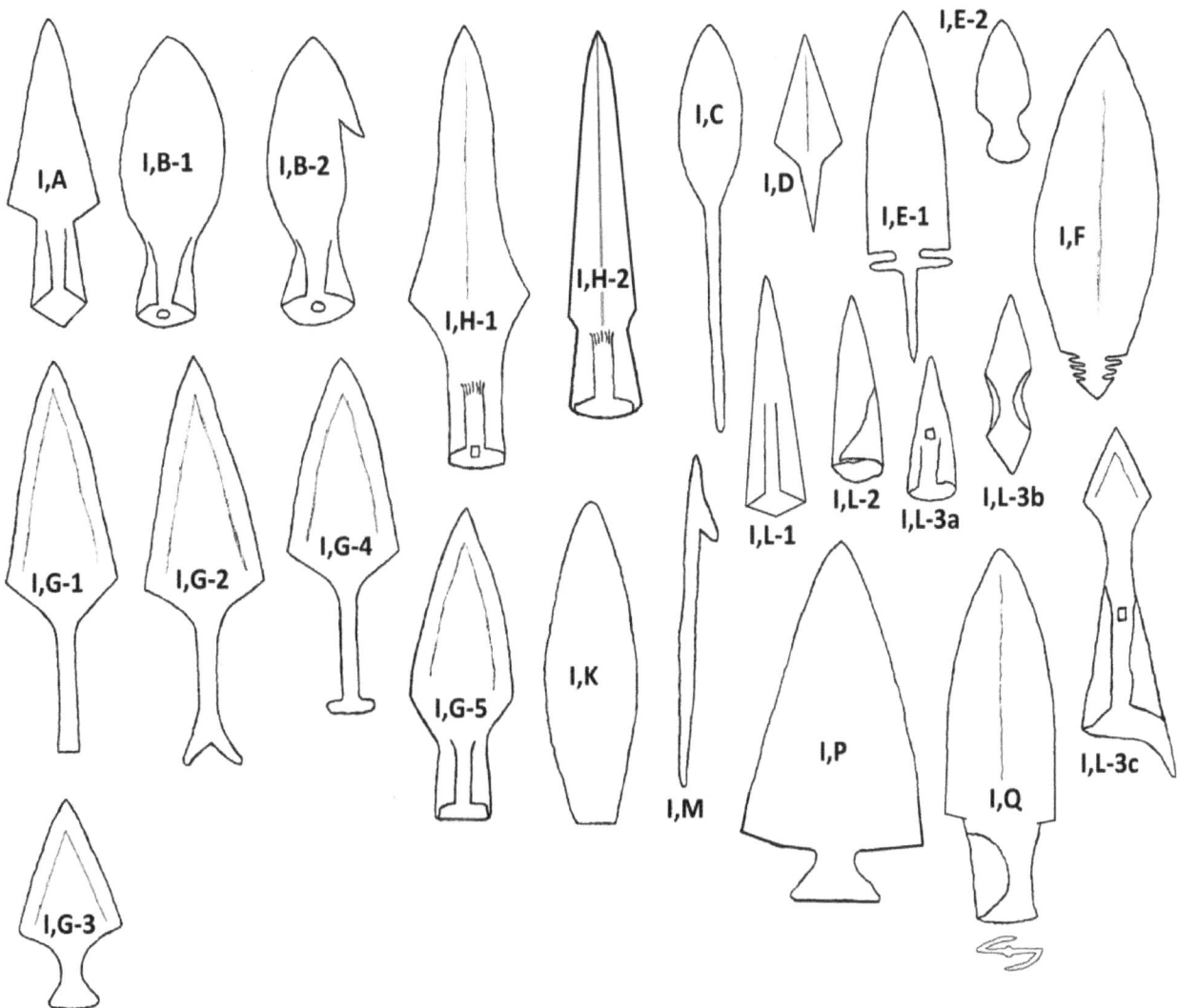

I,A Triangulate I,B-1 Common Ovate I,B-2 Barbed Ovate I,C Long Rattail I,D Short Rattail I,E-1 Barbed Tang I,E-2 Beavertail I,F Sawtooth Tang I,G-1 Straight Flat Tang I,G-2 Swallowtail I,G-3 Ace of Spades I,G-4 Pommel Tang I,G-5 Socketed Beveled Point I,H-1 Shouldered Northern Style Point I,H-2 Unshouldered Northern Style Point I,K Lanceolate I,L-1 Triangulate Conical I,L-2 Common Conical I,L-3a Holed Concial I,L-3b Pinch Point I,L-3c Minnesota Style Toggle Harpoon I,M Stick Harpoon I,P Pine Tree I,Q Winged Point

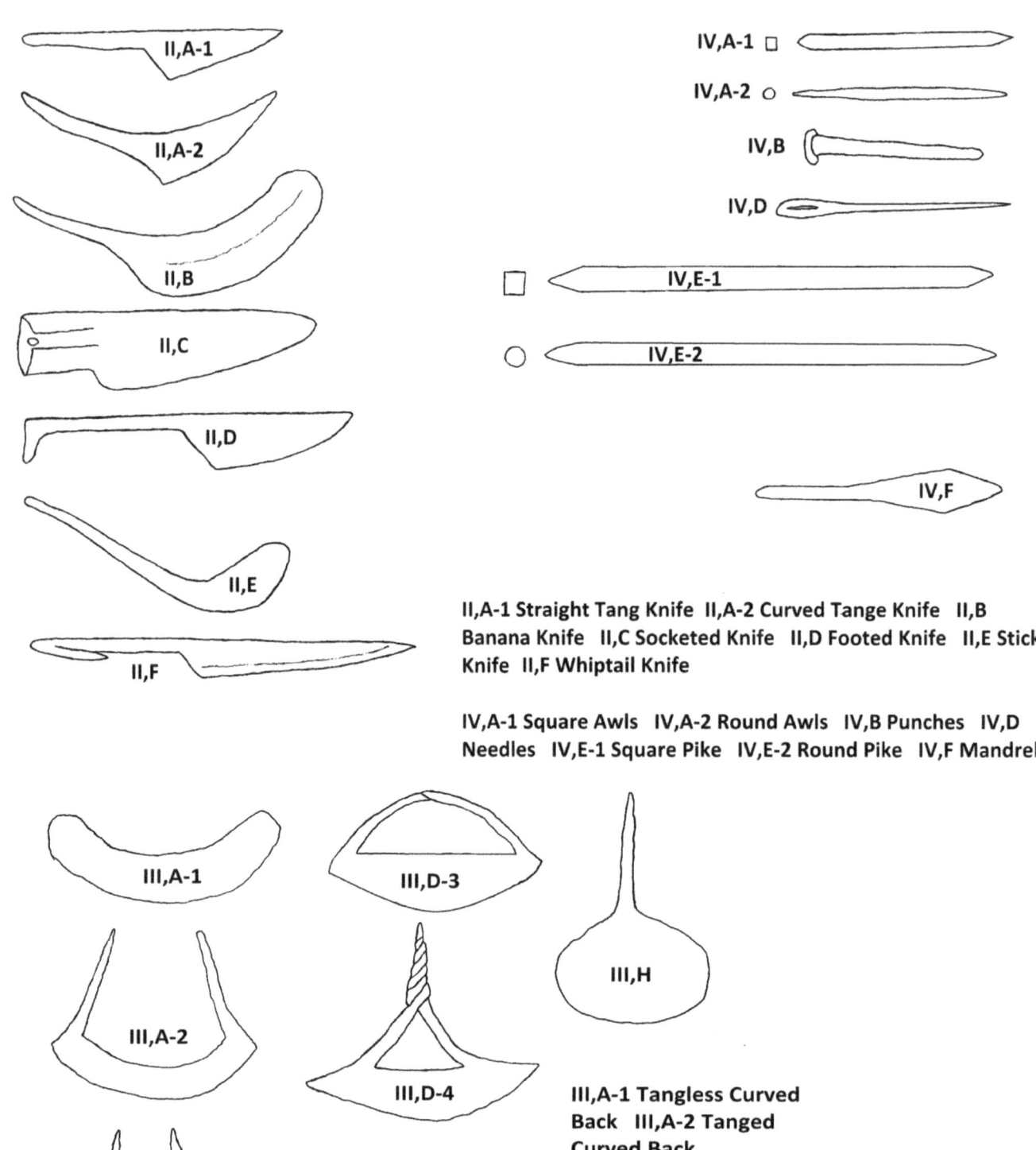

II,A-1 Straight Tang Knife II,A-2 Curved Tange Knife II,B Banana Knife II,C Socketed Knife II,D Footed Knife II,E Stick Knife II,F Whiptail Knife

IV,A-1 Square Awls IV,A-2 Round Awls IV,B Punches IV,D Needles IV,E-1 Square Pike IV,E-2 Round Pike IV,F Mandrel

III,A-1 Tangless Curved Back III,A-2 Tanged Curved Back
III,D-1 Back Tanged
III,D-2 Box Tanged
III,D-3 Bridge Tanged
III,D-4 Twisted Tang
III,G-1 Tangless Straight Back (Holed and not holed) III,G-2 Tanged Straight Back III,H Spatula

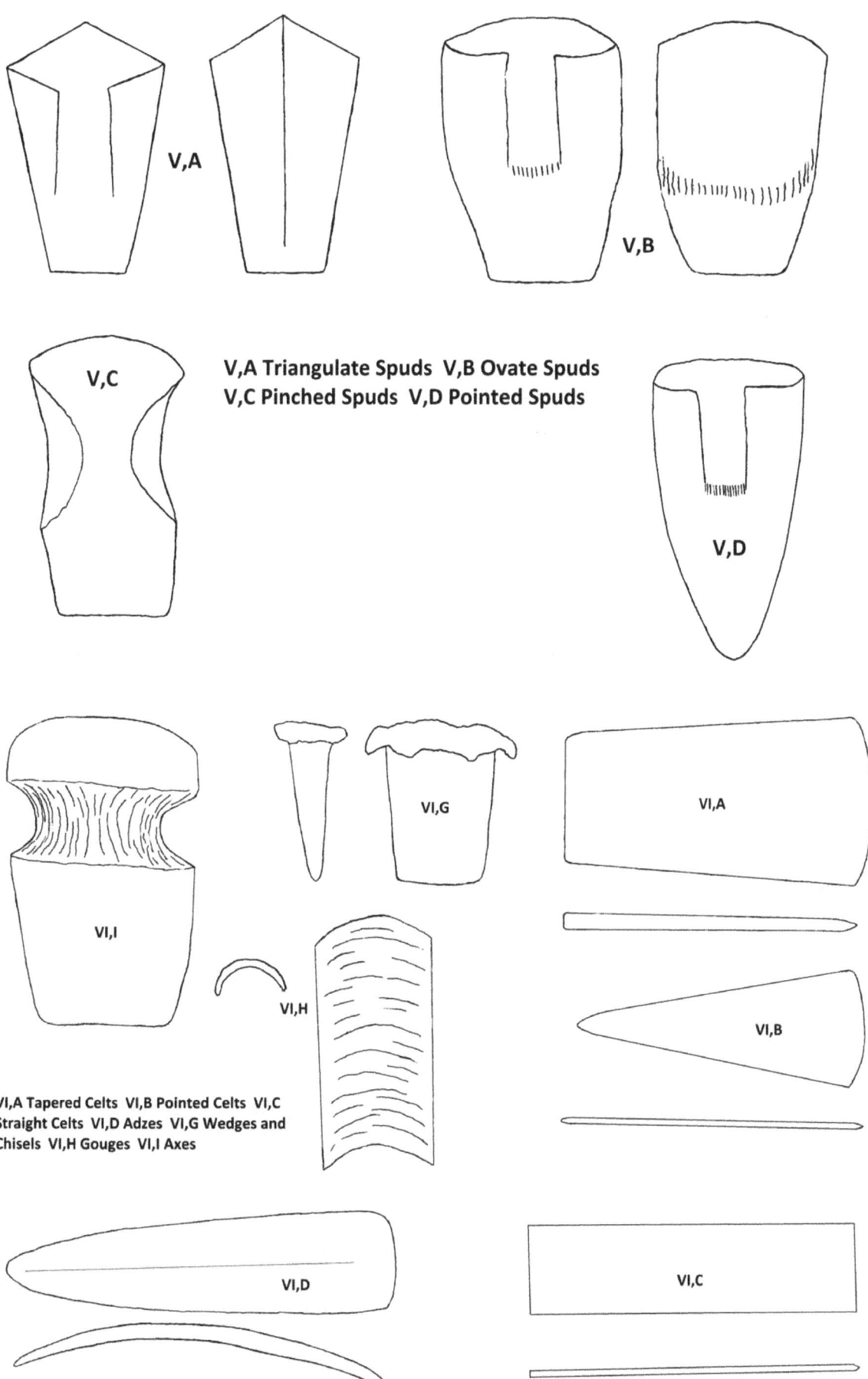

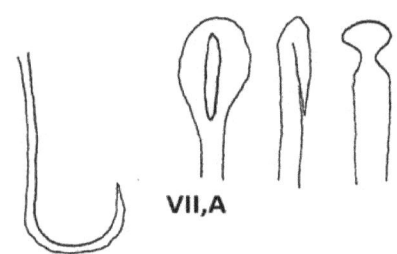
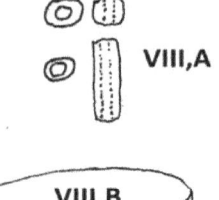
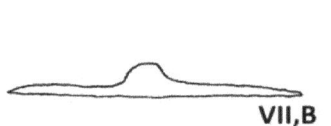
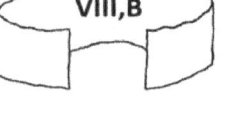

VII,A Hooks VII,B Gorges VII,C Leisters VIII,A Beads VIII,B Bracelets VIII,C Rings VII,D Pendants VIII,F Spirals

I
PROJECTILE FORMS

I,A Triangulates
I,B-1 Common Ovates
I,B-2 Barbed Ovates
I,C Long Rattails
I,D Short Rattails
I,E-1 Barbed Tangs
I,E-2 Beavertails
I,F Sawtooth Tangs
I,G-1 Straight Flat Tangs
I,G-2 Swallow Tails
I,G-3 Ace of Spades
I,G-4 Pommel Tangs
I,G-5 Socketed Bevels
I,H-1 Shouldered Northern Points
I,H-2 Unshouldered Northern Points
I,K Lanceolates
I,L-1 Triangulate Conicals
I,L-2 Ovate Conicals
I,L-3a Holed Conicals
I,L-3b Pinch Points
I,L-3c Minnesota Style Harpoons
I,M Stick Harpoons
I,P Pine Trees
I,Q Winged Points

Page 27

I,A Triangulates

Discussion Triangulates are one of the most wide-spread and consistent types in terms of shape and characteristics of all the copper types. Wittry's original system (Wittry, 1950) broke this system down into two distinct varieties, stepped and unstepped. Steinbring (Steinbring, 1975) however lumped the two groups into a single type based upon the observation that there appeared to be no noticeable distinction in the distributional patterns of either one. The distribution of stepped and un-stepped triangulates has not been explored by the author and it is assumed that Steinbring's observations are accurate. For this reason both varieties have been left as a single type here but it may very well prove necessary to seperate them into individual types if evidence shows either widely different distribution or some sort of temporal evolution from one type to another in the archaeological record.

Triangulates are most often made with fairly heavy, sturdy, construction methods. Both stepped and un-stepped Triangulates have strong median ridges that run from the tip to the tab. Median ridges were likely "swedged" early on in the production (this can be accomplished on just a flat rock with proper technique) and the socket construction would have been the last step. Preforms were likely long and diamond shaped. Triangular shaped notches would have been chisel cut from the preform at the desired height for the top of the socket and then the resulting wings could have been folded over with the use of a mandrel to finish the form of the socket. Surface and edge corrosion of artifacts can in some instances lead to the tab or nib feature of Triangulates being less consipicous, but it is necessary to use extreme caution in identifying any artifact as a I,A without this key feature. Triangulates in general are widely accepted as being developed early on and may have their origins in the Early to Middle Archaic time frame. Many Triangulates are made of heavy construction. The well formed median ridge, tab at the end of the socket, and angular socket shape are all universal signatures of the type. Blades are usually long triangular shaped and the shoulders are well formed at upword sloping angles. The socket normally comprises at least a 1/4 for the overall length and sometimes as much as 2/3 of the over all length. Sockets are never holed as they are with the I,B types.

Common names Triangulates, Ridged Sockets, Socketed Tangs, Ridge Backs.

Left, closeup of the upper socket on a Triangulate that has a well formed step. These steps undoubtedly helped prevent the shaft from slipping forward. *Courtesy of the M. Sainz Collection and the Little Eagler Arts Foundation of Wisconsin Dells.*

Left, 5" Triangulate point from Waukesha County Wisconsin. Note the well defined tab at the end of the socket, upward sloping shoulders, triangular shaped blade, triangular shaped socket, and presence of a step near the blade-socket junction. *D. Johnson Collection.*

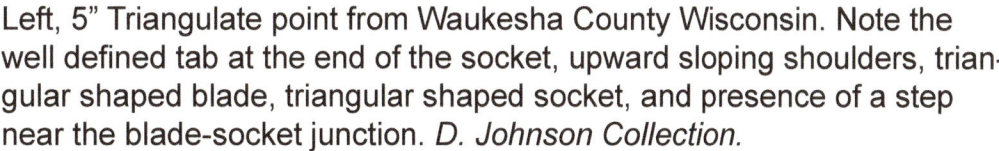

Left, 2 1/2" example from Iron County Wisconsin. Pieces exhibiting heavier corrosion like this may make key features like median ridges and tabs less pronounced. *D. Miller Collection.*

Below, 2 5/8" example from Oneida County Wisconsin. Note the well formed shoulders and strong median ridge, both typical features for the type. *D. Miller Collection.*

Right, 2 7/8" example from Ontario, Canada. *Private Collection.*

Right, 2 7/8" Triangulate from Keweenaw County Michigan. *D. Miller Collection.*

Left, 3" example from Lincoln County Wisconsin. *D. Johnson Collection.*

Left, 3" Triangulate from Vilas County Wisconsin. *D. Johnson Collection.*

Left, 3 1/2" example from Vilas County Wisconsin. *Courtesy of the D. Miller Collection.*

Left, 3 1/2" Triangulate from Vilas County Wisconsin with no step in the socket. *Private Collection*

Left, 3 1/8" example from Adams County Wisconsin. Piece has strong dorsal ridge, triangular shaped blade and socket, but weakly defined tab. Both dorsal and ventral sides shown. *D. Renner Collection.*

Left, 3 1/8" example from Marathon County Wisconsin. No step in the socket on this piece. *D. Miller Collection.*

Left, 3 3/4" Triangulate from Lincoln County Wisconsin. Note the heavy duty socket wall construction. *D. Johnson Collection.*

Left, 3 3/4" example from Mackinac County Michigan. *D. Johnson Collection.*

Left, 3 3/4" example from Vilas County Wisconsin. *Private Collection.*

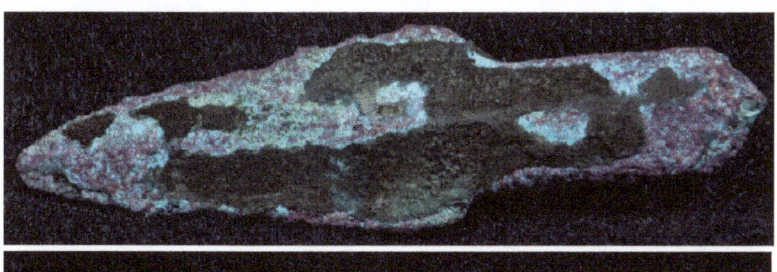

Left, 3 3/8" example from Vilas County Wisconsin. *Private Collection.*

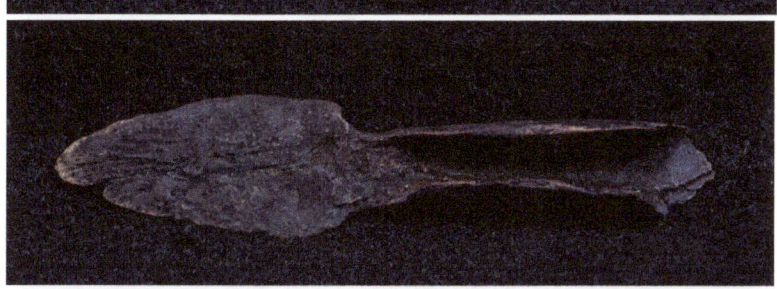

Left, 3 3/8" Triangulate from Winnebago County Wisconsin. No step in socket. *Private Collection.*

Left, 4" example from Lincoln County Wisconsin. *Private Collection.*

Left, 4" Triangulate from Mackinac County Michigan. *D. Johnson Collection.*

Left, 4" example from Oneida County Wisconsin. *D. Johnson Collecton.*

Left, 4" Triangulate from Ontario, Canada. *D. Johnson Collection.*

Left, very well preserved 4 1/2" Triangulate from Dodge County Wisconsin. *L. Born Collection.*

Left, 4 1/4" example from Mille Lacs County Minnesota. *D. Johnson Collection.*

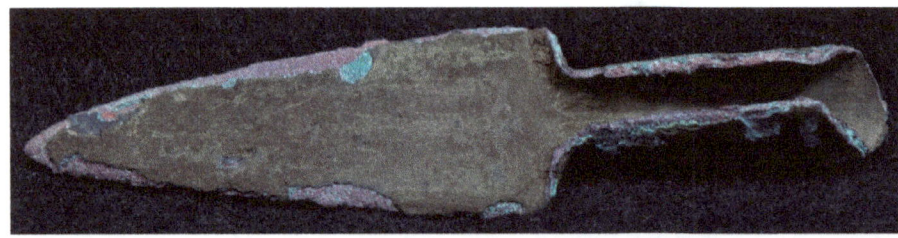

Left, classic 4 1/8" Triangulate from Vilas County Wisconsin. No step in the socket. *Private Collection.*

Left, 4 1/8" example from Winnebago County Wisconsin. *G. Weimer Collection.*

Above, 4 3/4" Triangulate with very short blade to socket ratio indicating extensive re-sharpening or a point that broke mid-blade and was re-tipped, resulting in a shorter point like this. Point found in Ontario, Canada. *Private Collection.*

Left, a well-worn example measuring 4 3/4" in length and from Ontario. *Private Collection.*

Left, 4 3/8" example from Winnebago County Wisconsin. *Private Collection.*

Left, 5 1/16" example from Sheboygan County Wisconsin. *Courtesy of the M. Sainz Collection and the Little Eagle Arts Foundation of Wisconsin Dells.*

Left, 5" Triangulate, classic form, Waukesha County Wisconsin. *D. Johnson Collection.*

Left, 5 1/2" example from Oconto County Wisconsin. *L. Born Collection.*

Left, 5 1/2" Triangulate from Roseau County Minnesota. *D. Johnson Collection.*

Left, 5 1/4" Triangulate from Columbia County Wisconsin. *D. Johnson Collection.*

Left, 5 1/8" example from Dane County Wisconsin. *L. Born Collection.*

Left, 5 3/4" Triangulate with well-formed step in socket. Oconto County Wisconsin. *J. Bussey Collection.*

Above, 5 3/8" Triangulate with hints of resharpening visible on the tip of the blade as well as some wood perserved in the socket. Winnebago County Wisconisn. *G. Weimer Collection.*

Above, 5 5/8" example with well-formed worm tracks from Manitowoc County Wisconsin. *T. Betka Collection.* Below, 6 5/8" example from Marquette County Wisconsin with a strong, well-formed step in the socket. *Courtesy of the Milwaukee Public Museum.*

6 1/4" Triangulate with exceptionally strong median ridge, tab, and angular shoulders, classic form. Unknown provenience. *J. Bussey Collection.*

Above, 7" Triangulate from Oconto County Wisconsin. *D. Johnson Collection.*

Above, exceptional example with portions of original surface still well-preserved. Shawano County Wisconsin. *L. Born Collection.*

Above, slender 8" example from Marathon County Wisconsin. *D. Johnson Collection.*

Above, 8 1/2" Triangulate with serious material flaws in blade from Otter Tail County Minnesota. *L. Born Collection.*

Above, 9 1/2" example lacking a step in the socket. Columbia County Wisconsin. *J. Bussey Collection.*

Above, incredible 10 3/4" Triangulate from Walworth County Wisconsin. *J. Bussey Collection.*

Above, 6 3/4" example that was found in Waupaca County Wisconsin in 1902. *Courtesy of the Logan Museum of Anthropology.*

Above, 8 3/4" Triangualte found in 1890 in Fond du Lac County Wisconsin. *Courtesy of the Logan Museum of Anthropology.*

Left, crude, thick-walled example found in Vilas County Wisconsin. *Private Collection.*

I,B-1
Common Ovates

Discussion There are a wide variety of ovates but all of them share a few traits. The sockets are always rounded or oval and always have a rivet hole. The sockets may have steps or not, and the socket itself can be inline with the dorsal plane or discontinuous. Blade shapes in the "classic" form of east central Wisconsin tend to be broadly oval. As one travels in distance and perhaps time, from east central Wisconsin the Common Ovate blade shapes range from oval to lanceolate. Overall sizes are equally as variable from just a couple of inches to eight or more. Common Ovates are sometimes punch marked on one or both blade faces. Common Ovates are without question one of the most common of spear types and their general characteristics appear to translate into other forms as well including harpoons, knives, and conicals.

Common Names Ovates, Classic Ovates, Socketed Tangs, Common Ovates

Below, classic form of Common Ovate from Door County Wisconsin. 5 1/2" in length with a ruptured rivet hole in socket. *Courtesy of the Milwaukee Public Museum*

Left, 1 7/8" Common Ovate with ruptured rivet hole. Found in Marathon County Wisconsin. *D. Miller Collection.*

Left, 2 1/8" Common Ovate also from Marathon County Wisconsin. Notice the two vertical lines on the blade face, evidence that the piece was found in bent condition and straightened. *Courtesy of the D. Miller Collection.*

Left, 2 1/8" example with ruptured rivet hole. In some instances the rupture may be the result of nothing more than corrosion but it is far too common of an occurence to account for them all. This example is from Oneida County Wisconsin. *Courtesy of the D. Miller Collection.*

Left, 2 3/4" Common Ovate which still has the rivet in the hole of the socket and can be seen protruding from the dorsal socket plain. Vilas County Wisconsin. The dorsal plane also has a series of linear punch marks but they are difficlut to see in the picture. *D. Miller Collection.*

Left, 2 3/4" example from Oneida County Wisconsin. *D. Johnson Collection.*

Left, 2 3/4" Common Ovate with square rivet hole in the socket. Found in Oneida County Wisconsin. *D. Johnson Collection.*

Left, 2 7/8" Common Ovate that was found in Winnebago County Wisconsin. *G. Weimer Collection.*

Left, 5" Common Ovate From Adams County Wisconsin. *Courtesy of the Chicago Field Museum.*

2 15/16" Common Ovate from Vilas County Wisconsin. Hole in socket is present but nearly corroded shut. *D. Miller Collection.*

Left, very nice 3" example from Ontario, Canada. *D. Johnson Collection.*

Left, 3" Common Ovate from Sheboygan County Wisconsin. *D. Johnson Collection.*

Left, 3 1/2" Common Ovate that was found in Lincoln County Wisconsin. *D. Johnson Collection.*

Left, 3 1/2" Common Ovate from Vilas County Wisconsin. *D. Miller Collection.*

Left, a well made 3 1/4" Common Ovate from St. Louis County Minnesota. *D. Johnson Collection.*

Left, 3 3/4" Common Ovate from Oneida County Wisconsin. Notice the red vertical lines on blade face, signs it was found in bent condition and straightened out. This is a common feature of artifacts in collections both public and private. *D. Johnson Collection.*

Left, 3 3/4" Common Ovate from Ontario, Canada. *Private Collection.*

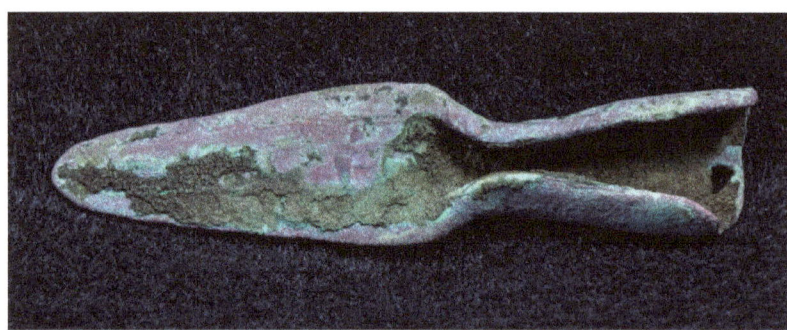

Left, 3 3/8" Common Ovate found in Vilas County Wisconsin. *Private Collection.*

Left, 3 5/8" example from Milwaukee County Wisconsin. Note the punch marks along the blade face consisting of two equal rows of marks that converge into a single row. *L. Born Collection.*

Left, 3 7/8" Classic form Common Ovate with square rivet hole. Found in Green Lake County Wisconsin. These large, broad-bladed forms are considered "Classic" by many and are typically found in the copper "Heartland" of eastern Wisconsin. *L. Born Collection.*

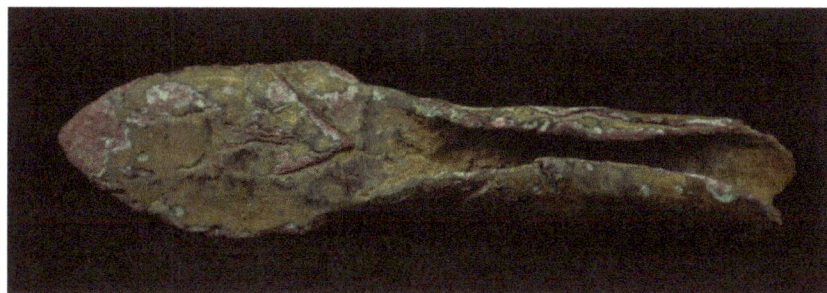

Left, 3 7/8" Common Ovate from Manitowoc County Wisconsin. *Courtesy of the T. Betka Collection.*

Left, 4" example from Houghton County Michigan. The flaring socket could be indicitive of the piece being used as a knife. *D. Johnson Collection.*

Left, 4 1/2" Common Ovate. This great example is from Columbia County Wisconsin. *Courtesy of the J. Bussey Collection.*

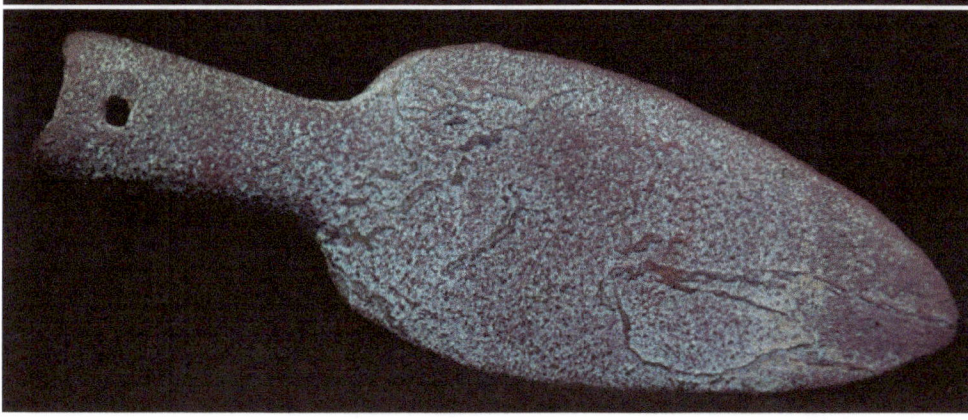

Left, another fantastic 4 1/2" example exhibiting classical features. This point was found in Portage County Wisconsin. *J. Bussey Collection.*

Below, 6" Common Ovate from Sheboygan County Wisconsin. *Courtesy of the Chicago Field Museum.*

Left, 4 1/4" Common Ovate from Marquette County Wisconsin. *Private Collection.*

Left, 4 1/4" example from Ontario, Canada. *D. Johnson Collection.*

Above, enlarged picture of a 4 3/4" example to better show the punch marks. The punch marks are in two rows which appear to merge into a single file but one mark nearest the tip is barely visible. Notice the piece also had a ruptured rivet hole but appears to have been used in spite of the damage. Unknown provenience. *J. Bussey Collecton.*

Left, both ventral and dorsal surfaces shown on a classic 4 3/4" Common Ovate. Found in Green Lake County Wisconsin. Note how the socket is offset from the dorsal blade face in this example, this worked the same as a steppped socket in preventing the shaft from sliding forward upon impact. *L. Born Collection.*

Above, very well made 4 5/8" example from Manitowoc County Wisconsin. *T. Betka Collection.*

Above, 4 15/16" Ovate with two rows of punch marks that extend from the blade-socket junction to near the point. Example has ruptured rivet hole and was found in Vilas County Wisconsin. *Private Collection.*

Above, 5" example from Roseau County Minnesota. *D. Johnson Collection.*

Above, very nice 5 1/2" example from Lincoln County Wisconsin. *D. Johnson Collection.* Below, punch marked 5 1/4" Common Ovate, unknown provenience. *L. Born Collection.*

Left, 5 1/8" punch marked example. Unknown provenience. *J. Bussey Collection.*

Above, 6 1/4" Common Ovate with classic form from Menominee County Wisconsin. *G. Weimer Collection.* Below, 6 1/2" example from Milwaukee County Wisconsin. Note the redened patina at the blade-socket junction, evidence that it was bent to some degree when first found. *L. Born Collection.*

Above, 6 1/8" Common Ovate with punch marks and the rivet still in place in the socket! Note that this exceptional example also has a redened patina near the blade-socket junction which is the result of the piece having been somewhat bent at that spot when it was found. Some of these old bends could have easily been the result of farming equipment or perhaps from rough use by the original owner. *L. Born Collection.*

Above, 6 1/8" Common Ovate with three punch marks in a row on the ventral blade surface near the blade-socket junction. This set of punch marks is rather unusual. Otter Tail County Minnesota, *L. Born Collection.* Below, large 6 7/8" example that was found near Mayville Wisconsin. *L. Born Collection.*

Above, huge 7" Common Ovate from Ontonagon County Michigan. Very few Ovates were made this large. *D. Johnson Collection.*

Above, 4" Common Ovate with classic form. Found in a garden bed in Washington County Wisconsin. *Courtesy the Marks Family Collection.*

Above, 5 3/4" Common Ovate from Ozaukee County Wisconsin. *Courtesy of the Milwaukee Public Museum*

Left, 2 3/8" Common Ovate with a punch marked dorsal plane as well as a ruptured rivet hole in the socket. Found in Lincoln County Wisconsin. *D. Miller collection.*

Right, 3 1/4" Common Ovate from Dane County Wisconsin, cleaned in modern times. *Courtesy of the M. Sainz Collection and the Little Eagle Arts Foundation of Wisconsin Dells.*

Below, 4 3/4" example from Fond du Lac County Wisconsin. *Courtesy of the M. Sainz Collection and the Little Eagle Arts Foundation of Wisconsin Dells.*

Left, Common Ovate with punch marks. It has been enlarged to show the detail of the punch marks that, in this particular case, appear to have been made with a chisel like tool. There are six marks total, the bottom two are sub-surface while the top four are slightly raised. It demonstrates on a micro scale how much of an effect weathering and corosion can have on an artifact, even on the same artifact just inches apart. Similar differences are often found from one side of a point to the other, with the side that was facing up in the ground being most heavily corroded. *Courtesy of the L. Born Collection*

Barbed Ovates
I,B-2

Discussion Barbed Ovates are for all practical purposes the same as Common Ovates except that they have a single barb on either side of the blade. These barbs are typically well executed. This demonstrates that at least some Common Ovates were adapted for specific uses, in this case, presumably spearing fish. Some of the smaller Common Ovates were likely used in similar fashion, even if they do not have the addition of a barb. While Barbed Ovates are tiny in number when compared to Common Ovates, it is assumed they share the same distribution patterns and cultural affiliations.

Common Names Barbed Ovates, Fish Spears, Barbed Sockets, Socket Tanged

Left, 2 1/4" Barbed Ovate. Unknown provenience. *J. Bussey Collection.*

Left, 2 3/4" Barbed Ovate from Vilas County Wisconsin. *D. Johnson Collection.*

Left, 3 3/4" example with unknown provenience. *J. Bussey Collection.*

Left, 3 3/4" Barbed Ovate from Oneida County Wisconsin. This example is unusual because the barb is set further back than it is on most. *D. Johnson Collection.*

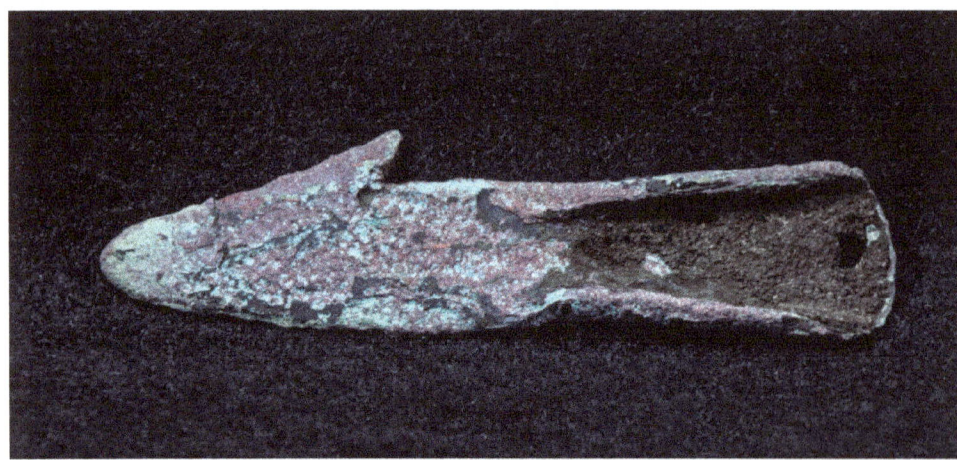

Left, 3 3/8" example from Vilas County Wisconsin. *Private Collection.* Below, 5 3/8" example from Sheboygan County Wisconsin. Long and narrow for the type. *L. Born Collection.*

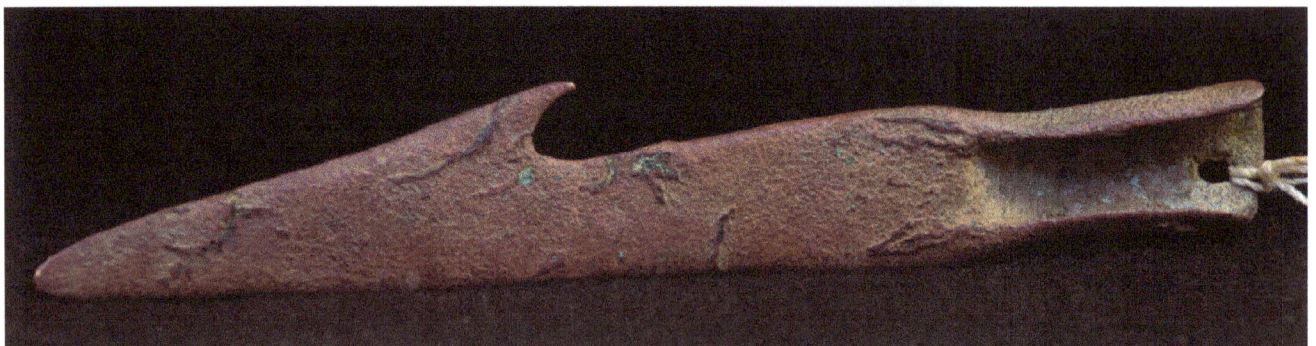

Below, 5 1/4" Barbed Ovate from Washington County Wisconsin. *Courtesy of the Milwaukee Public Museum*

Right, 3" example from Vilas County Wisconsin. *D. Miller Collection.*

Left, 3 3/8" Barbed Ovate from Vilas County Wisconsin. *D. Miller Collection.*

Left, 2 1/8" example from Vilas County Wisconsin. *N. Schanen Collection.*

Left, 3 5/8" Barbed Ovate. *N. Schanen Collection*

Right, 3" Barbed Ovate from Langlade County Wisconsin. *Courtesy of the Eugene and Cathy Schug Collection.*

Below, 4 1/8" example from Vilas County Wisconsin. *D. Miller Collection.*

Long Rattails
I,C-1

Discussion A long, often slender, willow leaf shaped blade with gently sloping shoulders that merges smoothly into a long cylindrical shaped tang. The thickest part of a Long Rattail is the blade-tang junction. Long Rattails from the Wisconsin "heartland" tend to be the largest examples. The farther from this region one travels the more the type shrinks in overall size demonstraiting an inverse proximal relationship with the heartland. While Long Rattails are among some of the most easily recognizable types very little is known about where they fit into the chronological order of copper use. What we do know for sure is that the long slender tang of the Long Rattails would have lent themselves best to hafting with soft woods (Steinbring 1975) in stark contrast to the socketed projectiles which would have been more sucessful with hardwoods for hafting.

Common Names Rattails, Long Rattails, Oval Tanged

Left, 2 1/4" Long Rattail from Oneida County Wisconsin. *D. Johnson Collection.*

Above, 4" Long Rattail from McHenry County Illinois. *D. Johnson Collection.*

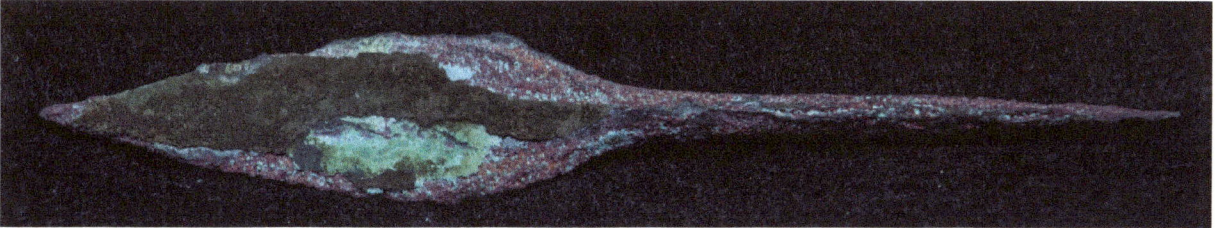

Above, 4 7/8" Long Rattail found in Vilas County Wisconsin. *Private Collection.*

Left, 2 3/4" example from Oneida County Wisconsin. *D. Johnson Collection.*

Page 53

Left, 4" Long Rattail from Vilas County Wisconsin. *D. Johnson Collection.*

Above, 4 1/2" example from Mackinac County Michigan. *D. Johnson Collection.*

Above, 4 1/4" Long Rattail found in Clayton County Iowa. *D. Johnson Collection.*

Above, 6 1/4" example found in Vilas County Wisconsin. *D. Johnson Collection.*

Above, remarkable 6 1/2" Long Rattail that is made almost entirely of native silver. This exceptionally rare piece was found in Ontario, Canada. *D. Johnson Collection.*

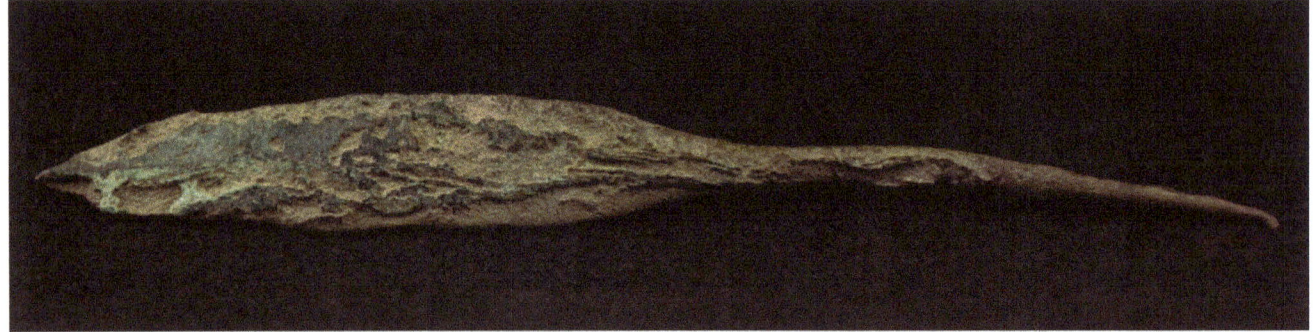

Above, 6 7/8" Long Rattail. Found in Adams County Wisconsin. *D. Renner Collection.*

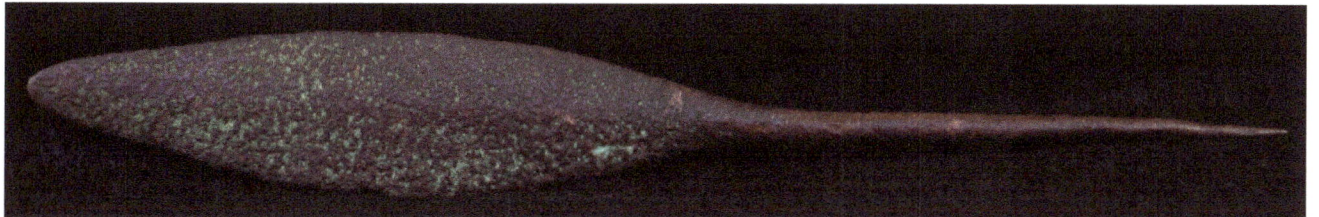

Above, 7 1/4" Long Rattail. While the provenience is unknown, we can assume it is a Wisconsin piece due to it's size and shape. *J. Bussey Collection.*

Above, huge 10 1/4" Long Rattail that was found in Brown County Wisconsin. *J. Bussey Collection.* Below, 6 5/8" example from Waupaca County Wisconsin. *Courtesy of the Milwaukee Public Museum.*

Below, 7 1/4" example from Washington County Wisconsin. *Courtesy of the Milwaukee Public Museum.*

Above, 8 1/2" example from Washington County Wisconsin. *Courtesy of the Milwaukee Public Museum.* Below, 8 1/8" long Rattail with well developed worm tracks. Found in Waukesha County Wisconsin. *Courtesy of the Milwaukee Public Museum.*

Above, 5 1/4" example from Vilas County Wisconsin. *N. Schanen Collection.*

Above, 9 1/8" Long Rattail from Kenosha County Wisconsin. *L. Born Collection*

Right, 5 1/4" Long Rattail from Whiteside County Illinois. *D. Miller Collection.*

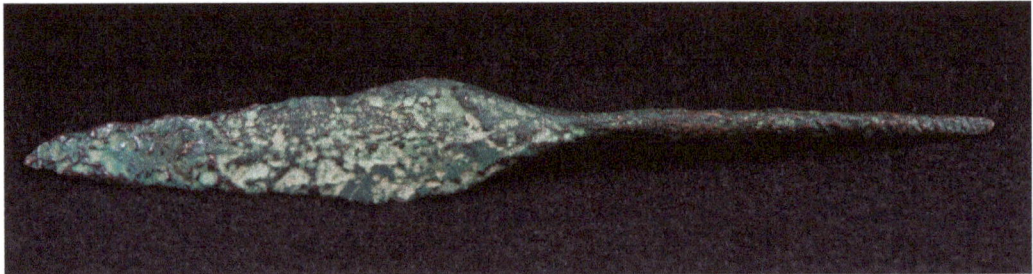

Below, close up of a Long Rattail point which has a large piece of silver composing half of the tip. The silver appears higher than the surrounding copper because it has not corroded away to the same degree as the copper. Unknown provenience but interesting study piece. *D. Miller collection.*

Above, 6" Long Rattail from Washington County Wisconsin. *Courtesy of the Chicago Field Museum.*

Left, classic 10" Long Rattail found near the city of Portage, Wisconsin. *James R. Beer Collection.*

Right, a nice Long Rattail from Ontario, Canada. Below, a smaller example from the same area, *both are courtesy of the O. Anttila Collection.*

I,C-2
Short Rattail

Discussion Short Rattails on average are shorter than their Long Rattail cousins. Short Rattails have no thickened reinforcement at the blade-tang junction and have stronger, more angular shoulders. The length of their blades is always longer than that of their tangs (not typically true for Long Rattails). Tangs are normally cylindrical and pointed and the blade faces are sometimes ridged.

Common Names Diamond Rats, Short Rattails, Short tails

Below, a Short Rattail found in Waupaca County Wisconsin. *Courtesy of the Quade-Hudson Family.*

Above, 4 3/4" Short Rattail from St. Louis County Minnesota. Notice the fold line in the middle of the blade, evidence that the piece was originally found in a bent condition. *D. Johnson Collection.* Below, 5" example with strong worm track development and strong shoulders. Found in Oneida County Wisconisn. *D. Johnson Collection.*

Above, 5 1/2" example from Mackinac County Michigan. *D. Johnson Collection.* Below, another example that is also 5 1/2" in length and from Mackinac County Michigan. *D. Johnson Collection.*

Above, 6 1/2" example from Iron County Wisconsin. *D. Johnson Collection.*

Above, 6 1/4" Short Rattail from Mackinac County Michigan. *D. Johnson Collection.*

Above, 6 1/4" very well made Short Rattail from Oconto County Wisconsin. *D. Johnson Collection.* Below, 6 3/4" example from Ontonagon County Michigan. *Courtesy the D. Johnson Collection.*

Above, 7 1/2" Short Rattail from Gogebic County Michigan. *D. Johnson Collection.*

Above, 7 1/4" example from Lincoln County Wisconsin. Notice incurvate blade edges, likely the result of resharpening. *D. Johnson Collection.*

Above, huge 8" example with classic form that was found in Brown County Wisconsin. *J. Bussey Collection.*

Left, the now famous Marquette County Spear. This enormous 12" Short Rattail was found by a person who was trout fishing in Marquette County Wisconsin. Not realizing what it was, the fisherman stuck it firmly into a fence post upon leaving the fishing hole. Quite some time passed before the fisherman was made aware of the piece's potential historical value. Upon returning to the fishing hole the finder found the point still stuck firmly in the fence post. This remarkable piece remains the largest known example. *J. Bussey Collection.*

Above, this two piece cache was found in Lincoln County Wisconsin. Both pieces are roughly five inches in length. These pieces, with their wide blades and very flat tangs are most likely from a later time period than the others shown in this type. Note that they also lack the strong worm track formation that is common. These are possibly Hopewell related. *Courtesy the J. Bussey Collection.*

Above, 6 3/8" example from Jefferson County Wisconsin. *Courtesy of the Logan Museum of Anthropology.*

Above, extra large 8" Short Rattail example from Dodge County Wisconsin. *Courtesy of the Logan Museum of Anthropology.*

Left, Short Rattail point from Ontario, Canada. *Courtesy of the T. Wilson Collection.*

Below, 6" example from Calumet County Wisconsin. *Courtesy of the Milwaukee Public Museum.*

Below, 7 3/4" Short Rattail point from Calumet County Wisconsin. *Courtesy of the Milwuakee Public Museum.*

Above, 8" example from Calumet County Wisconsin. *Courtesy of the Milwaukee Public Museum.* Below, 8 1/2" example from Waupaca County Wisconsin. *Courtesy of the Milwaukee Public Museum.*

Below, 9 3/8" Short Rattail from Calumet County Wisconsin. *Courtesy of the Milwaukee Public Museum.*

Left, 3 1/4" and 3 1/8" examples that were found together in Vilas County Wisconsin. *D. Miller Collection.*

Left, 4 13/16" example from Vilas County Wisconsin. *Private Collection.*

Barbed Tangs
I,E-1

Discussion Barbed Tangs have triangular-lanceolate shaped blades with shoulders that range from sharp and angular to soft and sloping. Most examples have a single, well-executed chisel cut to form a singular projection on both sides of the tang. The largest examples from the Wisconsin Heartland tend to be the "classic" examples and as one travels farther away these types tend to be slightly smaller and with less clear cut notches. In some cases excess material below the singular notch tapers gently and merges with the remainder of the tang, in classic examples there is no excess material below the single barb and the barb merges perpendicular to the tang. This is a very rare type. The large "classic" examples might be contemperaneous with Long Rattails and or Sawtooth Tanged Points.

Common Names Barbed Tangs, Notched Tangs

Below, 4 1/4" Barbed Tang from Vilas County Wisconsin. *Private Collection.*

Above, 6 1/4" Barbed Tang point with classic form. This fine example was found in Winnebago County Wisconsin. *G. Weimer Collection.* Below, 5 1/8" Barbed Tang that also shows the classic form. Unknown provenience. *J. Bussey Collection.*

Above, 5 1/8" example from Manitowoc County Wisconsin. *L. Born Collection.* Notice how the barbs on this example are slightly less pronounced and flow more smoothly into the tang element.

Above 6 5/16" Barbed Tang. *L. Born Collection.* Below, 5 1/2" example, unknown provenience. *J. Bussey Collection.*

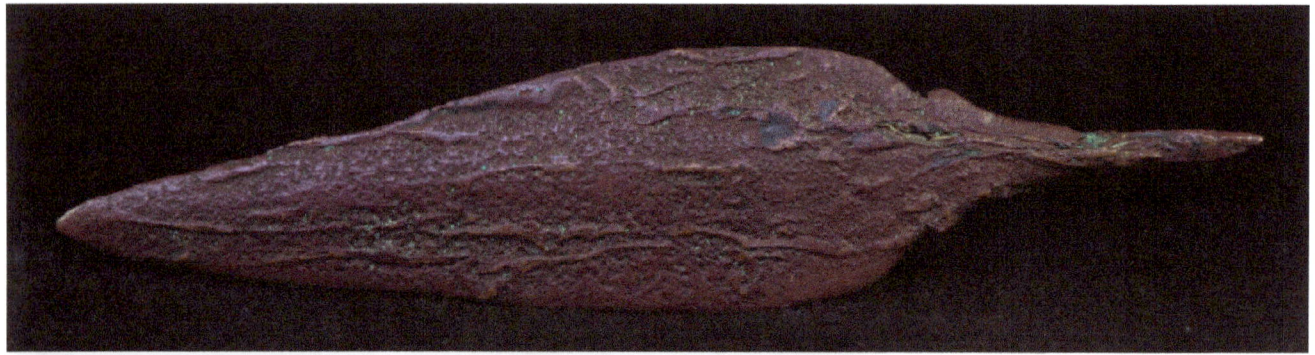

Left, 3 3/8" Barbed Tang from Lincoln County Wisconsin. *G. Weimer Collection.*

Left, 3 1/4" example from Mackinac County Michigan which has two diamond shaped holes in the blade, this is the only known example with this feature. *D. Johnson Collection.*

Left, 2 1/2" Barbed Tang from Mackinac County Michigan. *D. Johnson Collection.* Below, 5" example which has been harshly cleaned at some point since it's finding. Found in Fond du Lac County Wisconsin. *Courtesy of the Milwaukee Public Musuem*

Above, 3 15/16" example from Vilas County Wisconsin. *D. Miller Collection.*

Left, 2 3/8" Barbed Tang with the addition of a hole on the blade surface, the hole appears to be contemporary to the artifact. Unknown provenience. *Courtesy of the M. Sainz and Little Eagle Arts Foundation of Wisconsin Dells.*

Left, 3 3/8" example, unknown provenience, tang broken. *Courtesy of the M. Sainz Collection and the Little Eagler Arts Foundations of Wisconsin Dells.*

Beavertails
I,E-2

Discussion Beavertails are most likely atlatl projectile points. Age and cultural affiliation is not known but likely more recent than most. They are generally small to medium in size and have soft curving features that include a rougly oval to triangular blade followed by a flat rounded to oval tang similar to a Beaver's tail. Many examples appear to be weakly ridged on one or both-sides.

Common Names Beavertails, Turkey Tails

Left, Classic 2" example from Oneida County Wisconsin. *Courtesy of the D. Johnson Collection.*

Right, 2" example from Vilas County Wisconsin. *D. Miller Collection.*

Left, 2 1/2" example from Mackinac County Michigan. *D. Johnson Collection.*

Left, 3 1/2" Beavertail from Iron County Wisconsin. *D. Miller Collection.*

Right, 3 1/4" Beavertail from Lincoln County Wisconsin. *D. Miller Collection.*

Sawtooth
I,F-1

Discussion Sawtooth tangs are another easily recognizable type which we do not have a great deal of information for. These oval to lance shaped points typically have a well defined median ridge (on both sides) and a hafting element with multiple notches to facilitate a secure haft. Most examples are around five inches in length and these are fairly common in Wisconsin. Evidence of chisel cutting is often easy to spot in the tang's notches or "teeth".

Common Names Notched Tangs, Sawtooths, Sawtooth Tanged, Notched, Serrated Tang, Toothed Tangs

Above, 5 3/4" Sawtooth from Washingtonn County Wisconsin. *Courtesy of the Milwaukee Public Museum.*

Left, 3 5/8" example from Vilas County Wisconsin. *D. Miller Collection.*

Right, 3 7/8" Sawtooth from Vilas County Wisconsin. *D. Miller Collection.*

Left, a tiny 1 1/4" example from Shawano County Wisconsin. *Private Collection.*

Right, 3 3/16" example from Menominee County Michigan. Curved tip suggests potential use as a knife. *Courtesy of the S. Wasion Collection.*

Left, 1 3/4" Sawtooth Tang from Lincoln County Wisconsin. *D. Johnson Collection.*

Left, 2" Sawtooth from Lincoln County Wisconsin. *D. Miller Collection.*

Left, 2 1/4" Sawtooth from Bayfield County Wisconsin. *D. Johnson Collection.*

2 1/4" Sawtooth from Mackinac County Michigan. *D. Johnson Collection.*

2 1/4" example from Oneida County Wisconsin. *D. Johnson Collection.*

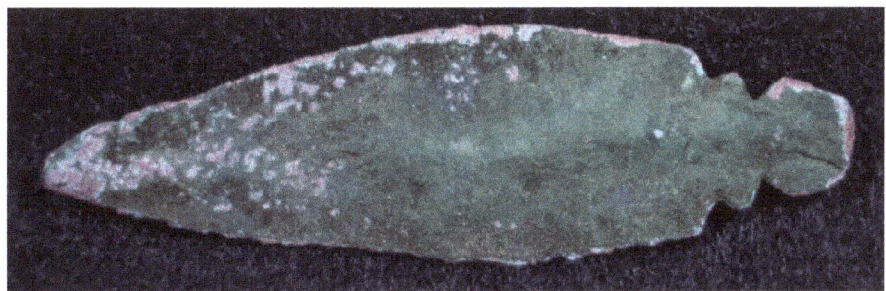

2 3/4" Sawtooth found in Wood County Wisconsin. *Private Collection.*

2 5/8" Sawtooth from Winnebago County Wisconsin. *G. Weimer Collection.*

2 13/16" Sawtooth from Columbia County Wisconsin. *J. Bussey Collection.*

Slender 3" example from Lincoln County Wisconsin. *D. Johnson Collection.*

3" Sawtooth from Lincoln County Wisconsin. *D. Johnson Collection.*

3 1/2" Sawtooth, unknown provenience. *J. Bussey Collection.*

3 1/4" example from Oneida County Wisconsin. *D. Johnson Collection.*

3 1/4" Sawtooth also from Oneida County Wisconsin. *D. Johnson Collection.*

3 1/4" with unusual patina, unknown provenience. *J. Bussey Collection.*

Slender 3 1/8" example. Unknown provenience. *J. Bussey Collection.*

3 3/4" Sawtooth point from Iron County Wisconsin. *D. Johnson Collection.*

3 3/4" Sawtooth from Mackinac County Michigan. *D. Johnson Collection.*

3 7/8" Sawtooth, unknown provenience. *J. Bussey Collection.*

3 9/16" example from Waukesha County Wisconsin. *J. Bussey Collection.*

4" Sawtooth from Cass County Minnesota. *Private Collection.*

4 1/4" example from Waupaca County Wisconsin. *J. Bussey Collection.*

4 3/4" Sawtooth that was found in Winnebago County Wisconsin in 1968. *G. Weimer Collection.*

Above, 4 7/16" Sawtooth from Marathon County Wisconsin. *G. Weimer Collection.*

Above, 5 1/4" Sawtooth from Portage County Wisconsin. *D. Renner Collection.*

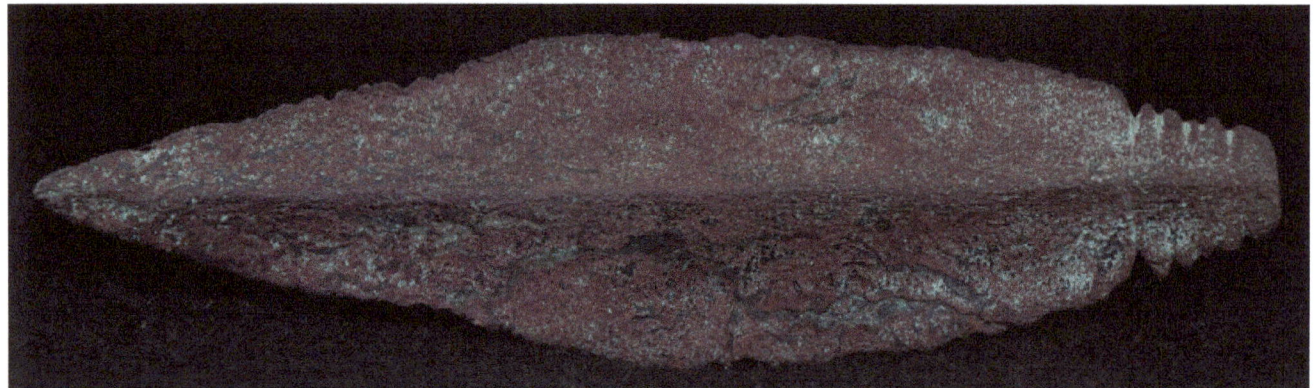

Above, 5 1/8" Sawtooth from Wisconsin. *J. Bussey Collection.*

Above, 6" example. Unknown provenience. *Courtesy of the J. Bussey Collection.*

6 1/8" Sawtooth from Sheboygan County Wisconsin. *J. Bussey Collection.*

Left, 3 3/4" Sawtooth point from Portage County Wisconsin. Below, large 6" Sawtooth, unknown provenience. *Courtesy of the Logan Museum of Anthropology.*

Above, 6 3/8" example from Oconto County Wisconsin. *L. Born Collection.*

Above, 6 3/8" from Vilas County Wisconsin. *Private Collection.* Below, 7 1/4" Sawtooth, unknown provenience. *J. Bussey Collection.*

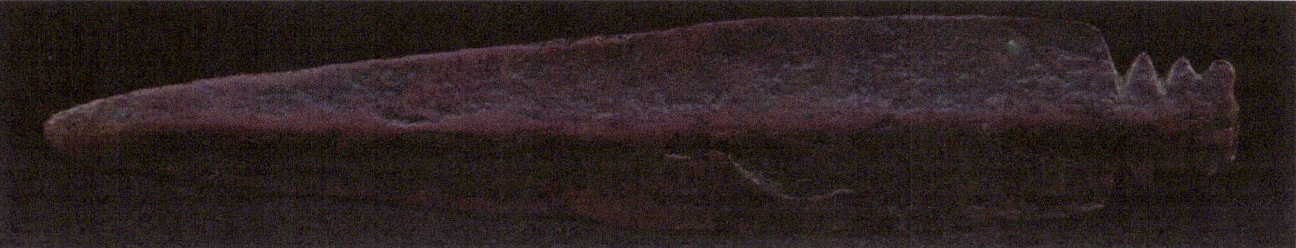

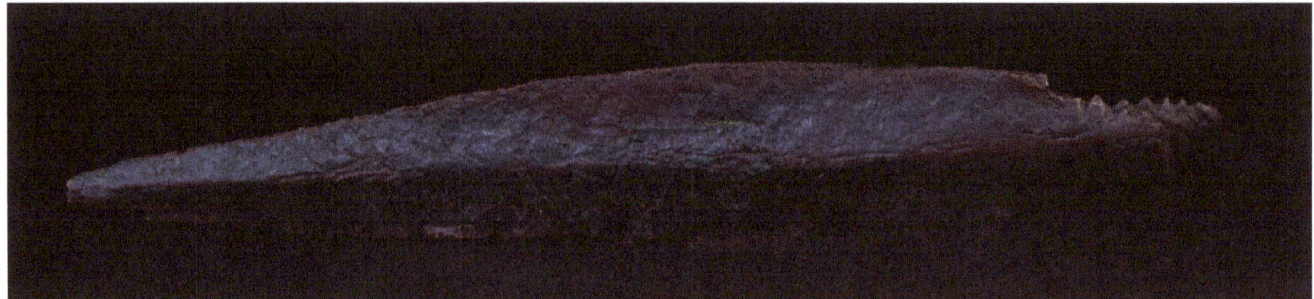

Above, 11 1/16" Sawtooth from Racine County Wisconsin, may be the largest known example. *J. Bussey Collection.*

Right, 4" example from Barry County Michigan. *Courtesy of the Milwaukee Public Museum*

Left, 4" Sawtooth tang from Washington County Wisconsin. *Courtesy of the Milwaukee Public Museum.*

Below, 4 3/8" Sawtooth from Waupaca County Wisconsin. *Courtesy of the Milwaukee Public Museum.*

Left, 9 5/8" Sawtooth from Kenosha County Wisconsin. *L. Born Collection.*

Right, an unfinished Sawtooth missinng only the chisel cut teeth at the base. Almost finished pieces like this are rare and make great study pieces that help us understand the manufacturing process. *Private Collection.*

Above center, 4 1/4" Sawtooth tang point from Keweenaw County Michigan. *D. Miller Collection.*

Straight Flat Tangs
I,G-1

Includes Ridged Flat Tangs Known as I,H by Wittry

Discussion Generally speaking this type consists of triangular shaped flat blades with strong shoulders that lead to a flat, squared tang. Ridged examples exist but are *exceptionally* rare. The rare ridged varieties do not appear to differ from regular flat tangs in any other way and for those two reasons they have been included in a singular type here. (Wittry listed the ridged variety as an idependant type I,H) Examples of regular Straight Flat Tangs range from less than two inches to ten inches or more. Blade beveling is often apparent on larger examples but may be difficult to see or non-existent on smaller examples. The high variability within the type might be evidence for a linear progression of the type over time or evidence of a popular type that had been reinvented by more than one group or more than one time. Tangs of the largest examples are usually neat and well-made with squared features while the tangs of smaller examples may be more tapering and even pointed. These, the Swallow Tails, Ace of Spades, and Socketed Beveled Points all appear to be very closely related. There also appears to be overlap between the smallest examples of these and the Ace of Spades. Like other types, the straight stem examples and the expanding stem examples might represent a temporal progression of the type.

<u>**Common Names**</u> Flat Tangs, Straight Flat Tangs, Beveled Lances, Tanged Points

Perfect, or "Classic" forms of the various copper types can be difficult to find. If we were to strictly follow Wittry's description of his I,G-1 the above 4 5/8" example would certainly fit the bill as the classic form. *J. Bussey Collection.*

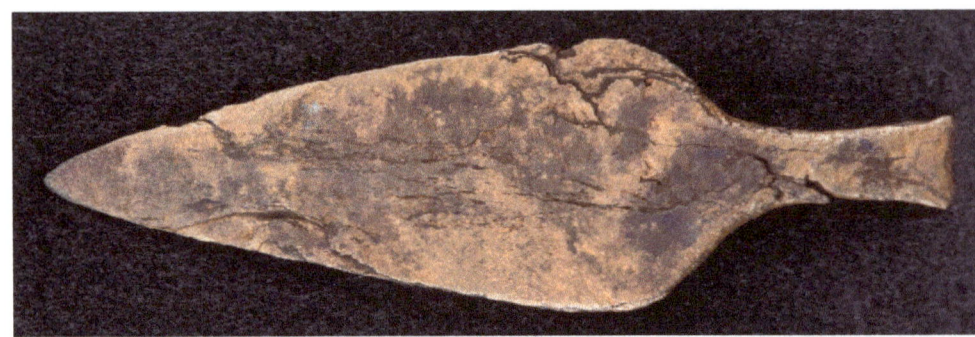

Left, 4 1/8" Straight Flat Tang point from Vilas County Wisconsin. *D. Miller Collection.*

Above, 5 1/8" Straight Flat Tang point from Vilas County Wisconsin. *D. Miller Collection.* Left, 1 13/16" example from Lincoln County Wisconsin. *N. Schanen Collection.*

Left, 2" example which was found in Marathon County Wisconsin. *D. Miller Collection.*

2" Straight Flat Tang from Oneida County Wisconsin. *D. Johnson Collection.*

2" Straight Flat Tang point made almost exclusively of silver. A small, thin portion of the lower blade edge and base were apparently made from copper that has completely coroded away. Lincoln County Wisconsin. *J. Bussey Collection.*

Left, a 2 1/2" example from Mackinac County Michigan. *D. Johnson Collection.*

Left, 2 1/2" Straight Flat Tang point from Oneida County Wisconsin. *D. Johnson Collection.*

2 1/4" example from Hennepin County Minnesota. *D. Johnson Collection.*

2 1/4" Straight Flat Tang from Mackinac County Michigan. *D. Johnson Collection.*

2 3/4" example from Gogebic County Michigan. *D. Johnson Collection.*

2 3/4" Straight Flat Tang from Hennepin County Minnesota. *D. Johnson Collection.*

2 7/8" example from Vilas County Wisconsin. *Private Collection.*

3" example from Rock County Wisconsin. *D. Johnson Collection.*

Left, 3" Straight Flat Tang from Sherburne County Minnesota. *D. Johnson Collection.*

Above, longest point is 2 3/8" in length. This cache was found under an uprooted tree in Vilas County Wisconsin. *Private Collection.*

Left, 3" Straight Flat Tang point from Winnebago County Wisconsin. This is the only example encountered with holes punched side by side in the blade, the function or purpose of which is unknown. *G. Weimer Collection.*

3 1/2" example from Crow Wing County Minnesota. *D. Johnson Collection.*

3 1/2" Straight Flat Tang from Vilas County Wisconsin. *Private Collection.*

3 1/4" example from Oneida County Wisconsin. *D. Johnson Collection.*

Left, 3 1/4" example from Vilas County Wisconsin. *D. Miller Collection.*

3 3/4" Straight Flat Tang point from Mackinac County Michigan. *D. Johnson Collection.*

3 3/8" example from Vilas County Wisconsin. *Private Collection.*

3 3/8" Straight Flat Tang from Winnebago County Wisconsin. *G. Weimer Collection.*

Above and below, both faces of a 3 5/8" Straight Flat Tang point adorned with punch marks on both sides. On one surface the punch marks form a straight line and on the opposite side the marks form a crescent shaped line. This example was found in Waukesha County Wisconsin. *L. Born Collection.* (enlarged to better show punch marks)

Left, 3 5/" Straight Flat Tang from Vilas County Wisconsin. *Private Collection.*

3 5/16" Straight Flat Tang point from Vilas County Wisconsin. *Private Collection.*

4" example from Winnebago County Wisconsin. *Private Collection.*

4 1/4" Straight Flat Tang from Jefferson County Wisconsin. *D. Johnson Collection.*

4 1/8" example from Ontario, Canada. *Private Collection.*

4 3/4" Straight Flat Tang from Green Lake County Wisconsin. *D. Johnson Collection.*

Above, 4 5/8" example from Oconto County Wisconsin. Classic form with well developed edge beveling. *L. Born Collection.*

Above, 5" Straight Flat Tang from Marquette County Wisconsin. *D. Johnson Collection.* Below, 5 1/4" piece from Mackinac County Michigan. *D. Johnson Collection.*

Above, 5 3/4" Straight Flat Tang, unknown provenience. *J. Bussey Collection.* Below, 6" example from Marquette County Wisconsin. *Private Collection.*

Above, 6" Straight Flat Tang from Vilas County Wisconsin. *D. Johnson Collection.*

The Itasca Flat Tang, this 10" Straight Flat Tang artifact was found in Itasca County Minnesota as part of a small cache. It is classic in form and one of the finest examples known. *Courtesy of the D. Miller Collection.*

Longest point is 3 1/4" in length, all four are from Oneida County Wisconsin. *D. Johnson Collection.*

Left, 4" example from Milwaukee County Wisconsin that has a hole in the tang, function is uncertain, but this is a rare attribute. *Courtesy the Logan Museum of Anthropology.*

Below, interesting holed example from Wisconsin, measures 5 7/8" in length, again, these holes are a rare attribute for the type. *Courtesy of the Milwaukee Public Museum.*

Left, a large 10" example. *L. Born Collection.*

Right, 5 7/8" Straight Flat Tang from Keweenaw County Michigan. *D. Miller Collection.*

Below, 6" Straight Flat tang from Vilas County Wisconsin. Piece has well defined beveled edges. *D. Miller Collection.*

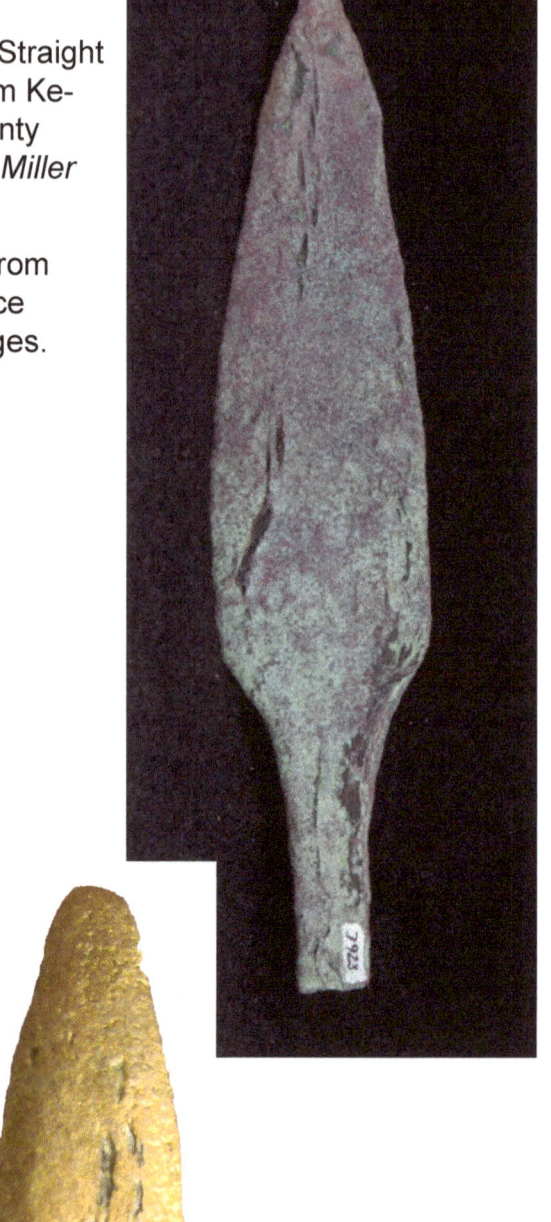

Left, 3 1/2" example from Winnebago County Wisconsin. *Private Collection.*

I,G-2
Swallowtails

Discussion Swallowtails differ little from most Straight Flat Tangs except that they have a split base that ranges from small bilobate examples to long tendrils in others. It has been theorized that the basal notch formed by the split was used to butt up against a rivet to aid in hafting (Spohn 2012). The length of the tendrils formed by the split in some examples is long enough that they may have actually stuck out beyond the hafting material. Many examples are beveled and only rarely may be ridged. To see a remarkably similar ground slate point visit pg 155 of "The Shield Archaic" by J.V. Wright, 1972.

Common Names Swallowtails, Split Tangs, Fish Tails, Orientals, Eye Tangs

Left, 3 1/2" Swallowtail from Keweenaw County Michigan. *D. Miller Collection.*

Left, 2 1/2" example from Carlton County Minnesota. *Private Collection.*

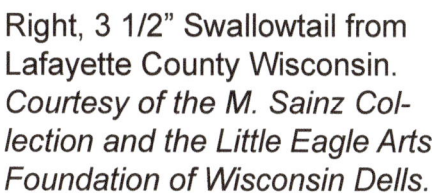

Right, 3 1/2" Swallowtail from Lafayette County Wisconsin. *Courtesy of the M. Sainz Collection and the Little Eagle Arts Foundation of Wisconsin Dells.*

Above, 6 1/8" example from Langlade County Wisconsin. Edge beveling is not as obvious in this picture as it is in hand. *D. Miller Collection.*

Pictured here are the two slightly different Swallow Tail points, the Beveled (Left) and the Ridged (Right). The example on the left was found in Outagamie County Wisconsin. Measures 6 1/2" in length. *Courtesy of the Logan Museum of Anthropology.* The example on the right was found in Marquette County Wisconsin and measures roughly 6 1/2" in overall length. This ridged variety is quite rare. *Private Collection.*

Below, 5 9/16" Swallowtail from Vilas County Wisconsin. *Private Collection.*

Right, 2 15/16" example from Vilas County Wisconsin. *D. Miller Collection.*

Swallow Tails can vary considerably in size, this example is just 2" in length and found in Lincoln County Wisconsin. *D. Johnson Collection.*

Left, 2 3/4" Swallow Tail from Mackinac County Michigan. Minus the "tails" this would be indistinguishable from a Straight Flat Tang. This point type as a whole is very closely related to the rest of the flat tang family of points. *D. Johnson Collection.*

Left, 2 7/8" Swallow Tail from Oneida County Wisconsin. *J. Bussey Collection.*

Left, 2 7/8" example from Vilas County Wisconsin. On this particular example the tails are little more than a notch in the base of an otherwise typical flat tang projectile. *D. Miller Collection.*

Left, 3 1/2" Swallow Tail from Keweenaw County Michigan. *D. Miller Collection.*

Left, 3 1/4" example from Ontario, Canada. It's unclear if one of the tails broke off or if its indicative of a single pronged variety. All other characteristics are the same. *Private Collection.*

Left, 3 3/4" Swallow Tail from Oneida County Wisconsin with a wide tail. *J. Bussey Collection.* Below left, a 4" Swallow Tail with lobed tails that appear to be almost as much the result of an indentation caused by a pin or rivet as much as it was intentionally. This one was found in Mackinac County Michigan. *D. Johnson Collection.*

Left, 4" Swallow Tail that has small angular notch dividing the tails. The piece on the right is 4 1/8" in length and stands in stark contrast, having a wide spread notch in the base with two comparatively long and sharp tails. The example on the left has unknown provenience, the example on the right was found in Oneida County Wisconsin. *Both examples come courtesy of the J. Bussey Collection.* Below, 2" example from Oneida County Wisconsin. *D. Miller Collection.*

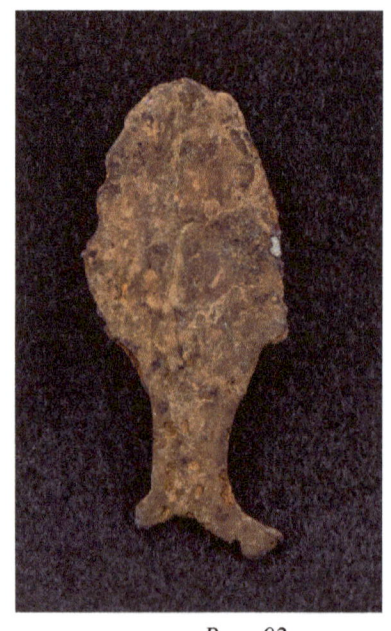

Above, 4 1/2" Swallow Tail from Sheboygan County Wisconsin. Below, 4 1/2" example from Winnebago County Wisconsin. *Both artifacts are courtesy of the Milwaukee Public Museum*

Below, 7" Swallow Tail from Outagamie County Wisconsin. *Courtesy of the Milwaukee Public Museum.*

Above, 7 1/4" Swallowtail with barely noticeable indentation on the base. Fond du Lac County Wisconsin. *Courtesy of the Milwaukee Public Museum.*

Above, 9" Swallowtail from Kenosha County Wisconsin. *L. Born Collection.*

Left, and below, two classic Swallow Tail points, both from Ontario, Canada. *Courtesy of the T. Wilson Collection.*

Above, nice example from Ontario, Canada. *Courtesy of the T. Wilson Collection.*

Left and below, three Swallow Tail examples, all from Ontario, Canada. *Courtesy of the T. Wilson Collection.*

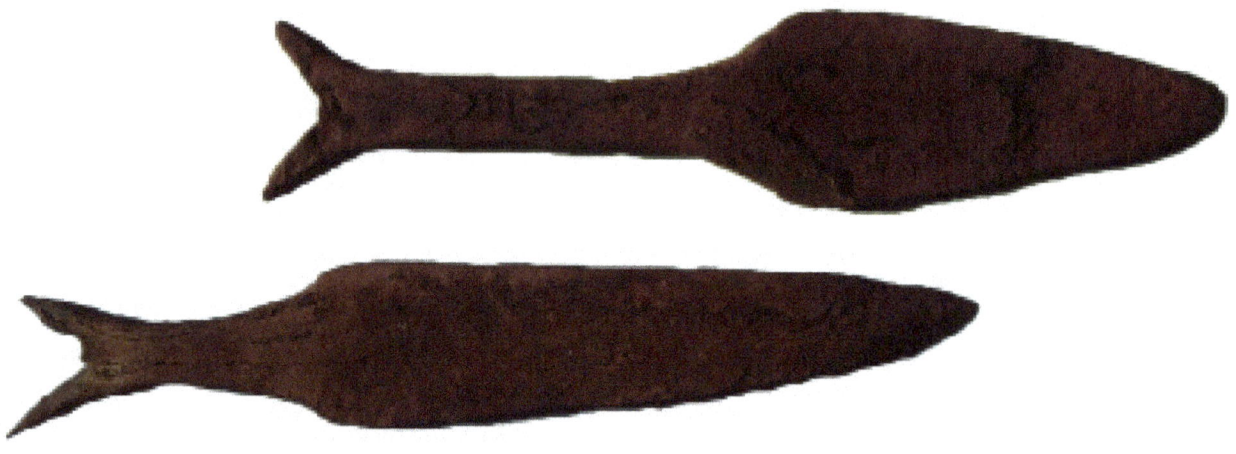

I,G-3
Ace of Spades

Discussion The Ace of Spades type might also be called simply expanding flat stems because the're nearly identical to the Straight Flat Stems with a few important exceptions. Ace of Spades types are typically shorter and with fewer long knife-like examples known. Blade beveling is frequently conspicuous. The size of most of these would suggest use as a projectiles. These probably fit near the end of the chronological order of major copper types (Steinbring 1975).

Common Names Ace of Spades, Expanding Flat Tangs, Pommel Tangs

Above, classic form, found in Winnebago County Wisconsin and measuring 3 7/8" in length. This exceptional piece is larger than the average Ace of Spades, but it has identical attributes. These larger examples, though differenciated by some, are here considered as a single type because of their assumed contemperaneous nature. *Courtesy the G. Weimer Collection.*

Right, 1 1/4" Ace of Spades from Koochiching County Minnesota. *D. Johnson Collection*. These small and well formed examples like this were almost certainly atlatl points.

Left, classic 2" Ace of Spades from Koochiching County Minnesota. *Courtesy of the D. Johnson Collection.*

Left, nice little example from Ontario, Canada. *O. Anttila Collection.*

Right, 2 1/2" example from Marathon County Wisconsin. *D. Miller Collection.*

Left, 2 1/8" example from Winnebago County Wisconsin. Wether the single basal tang was intentional or the result of a material flaw that caused the opposite side to break off is unknown, but it is most likely the latter of the two that caused this unusual piece. *G. Weimer Collection.*

Right, nice 2 3/4" Ace of Spades with beveling still visible. Found in Koochiching County Minnesota. *D. Johnson Collection.*

Above, 2 13/16" Ace of Spades from Winnebago County Wisconsin. Beveling is still clearly visible alogn blade edges, neat example. *G. Weimer Collection.*

Left, Ace of Spades measuring 3" in length, found in Winnebago County Wisconsin. Strong, wide beveling clearly visible. *Courtesy of the Lee Born Collection.*

Right, 3 1/2" example from Vilas County Wisconsin. *D. Johnson Collection.*

Left, 3 1/4" Ace of Spades from Keweenaw County Michigan. *D. Johnson Collection.*

3 1/8" Right, Ace of Spades, beveling is obvious as it is on most examples of this type. Found in Winnebago County Wisconsin. *G. Weimer Collection.*

Left, a classic Ace of Spades example from Wisconsin. *Courtesy of the Milwaukee Public Museum.*

Left and Below, both are classic forms of the Ace of Spades type porjectile point. Both of these examples, as most, are close to three inches in length. Both were found in Wisconsin but precise county was unknown. *Courtesy of the Milwaukee Public Museum.*

Left, 2 1/2" example from Marathon County Wisconsin. *D. Miller Collection.*

Below, unusual 3 3/4" example from Jefferson County Wisconsin, it has been punch marked on both faces. *Courtesy of the Milwaukee Public Museum*

Above, nice 2 1/2" Ace of Spades. *D. Johnson Collection.*

Left, 4 1/4" example from Washington County Wisconsin. *Courtesy of the Milwaukee Public Museum*

Left, 4 1/2" example from Menominee County Michigan. A portion of the tip is missing from previous research, *Courtesy of the Chicago Field Museum.*

Above, 6 1/8" example with a strong median ridge, Adams County Wisconsin. *J. Bussey Collection.* This particular example appears to be more of an anomoly than a typical point for this type. Most examples are not ridged nor do most examples have tangs as thick as this example. Could represent a different type or be a unique item. This category seemed most fitting for the time being however.

Below, 4 7/8" example from Dane County Wisconsin. *Courtesy of the Logan Museum of Anthropology.*

I,G-4
Pommel Tangs

Discussion The difference between Pommel Tangs and some Ace of Spades isn't all that clear. Pommel Tangs might be more of a regional variant than truly different type but more examples, along with distribution patterns, would need to be looked at in greater detail to determine. Regardless of placement or the appropriateness of this type it is rare by any standard and it is undboutedly very closely related to the other types in this group.

Left, Pommel Tang from Ontario, Canada. *Courtesy of the T. Wilson Collection.*

Left, 3 3/4" example of a Pommel Tang. Koochiching County Minnesota. *D. Johnson Collection.*

Left, 2 1/2" Ace of Spades or Pommel Tang? All of the types in this group are closely realted that attributes appear to overlap at times. Koochiching County Minnesota. *Courtesy of the D. Johnson Collection.*

I,G-5
Socketed Beveled Points

Discussion Socketed Beveled Points are similar to other members of the I,G family. These were mistankenly included with the Ovate family of points by Wittry. They however have far more in common with the I,G family than the former including beveled edges, blade shape, size, and possibly even distribution. These might represent a transitional type between Straight Flat Tangs and other socketed types.

Common Names Bifacially Beveled Ovates, Beveled Ovates, Socketed Beveled Points, Beveled Sockets.

Below, 4 5/8" Socketed Beveled Point from Wisconsin. Provenience unknown. *Courtesy of the Milwaukee Public Museum*

Left and right, the obverse and reverse of a Socketed Beveled Point. Found in Winnibago County Wisconsin and measuring 7 1/16" in length. *Courtesy of the Milwaukee Public Museum.*

Above, 4 1/2" example from Ontario, Canada. *D. Johnson Collection.*

I,H-1 and I,H-2
Northern Style Points
Shouldered and Unshouldered

Discussion Northern Style Points, both shouldered and unshouldered are quite distinctive. They also have a more restricted distribution pattern than many other types. The I,H-1 Shouldered Northern Style Points are found in areas from north eastern Minnesota and the U.P. of Michigan and north while the Unshouldered variety is found a little further south into Wisconsin. The larger shouldered types are frequently very well made. Sockets on Shouldered types are set back a ways from the blade while the Unshouldered Northern Points have a socket closer to the blade. Some of the Unshouldered types have median ridges and some do not.

Left, 3 1/2" A Shouldered Northern Style Point from Koochiching County Minnesota. *D. Johnson Collection.*

Above, 5 3/4" a Shouldered Northern Style Point also from Koochiching County Minnesota. This is probably the single finest example the author encountered while researching the book. Note the incurvate blade edges, diamond shaped blade, holed socket, and the socket is set back some distance from the widest portion of the blade. *D. Johnson Collection.*

Above, very large 8" example from Pine County Minnesota. *D. Johnson Collection.* Left, 4" Unshouldered Northern Style Point from Oneida County Wisconsin. *D. Miller Collection.*

Right, four more examples of Unshouldered Northern Style Points. These are a fairly rare type. While they do not show up well in these pictures, all four examples have easy to see median ridges on their ventral sides (top picture) and very weak or no ridge on the dorsal side. From left to right the first three were all found in Vilas County Wisconsin while the example at the far right was found in Oneida County Wisconsin. *D. Miller Collection.*

Left, 5 3/4" Shouldered Northern Point from Cass County Minnesota. *Private Collection.*

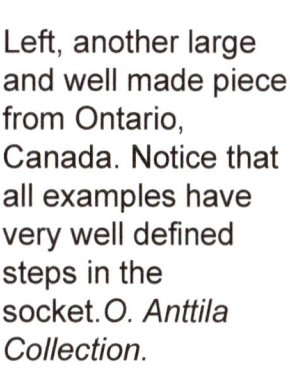

Left, two nice examples from Ontario, Canada. *Courtesy of the O. Anttila Collection.* Below, an unusually large and well made example, also from Ontario, Canada. *Courtesy of the O. Anttila Collection.*

Left, another large and well made piece from Ontario, Canada. Notice that all examples have very well defined steps in the socket. *O. Anttila Collection.*

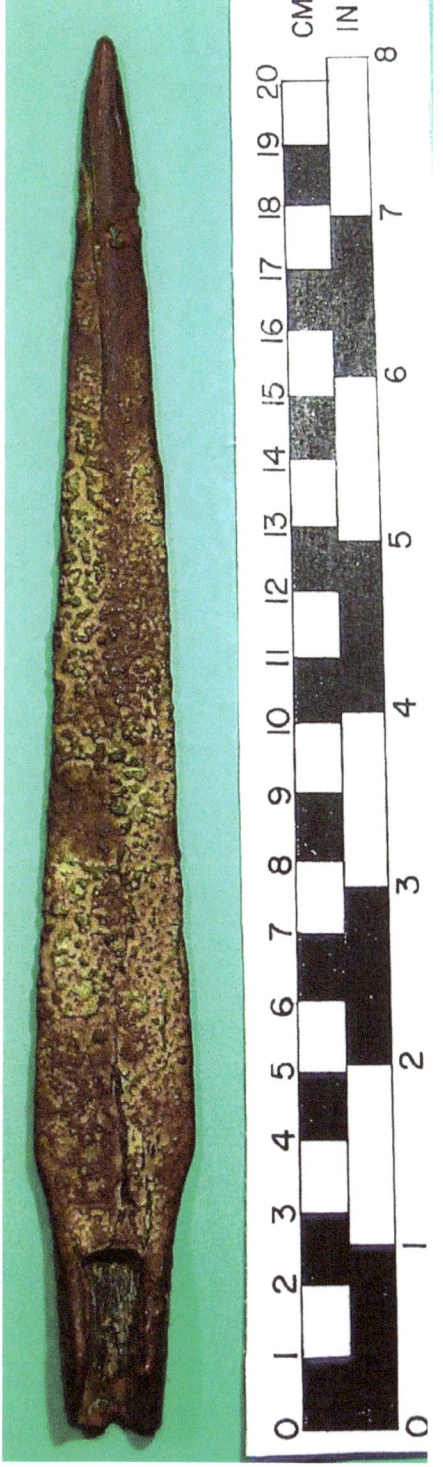

I,L-1
Triangulate Conicals

Discussion Wittry, Steinbring, Flaskard, and others have all included conical points in some form in their typeology discussions but none have thus far made any attempt to disect this diverse group in detail. Conicals as a whole represent the single most common group of copper projectiles. Their distribution covers the entire Western Great Lakes Region and beyond. Any large sampling of conicals immediately uncovers some general trends. Many conicals mimic other point types, ovates and triangulates in particular. Triangulate conicals have angular sockets, dorsal median ridges, and socket tabs like thier full sized socketed cousins.
<u>**Common Names**</u> Conicals, Triangulate Conicals.

Left, 2 3/4" Triangulate Conical from Vilas County Wisconsin. *D. Miller Collection.*

Right, 2 5/8" example from Vilas County Wisconsin. *D. Miller Collection.*

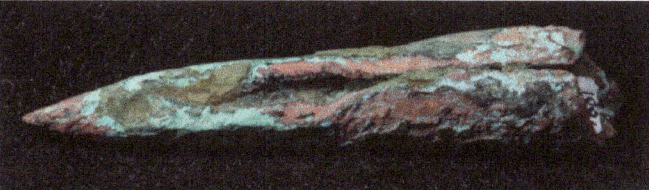

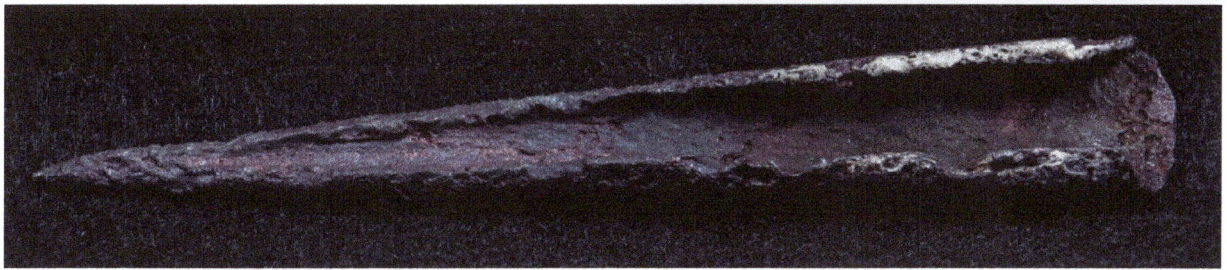

Above, large 5 3/16" Triangulate Conical from Winnebago County Wisconsin. *Private Collection.*

Left, 1 3/4" example from Mararthon County Wisconsin. *D. Miller Collection.* Below, 1 7/8" from Lee County Illinois. *D. Miller Collection.*

Below, very well made 2 3/4" Triangulate Conical from Marquette County Wisconsin. *Private Collection.*

Left, 2 3/4" example from Vilas County Wisconsin. *D. Miller Collection.*

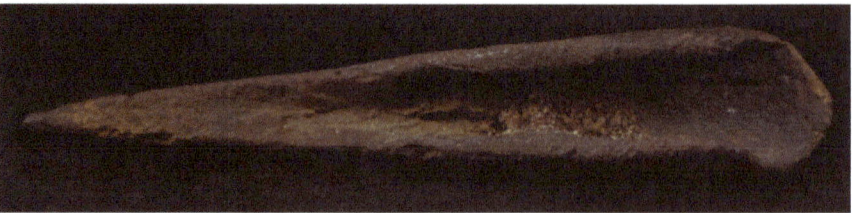

Right, 3" example from Winnebago County Wisconsin. *G. Weimer Collection.*

Left, 3 3/8" Triangulate Conical from Columbia County Wisconsin. *B. Wasemiller Collection.*

Left, 4 1/2" Triangulate Conical from Lincoln County Wisconsin. *D. Johnson Collection.*

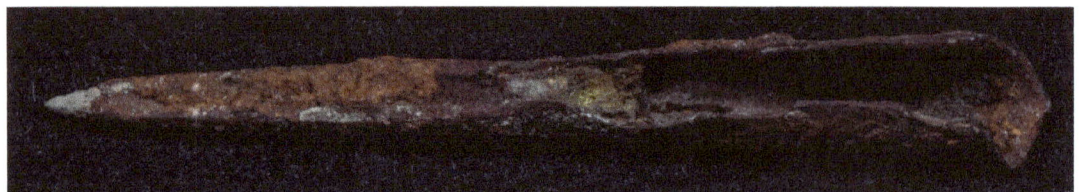

Above, 4 1/4" example from Winnebago County Wisconsin. *Private Collection.*

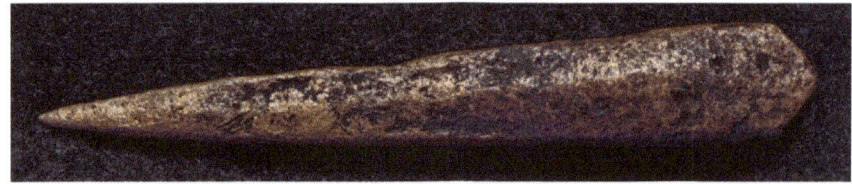

Left, 3 3/4" Triangulate Conical from Vilas County Wisconsin. *D. Miller Collection.*

Left, 2 7/8" Triangulate Conical from Vilas County Wisconsin. *N. Schanen Collection.* Below, 4" Triangulate Conical from Marathon County Wisconsin. *Courtesy of the D. Miller Collection.*

I,L-2
Ovate Conicals

Discussion Ovate Conicals represent not only the most common type of conical point, but also one of the most common types of copper artifact. They are surpassed in numbers by only awls. The type as a whole has tremendous variation from the very crude to the very fine and from tiny to large and heavy. They all appear to have been made in similar fashion, and perhaps by the same people as the Ovate family of points. Ovate Conicals typically have a socket that leads to a flat, rectangular projection which ends in a point. Examples of Ovate Conicals in which this trait is short or missing may in some cases be indicitive of use-wear. These should not be confused with the post contact tinkler cones that are most often made from kettle brass. Many examples are shown larger than actual size to show details better.

Common Names Conical, Common Conical

Left, 1 1/2" Ovate Conical from Houghton County Michigan. *D. Johnson Collection.*

Right, 1 1/8" Ovate Conical fromf Vilas County Wisconsin. *Private Collection.*

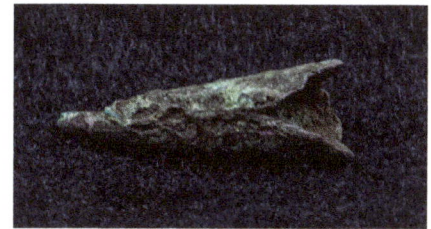

Below, 1 3/4" example from Koochiching County Minnesota. *D. Johnson Collection.*

Left, 1 3/4" example from Lincoln County Wisconsin. *Private Collection.* Above, 1 3/4" example from Oneida County Wisconsin. *D. Johnson Collection.*

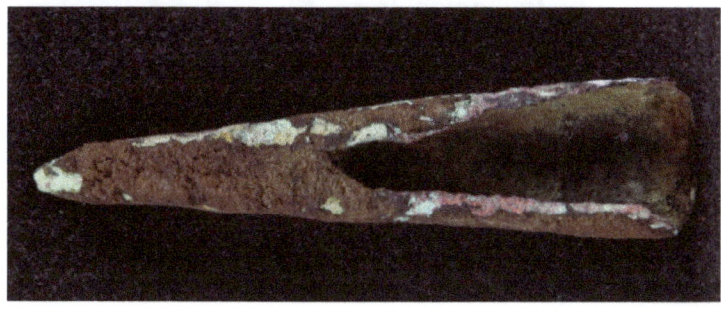

Left, a nice 3" example from Vilas County Wisconsin. *N. Miller Collection.*

Left, 2 1/2" Ovate Conical from Winnebago County Wisconsin. *Courtesy of the M. Sainz and the Little Eagle Arts Foundation of Wisconsin Dells.*

Below, 1 5/8" Ovate Conical from Crow Wing County Minnesota. *L. Manthison Collection.*

Left, 1 3/4" example from Vilas County Wisconsin. *Private Collection.* Right, 1 3/4" Ovate Conical from Vilas Co Wisconsin. *Private Collection.*

Right, 1 3/4" example from Vilas County Wisconsin. *D. Miller Collection.*

Left, 1 5/8" Ovate Conical from Marathon County Wisconsin. *D. Miller Collection.*

Right, 1 7/8" example from Oneida County Wisconsin. *D. Miller Collection.*

Above, 1 15/16" Ovate Conical from Vilas County Wisconsin. *D. Miller Collection.*

Left, 2" example from Lincoln County Wisconsin. *D. Johnson Collection.*

Left, a nice 2" example from Oneida County Wisconsin. *D. Johnson Collection.*

Right, 2" Ovate Conical from Ontario, Canada. *Private Collection.*

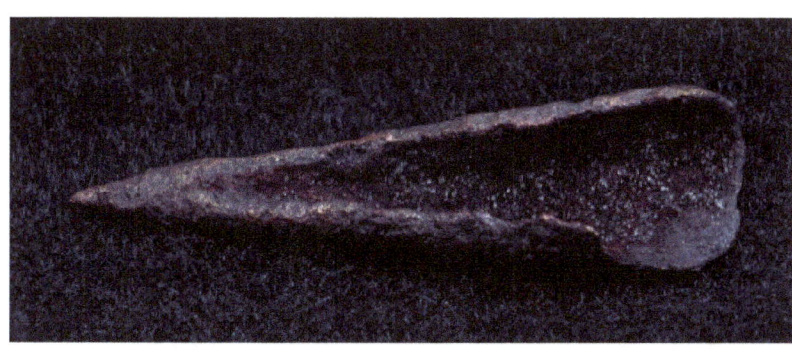

Left, 2" example from Winnebago County Wisconsin. *Private Collection.*

Right, 2 1/2" holed example from Marathon County Wisconsin. *D. Miller Collection.*

Left, 2 1/2" Ovate Conical from Oneida County Wisconsin. *D. Johnson Collection.*

Right, 2 1/2" example with a slight hint of a tail, Vilas County Wisconsin. *D. Miller Collection.*

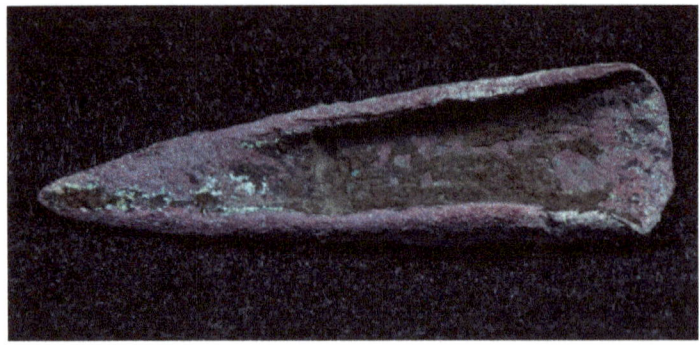

Left, 2 1/2" Ovate Conical from Vilas County Wisconsin with a slight step formed in the socket, this is fairly unusual. *Private Collection.*

Right, 2 1/4" Ovate Conical point from Mackinac County Michigan. *D. Johnson Collection.*

Left, 2 1/4" Ovate Conical from Iowa County Wisconsin. *D. Johnson Collection.*

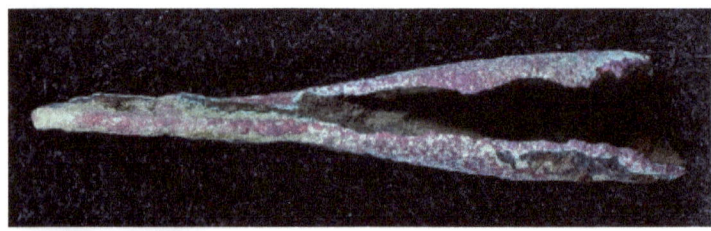

Right, 2 1/4" Ovate Conical from Vilas County Wisconsin. *Private Collection.*

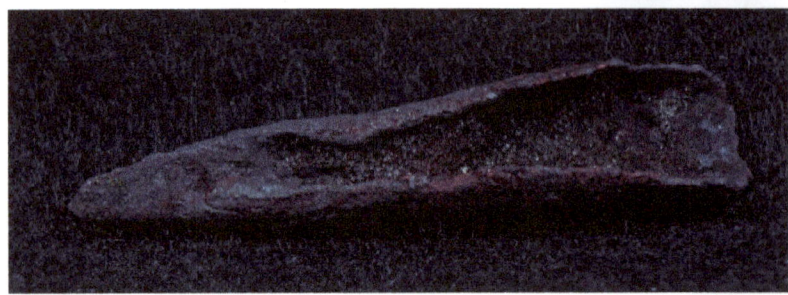

Left, 2 1/4" example from Winnebago County Wisconsin. *Private Collection.*

Right, 2 1/8" Ovate Conical from Gogebic County Michigan. *D. Miller Collection.*

Left, 2 1/8" example from Oneida County Wisconsin. *D. Miller Collection.*

Left, ventral and profile view of a 2 3/4" Ovate Conical with an offset socket and the remains of a ruptured rivet hole in the socket, both attributes are also frequently found with Common Ovates. It's possible that this piece may have once been part of a larger Common Ovate piece that broke and was salvaged. Found in Vilas County Wisconsin. *Courtesy of the D. Miller Collection.*

Right, 2 3/8" example from Green Lake County Wisconsin. *Private Collection.*

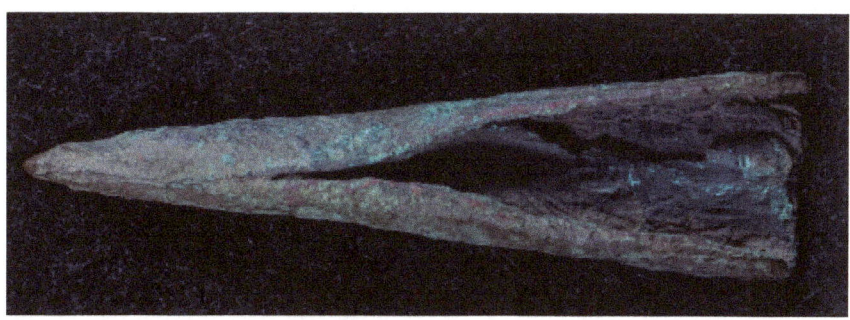

Left, 2 5/8" example from Vilas County Wisconsin. *Private Collection.*

Right, 2 5/8" example from Vilas County Wisconsin. *D. Miller Collection.*

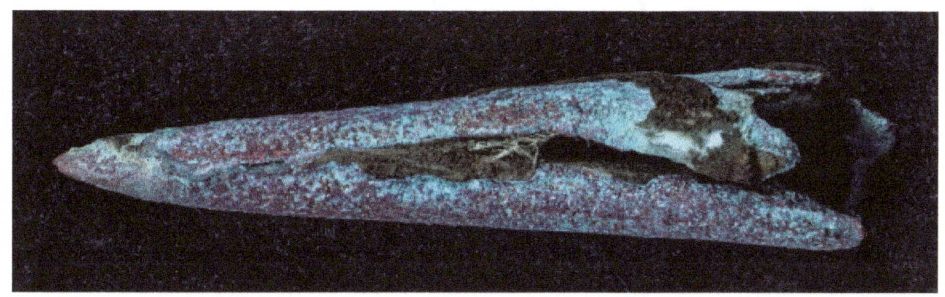

Left, 2 7/8" Ovate Conical from Vilas County Wisconsin. *Private Collection.*

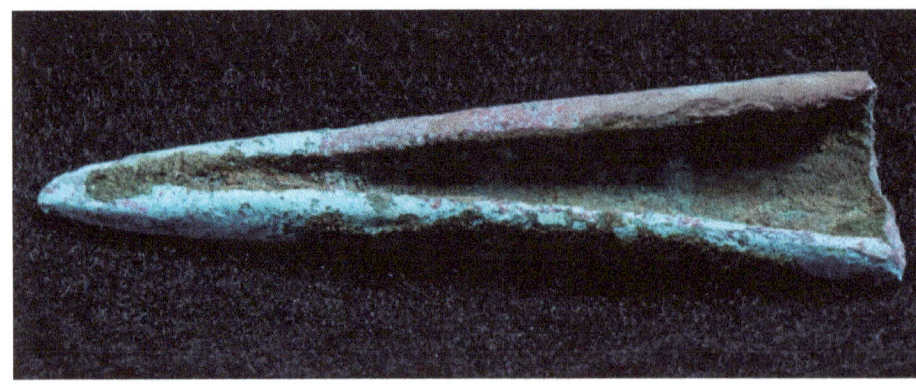

Left, 2 13/16" example from Vilas County Wisconsin. *Private Collection.*

Right, 2 15/16" holed example from Winnebago County Wisconsin. *G. Weimer Collection.*

Left, 3" examplel from Lincoln County Wisconsin. *D. Johnson Collection.*

Right, 3" holed conical from Mackinac County Michigan. *D. Johnson Collection.*

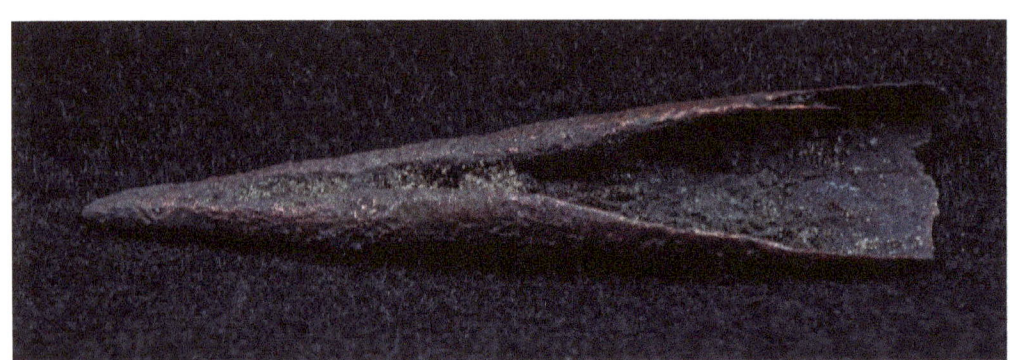

Left, 3" example from Winnebago County Wisconsin. *Private Collection.*

Left, 3" example from Lincoln County Wisconsin that has been enlarged to show preserved wood within the socket. *D. Johnson Collection.*

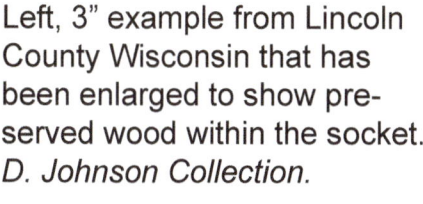

Right, 3 1/2" Ovate Conical from Koochiching County Minnesota. *D. Johnson Collection.*

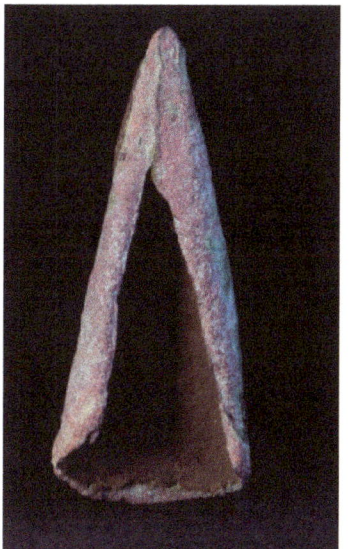

Left, 1 3/4" Ovate Conical from Vilas County Wisconsin. *Courtesy of the N. Schanen collection.*

Below, 3 1/4" example from Lincoln County Wisconsin. *D. Johnson Collection.*

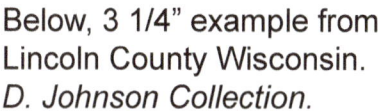

Right, 3 1/8" Ovate Conical from Winnebago County Wisconsin. *G. Weimer Collection.*

Above, 4" Ovate Conical from Vilas County Wisconsin. *Private Collection.*

Above, 5 1/4" holed example from Dane County Wisconsin. *Courtesy of the L. Born Collection.*

Above, 4 5/16" heavy duty example from Winnebago County Wisconsin. *Private Collection.*

Below, 6 1/4" example from Ontario, Canada. *Private Collection.*

Left, 3 1/2" example from Vilas County Wisconsin, Below, 3 1/4" Ovate Conical, also from Vilas County Wisconsin. *Both courtesy of the N. Schanen Collection.*

Left, a large 6" example. *N. Schanen Collection.*

Below, 5" Ovate Conical from Green Lake County Wisconsin. *Courtesy of the J. Ruth Collection.*

Right, 1 3/4" example from Oneida County Wisconsin. *Courtesy of the D. Johnson Collection.*

Left, 2" Ovate Conical from Vilas County Wisconsin. *Courtesy of the D. Miller Collection.*

I,L-3a
Holed Conicals

Discussion This type, prior to consultation with Ron Mullins, a leading expert in all things related to spear fishing, had been labeled "Toggeling Conicals". The smallest examples would simply not work as toggel heads according to Mr. Mullins and some of the larger tailed examples *might* have worked as such but we are far from certain. Calling them Holed Conicals leaves this mystery open for future research and classification. The holes may have been made simply to attach the point to the shaft rather than for line attachment. More than likely they represent both types that were nailed to the shaft *and* small toggeling harpoons. More research is needed on this interesting type.

Common Names Holed Conicals, Toggle Heads, Toggling Conicals

Right, the largest piece is 2 7/8" in length, both of these were found within ten feet of each other in Menominee County Michigan. Note the constriction around the mid point with the hole, these might just as easily be called Pinch Points. *S. Wasion Collection*

Left, 3 11/16" Holed Conical from Vilas County Wisconsin. *Private Collection.*

Left, 2 1/2" Holed Conical from Rock County Wisconsin. *D. Johnson Collection.*

Left, 1 1/4" example from Manitowoc County Wisconsin. *T. Betka Collecton.* Right, 1 3/8" example from Vilas County Wisconisn. *D. Miller Collection.*

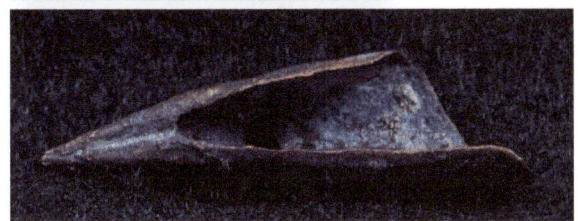

Left, 1 5/8" Holed Conical from Winnebago County Wisconsin. *Private Collection.*

Page 119

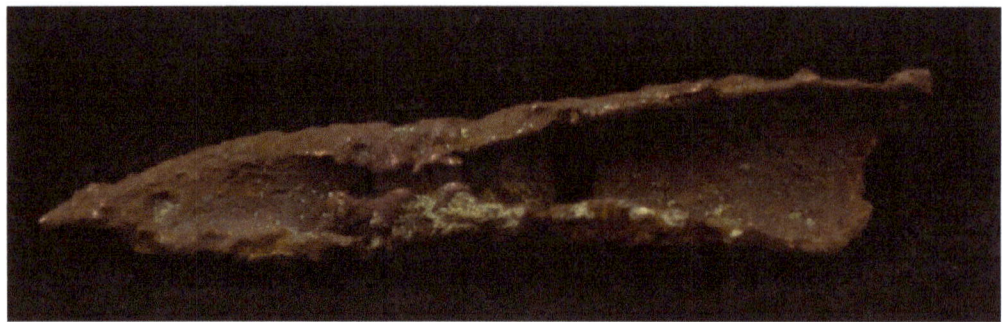

Above, 2 5/8" Holed Conical point from Winnebago County Wisconsin. *G. Weimer Collection.*

Right, 1 15/16" Holed Conical that was found in Winnebago County Wisconsin. *G. Weimer Collection.*

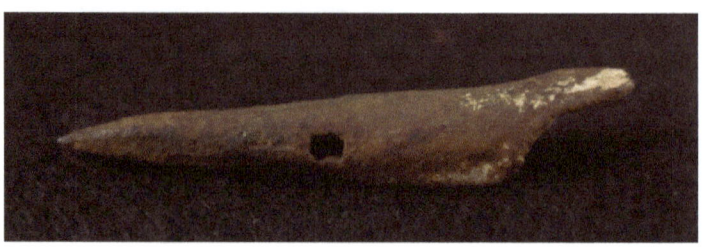

Left, a fine 2" example from Koochiching County Minnesota. *D. Johnson Collection.*

Left, 2 1/4" example from Dickinson County Michigan. *D. Johnson Collection.*

Left, 2 1/4" Holed Conical from Winnebago County Wisconsin. *G. Weimer Collection.*

Left, 2 1/16" example from Winnebago County Wisconsin. *Courtesy of the M. Sainz Collection and the Little Eagle Arts Foundation of Wisconsin Dells.*

Left, 2 1/4" example from Mackinac County Michigan. Unusual because it is double holed. *Courtesy of the D. Johnson Collection.*

I,L-3b
Pinch Points

Discussion Steinbring suggested that these points were evidence for twin copper tool production, that is, that a single copper piece was manufactured with a tip at either end and then by cutting in the middle two identical copper points might be made (Steinbring pg 95). Martin points out that material evidence is lacking (Martin pg 131) to support this hypothesis. I have come to the conclusion that these are a toggling style harpoons with a line that was secured around the indented middle section of the point, making the lower end a tail rather than a duplicate point. That tail would've facilitated the toggling motion inside the prey. Such points might have been effective with small aquatic species only.

Common Names Pinch Points, Toggle Heads

The example at left is 1 3/4" in length and from Keweenaw County Michigan. *D. Johnson Collection.*

Right, 1 7/8" Pinch Point from Marathon County Wisconsin. Most examples of this type have a well defined, pointed, tail and an open face. *D. Miller Collection.*

Left, a 2 1/8" example from Marathon County Wiscons. *D. Miller Collection.*

Below, Pinch Point from Winnebago County Wisconsin. *G. Weimer Collection.*

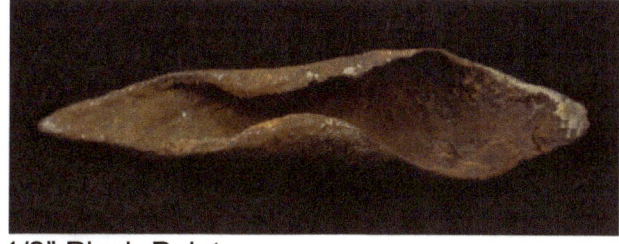

Left, 2 1/2" Pinch Point from Winnebago County Wisconsin. *G. Weimer Collection.*

Right, 2 1/2" example from Mackinac County Michigan. *D. Johnson Collection.*

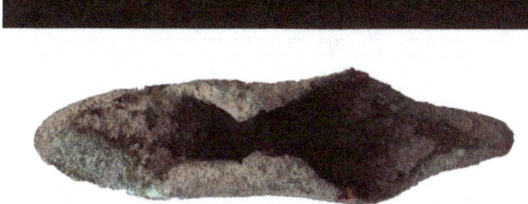

Left, two classic Pinch Points, both measure 2" in length and both were found in Mackinac County Michigan. *Courtesy of the D. Johnson Collection.*

Page 121

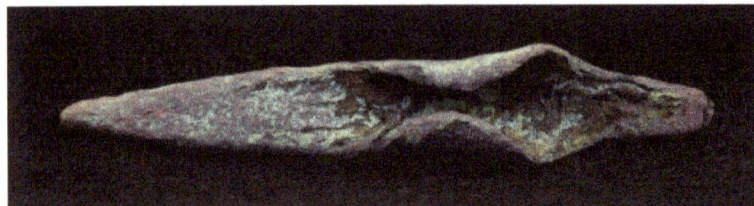

Left, 2 3/4" Pinch Point with classic form, unknown provenience. *J. Bussey Collection*. Below, 2 3/4" Pinch Point from Winnebago County Wisconsin. *Private Collection*.

Below, 3 1/2" example from Mackinac County Michigan. *D. Johnson Collection*.

Below, 3 1/4" Pinch Point from Winnebago County Wisconsin. *Private Colleciton*.

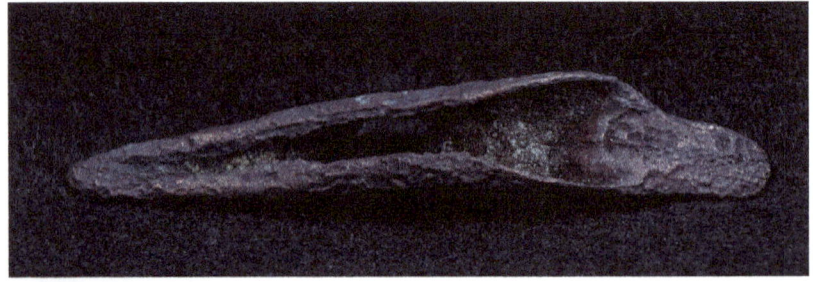

Below, 3 1/8" example from Vilas County Wisconsin. *D. Miller Collection*.

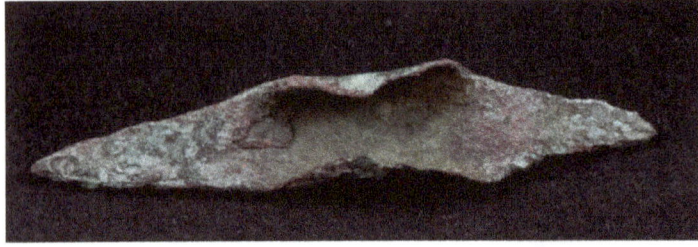

Below, 3 5/8" Pinch Point from Winnebago County Wisconsin. *G. Weimer Collection*.

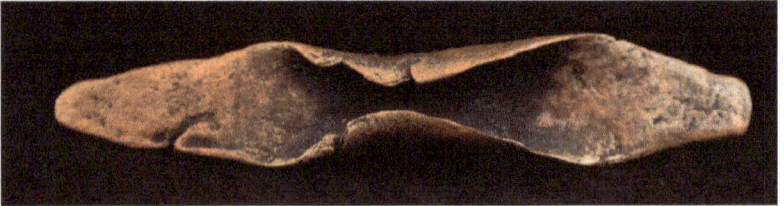

Left, 2 7/8" Pinch Point from Keweenaw County Michigan. *D. Miller Collection*.

I,L-3c
Minnesota Style Harpoon

Discussion The Minnesota Style Harpoons are lumped in here with Holed Conicals and Pinch Points because of their similarity of function. This type of harpoon, as one may have guessed by the name, is found in the highest concentrations in north eastern Minnesota. Other examples have also been found into the U.P. of Michigan as well as Ontario but the type is all but absent from the Wisconsin heartland. These harpoons usually have small beveled blades, tails on the socket, and square holes.

Common Names Minnesota Harpoons, Toggeling Harpoons

Above, classic Minnesota Style Harpoon. This particular example is 3" in length and from Koochiching County Minnesota. It is exceptionally well made and well preserved, note the clearly visible bevels on the blade. Below, another classic Minnesota Style Harpoon, it is 2 1/2" and from Koochiching County, both examples are tailed and have square holes around the midpoint of the blade. *Both are courtesy of the D. Johnson Collection.*

Right, another absolutely classic Minnesota Style Harpoon measuring 2 3/4" from Koochiching County Minnesota. *D. Johnson Collection.*

Left, 2 3/4" example from Mackinac County Michigan. *D. Johnson Collection.*

Left, 3 3/4" Minnesota Style Harpoon from Mackinac County Michigan. *D. Johnson Collection.*

Above, 3" classic example from Koochiching County Minnesota. *D. Johnson Collection.*

Above, 3 1/4" double holed example from Koochiching County Minnesota. *D. Johnson Collection.*

Above, 3 1/4" example from Koochiching County Minnesota. *D. Johnson Collection.* Below, a large but crude example, 3 3/4" in length, Koochiching County Minnesota. *D. Johnson Collection.*

Above, 4 3/8" Harpoon that doesn't match the classic form of a Minnesota Style, but doesn't quite match anything else either. I would be more comfortable leaving it in this category if it were holed but it is not. The long tails are indicitive of a point you would think was used to toggle but without a positive point to attach a line we can't say. I belive the constriction near the blade/socket junction would be sufficient to attach a line for toggling. Without evidence to dissuade me to the contrary it will remain here although arguements for a modified Common Ovate easily be made as well. Lincoln County Wisconsin. *D. Miller Collection.*

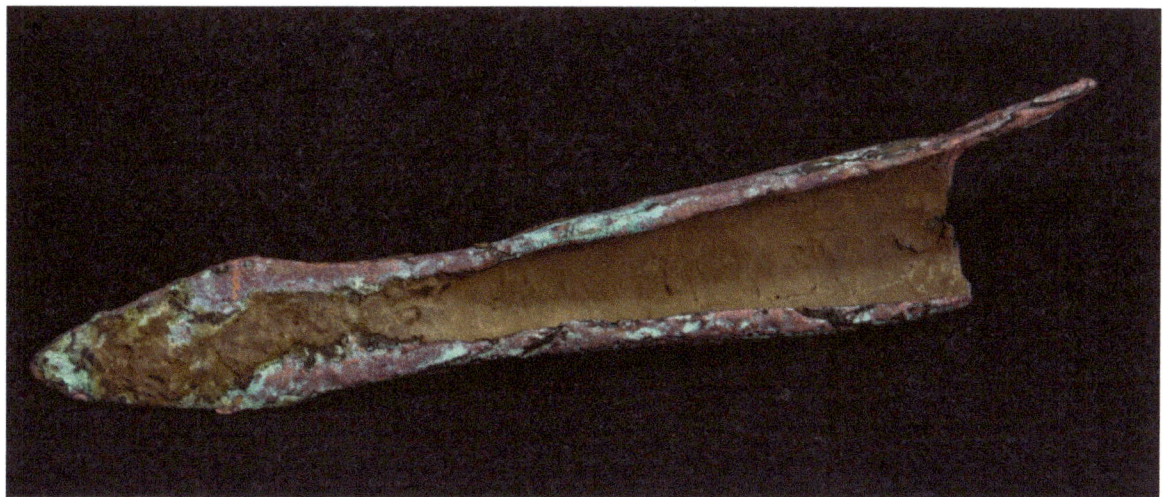

Above, 5 1/2" Minnesota Style Harpoon point minus the typical mid point hole for toggeling. The hole could be corroded shut or the line may have been attached around the constriction behind the blade. It's also possible, though unlikely, that it represents an unfinished piece. *D. Miller Collection.*

Below, 5 1/8" example from Vilas County Wisconsin, this particular example has a bifacially beveled blade and again, lacks a toggel line hole. Given that the constriction at the blade socket junction is near the center point it's assumed that this was where a line may have attached or, perhaps, it was not a toggeling type at all and used only as a harpoon. *D. Miller Collection,*

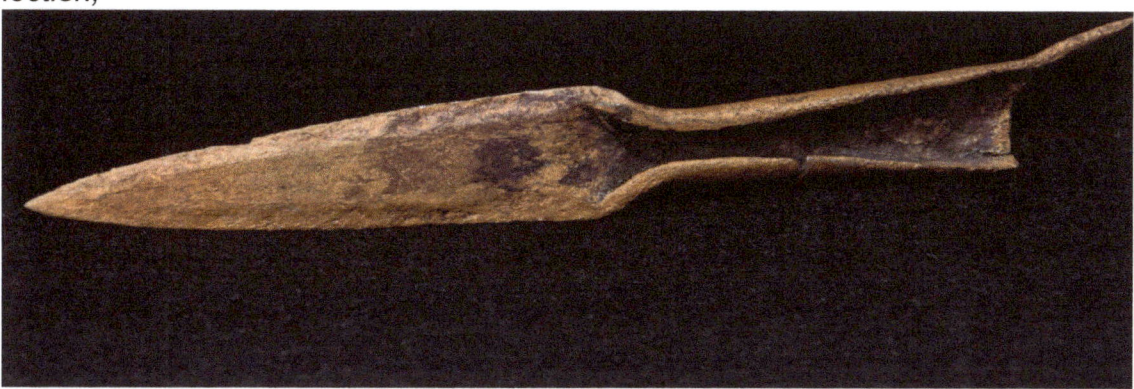

I,M
Stick Harpoons

Discussion Single barbed Stick Harpoons are by far the most common type of stick harpoon, their construction is simple and consists of a single flat bar or round shaped shaft that is pointed on one or both ends and has a single projection or barb. These were not noted as being common by Steinbring and not discussed in any length by Wittry, but this has proven to be a fairly common type. Only rarely do they show any obvious signs of line attachment by means of a groove around the shaft or a flatened hump that could stop the line from sliding off. They range in size considerably and appear to have been used to harpoon game of all sizes. Multi-barbed examples are much more rare and differ only in the number of barbs. Bone and antler examples of these multi-barbed harpoons are also known (Ritzenthaler, 1953)

Common Names Stick Harpoons

Left, 3" example from Door County Wisconsin. *Courtesy of the Milwaukee Public Museum.*

Right, 4 5/8" multi-barbed Stick Harpoon from Vilas County Wisconsin. *D. Miller Collection.*

Left, 1 5/8" Stick Harpoon from Vilas County Wisconsin. *D. Miller Collection*

Right, 2" example from Keweenaw County Michigan. *D. Johnson Collection.* Below, 2" stick harpoon from Vilas County Wisconsin. *D. Johnson Collection.*

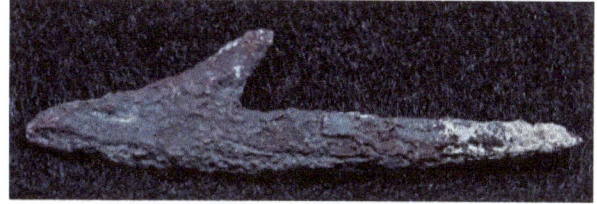

Above, 2" example found in Winnebago County Wisconsin. *Private Collection.*

Above, 2" Stick Harpoon from Winnebago County Wisconsin. *G. Weimer Collection.*

Right, 2 1/2" Stick Harpoon from Ontario, Canada. *D. Johnson Collection.*

Above, 2 1/2" example from Keweenaw County Michigan. *D. Miller Collection.* Below, 2 1/2" example from Lincoln County Wisconsin. *G. Weimer Collection.*

Left, 2 3/4" Stick Harpoon from Mackinac County Michigan. *D. Johnson Collection.*

Left, 2 1/4" example from Vilas County Wisconsin. *D. Miller Collection.*

Left, 2 3/4" example from Oneida County Wisconsin. *D. Johnson Collection.*

Left, 3" Stick Harpoon from Delta County Michigan. *D. Johnson Collection.*

Left, 3" example from Vilas County Wisconsin. *Private Collection.*

Left, 3" example from Washburn County Wisconsin. *D. Johnson Collection.*

Left, 3 3/8" example from Ontario, Canada. *Private Collection.*

Left, 3 1/4" Stick Harpoon from Oneida County Wisconsin. *D. Johnson Collection.*

Left, 3 3/4" Stick Harpoon from Vilas County Wisconsin. *D. Miller Collection.*

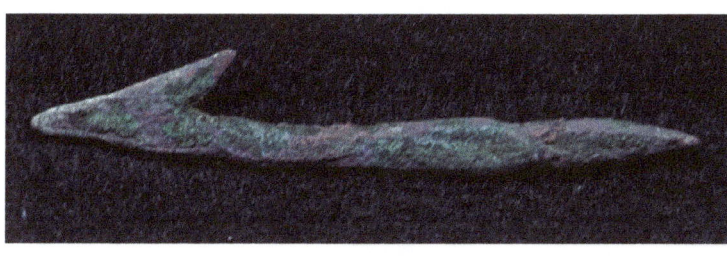

Left, 3 1/16" Stick Harpoon from Vilas County Wisconsin. *Private Collection.*

Left, unusual 4" harpoon with a socket, while not unique, it is a rare variety. This example was found in Ontario, Canada. *Private Collection.*

Left, 4" example from Rock County Wisconsin. *D. Johnson Collection.*

Above, 4 1/2" Stick Harpoon with flat spot that aided with line attachment. Mackinac County Michigan. *D. Johnson Collection.*

Above, heavy duty 5" Stick Harpoon with round form from Vilas County Wisconsin. *B. Wasemiller Collection.* Below, Canadian example with preserved cordage, This is an exceptional artifact. *O. Anttila Collection.*

Above, heavy 5" Stick Harpoon, round form, Vilas County Wisconsin. *Private Collection.*

Above, 5 1/4" Stick Harpoon from Koochiching County Minnesota. *D. Johnson Collection.* Below, massive 11" Stick Harpoon. Unknown provenience. *J. Bussey Collection*

Above, huge 12 1/8" Stick Harpoon from Jeffferson County Wisconsin. *J. Bussey Collection.*

Left, two stick harpoons from Keweenaw County Michigan that have both been modified to facilitate a secure line attachment, longest one is 4" in length. *D. Johnson Collection.*

Right, 3 1/2" Stick Harpoon from Sheboygan County Wisconsin. *Courtesy of the Milwaukee Public Museum*

Left, 2 1/2" multi-barbed Stick Harpoon from Ontario, Canada. Multi-barbed examples are nowhere near as numerous as their single barbed cousins. *D. Johnson Collection.*

Below, 6 1/4" Stick Harpoon from Vilas County Wisconsin. *N. Schanen Collection.*

Left, 4 1/2" example from Menominee County Michigan. *S. Wasion Collection.*

Below, 7 3/8" heavy duty Stick Harpoon, *N. Schanen Collection.*

I,P
Pine Trees

Discussion This category appeared to have a broader definition in Wittry's eyes (1951) and perhaps a bit of a dumping ground in Steinbring's eyes (1975). In this system they are considered a viable independant type which actually has remarkable consistency in both attributes and distribution, being found almost exclusively in upper and lower Michigan. Most examples are medium to large sized, thin, and exceptionally flat. Base form is variable. Bladed edges are sometimes incurvate, presumably from resharpening.

Common Names Pine Trees, Christmas Trees, Flats

Right, 3 3/4" example with well developed worm tracks. Unknown provenience. *J. Bussey Collection.*

Left, 4" example from Newaygo County Michigan. *D. Miller Collection.*

Left, 2 3/4" a classic Pine Tree type point, classic in every respect except where it was found. This particular example was found in Sheboygan County Wisconsin, the vast majority of examples with known provenience are from points further north. *J. Bussey Collection.*

Left, 4 1/4" example thought to be from the U.P. of Michigan but the county is unknown. *J. Bussey Collection.*

Left, 3 7/8" example, unknown provenience. *J. Bussey Collection.*

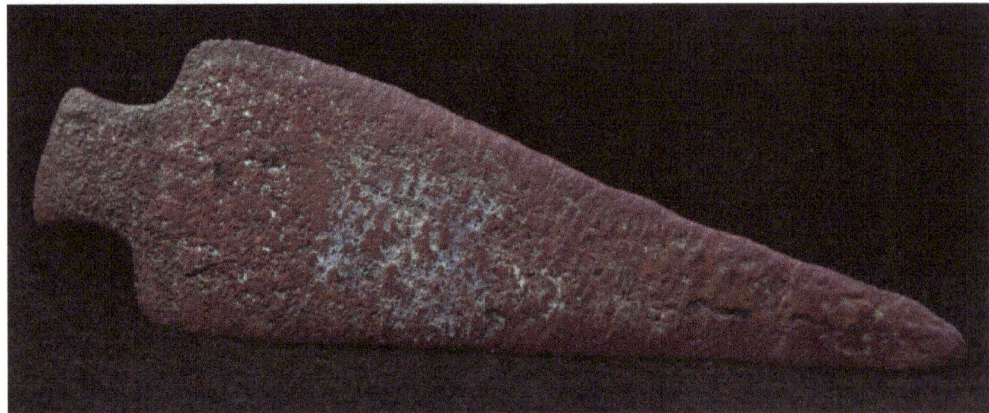

Right, 3 15/16" Pine Tree type point, thought to have been from the U.P. of Michigan but county unknown. *J. Bussey Collection.*

Left, 5 1/4" Pine Tree type from the U.P. of Michigan. *J. Bussey Collection.*

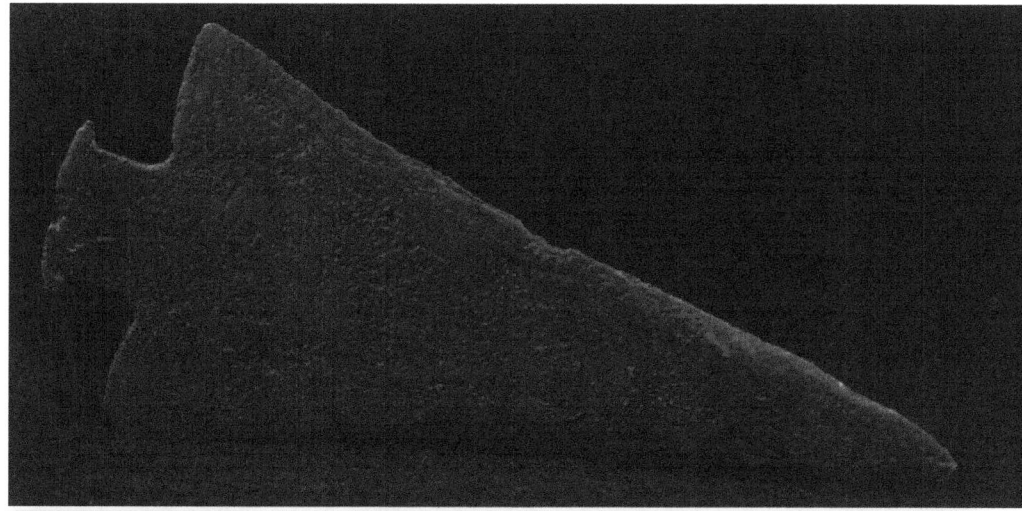

Left, 4 5/8" Pine Tree, unknown provenience. *J. Bussey Collection.*

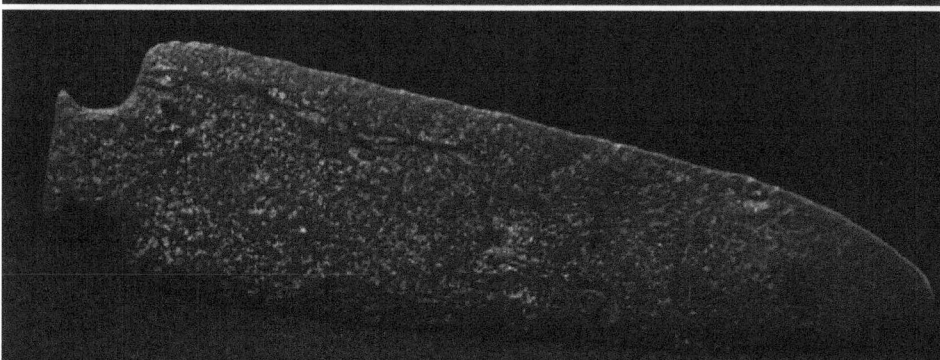

Left, slender 4 9/16" example. Provenience unknown. *J. Bussey Collection.*

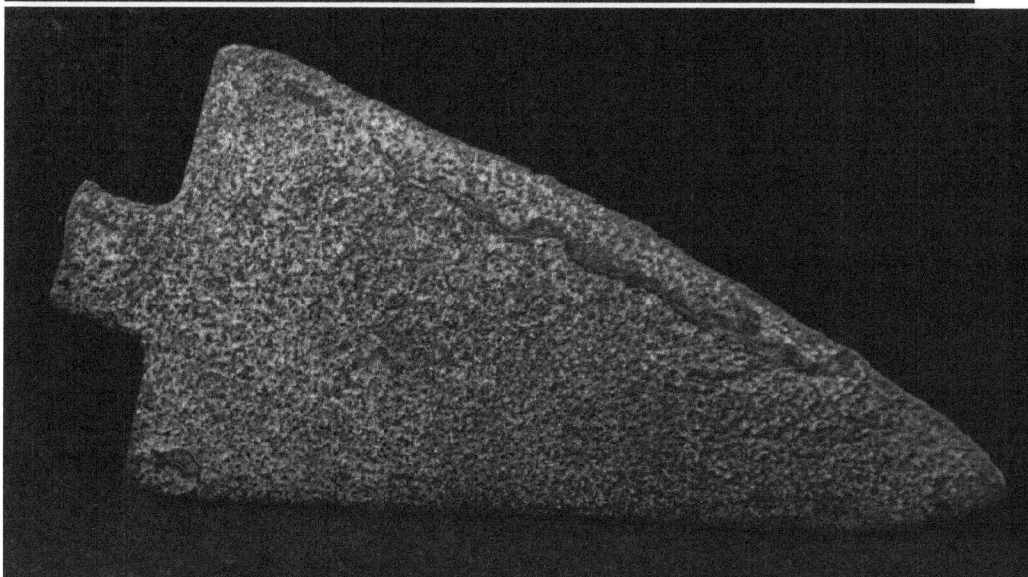

left, 4 9/16" Pine Tree from the U.P. of Michigan, county unknown. *Courtesy of the J. Bussey Collection.*

Below 5 3/4" example from the U.P. *J. Bussey Collection.*

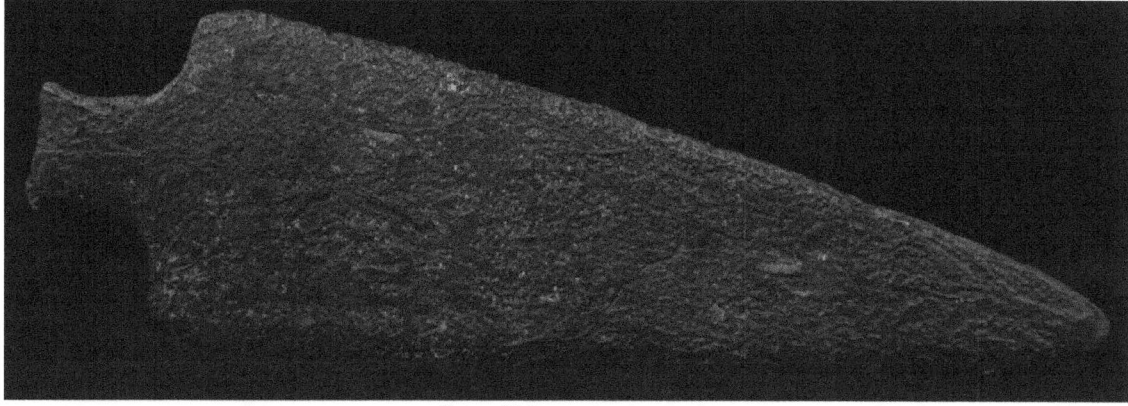

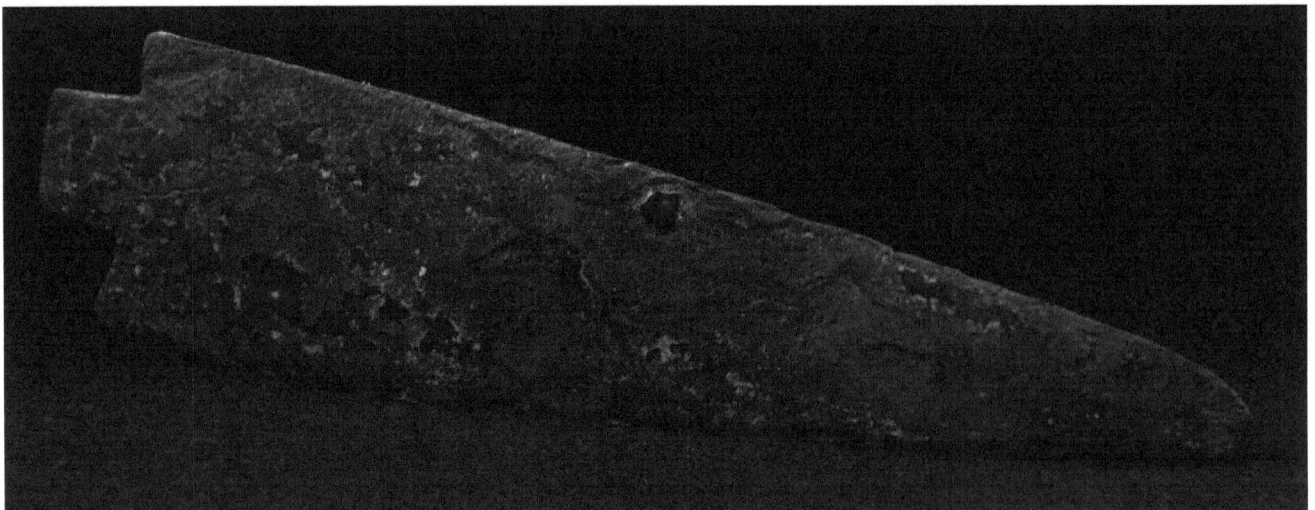

Above, 7" example with an unknown provenience. *J. Bussey Collection.*

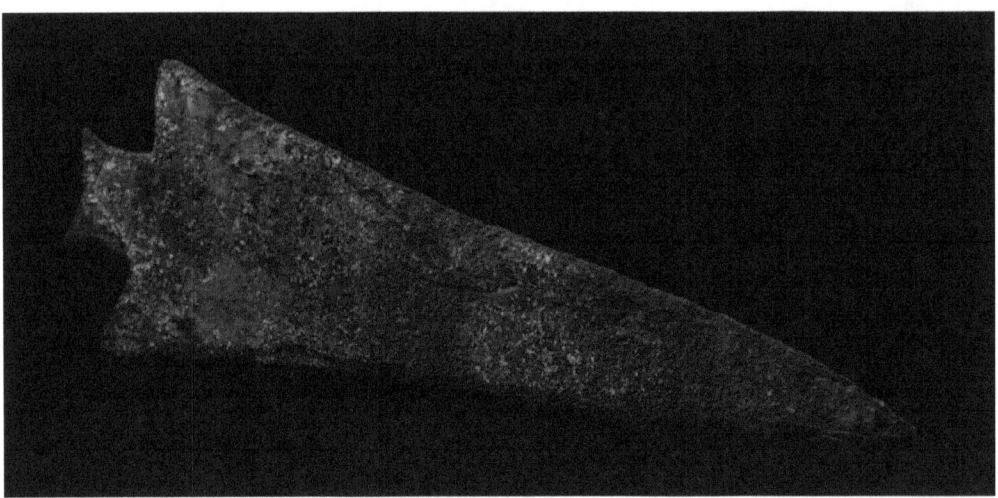

Left, beautiful 6" example from the U.P. of Michigan. *Courtesy of the J. Bussey Collection.*

Below, 5 7/8" example found in Lake County Illinois, it stands out as a southern anomaly amongst a predominantly northern group. *L. Born Collection.*

5" long Pinetree Point from Muskegon County Michigan. *Courtesy of the Chicago Field Museum.*

Below, another fine example, this one from Montcalm County Michigan. *Courtesy of the Chicago Field Museum.*

I,Q
Winged Points

Discussion These three examples have all been found in recent years from a couple of different counties in Northern Wisconsin. All three are fairly thin but have median ridges and "wings" on the base that are folded, one up, and one down. In the largest example directly below one of the wings is missing, having been broken off, but on the other two smaller examples both wings are still there. Al have triangular shaped blades and none have very heavy worm track development. Chisel cutting techniques have been used to make all three examples.

Common names; Winged Points, Butterfly Points

7 1/4" Winged Point from Oneida County Wisconsin. 1 of 3 known examples found in recent years. *L. Born Collection.*

Above, 5" Winged Point from Vilas County Wisconsin. *D. Miller Collection.*

Above and below, both faces of the same Winged Point. *Private Collection*

II
Knife Forms

II,A-1 Straight Back
II,A-2 Curved Back
II,B Banana Knives
II,C Socketed
II,D Footed
II,E Stick
II,F Whiptails

II,A-1
Straight Back Knives

Discussion Straight Backed Knives appear to have been one of the longest used types of copper artifact. Whether or not the same type was reinvented or it enjoyed continuous use is not known for sure but many large, heavy, examples with advanced cororsion and worm track development are almost certainly atrributable to the Archaic and we know that much smaller and often times, better preserved examples, have shown up at later Woodland sites. Straight Backs, as the name implies, have a straight back but some examples may show the slightest hint of curvature. Deliniation between Straight Backs and Curved Backs can be difficult and most likely not important. The overlap between the two may be the result of a gradual shift in style over time or perhaps a case of individual preference. Both types may have been used contemperaneous with one another. Future distributional studies on the Straight Backs and Curved Backs might help shed some light on their relationship with one another. Straight Backs are one of the few types of copper artifacts where we encounter punch marks. Tangs are frequently bent up or down at steep angles to aid in hafting.

Common Names Straight backs, Tanged knives

Above, 6 1/4" Straight Back Knife found in Marathon County Wisconsin. *D. Miller Collection.*

Above, 6 3/4" example from Oneida County Wisconsin with good worm track development. *D. Johnson Collection.* Below, 6 3/4" example from Waushara County Wisconsin that is also punch marked with two staggered parallel lines of dots. *L. Born Collection.*

Left, 2 1/2" Straight Back Knife from Iron County Wisconsin. *D. Johnson Collection.*

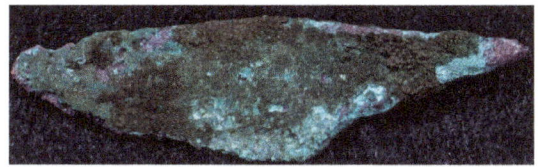

Left, example that measures just 2 1/8" in length from Vilas County Wisconsin. *Private Collection.*

Left, 2 3/4" Straight Back from Keweenaw County Michigan. Tang may have been shortened due to a material flaw. *D. Johnson Collection.*

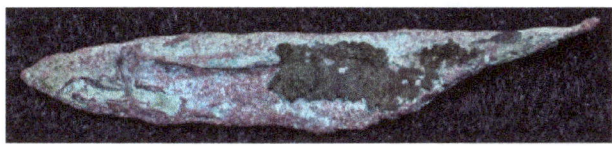

Left, 2 3/8" Straight Back from Vilas County Wisconsin. *Private Collection.*

Left, 3 1/2" example from Rock County Wisconsin. A natural imperfection in the raw material has caused the lamination-looking split in the tang. *D. Johnson Collection.*

Left, 3 1/4" Straight Back Knife from Houghton County Michigan. *D. Johnson Collection.*

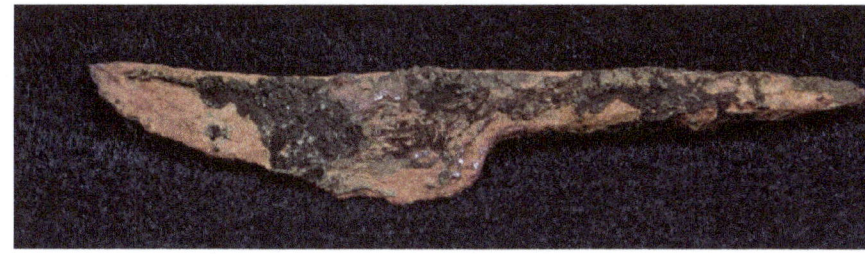

Left, 3 3/4" Straight Back Knife from Vilas County Wisconsin. *Private Collection.*

Left, 3 3/8" example from Marathon County Wisconsin. *D. Miller Collection.*

Left, 3 5/16" Straight Back, this slender example was found in Ontario, Canada. *Private Collection.*

Right, 3 7/8" from Vilas County Wisconsin. *G. Weimer Collection.*

Left, 3 7/8" Straight Back with punch marks on both faces of the blade. (Both faces shown) Vilas County Wisconsin. *Private Collection.*

Right, 3 9/16" example from Vilas County Wisconsin. *Private Collection.*

Left, 3 13/16" from Ontario, Canada. *Private Collection.*

Left, 3 15/16" Straight Back Knife from Ontario, Canada. *Private Collection.*

Right, 4" example from Cook County Minnesota. *D. Johnson Collection.*

Left, 4" example from Iron County Wisconsin. *D. Johnson Collection.*

Right, 3 3/4" "Hump Back" example from Koochiching County Minnesota. *D. Johnson Collection.*

Left, 3 3/4" example from Mackinac County Michigan. *D. Johnson Collection.*

Right, 4" exampel from Sawyer County Wisconsin. *D. Johnson Collection.*

Left, 4" Straight Back Knife from Ontonagon County Michigan. *D. Johnson Collection.*

Right, 4" example from Thunder Bay Ontario, Canada. Hooked tail was likely a hafting aid. *D. Johnson Collection.*

Left, 4" example from Vilas County, note the tip of the tang is bent perpendicular to the blade, this is also a hafting aid that prevented slippage of the handle. *Private Collection.*

Right, 4 1/2" Straight Back Knife from Florence County Wisconsin. *D. Johnson Collection.*

Above, 4 1/2" Straight Back Knife from McHenry County Illinois. *D. Johnson Collection.*

Above, 4 1/2" example from Oneida County Wisconsin. *D. Johnson Collection.*

Left, 4 1/2" Straight Back from St. Louis County Minnesota. *D. Johnson Collection.*

Right, 4 1/2" example from Vilas County Wisconsin. *Private Collection.*

Left, 4 1/4" example with hooked tang from Keweenaw County Michigan. *D. Johnson Collection.*

Right, 4 1/2" hooked Straight Back Knife from Vilas County Wisconsin. *D. Johnson Collection.*

Left, 4 1/4" example from Ontario, Canada. *Private Collection.*

Right, 4 1/4" example from Sawyer County Wisconsin. *D. Johnson Collection.*

Left, 4 1/4" Straight Back Knife from Vilas County Wisconsin. *Private Collection.*

Right, 4 3/4" example from Cook County Minnesota. *D. Johnson Collection.*

Left, 4 3/4" example from Mackinac County Michigan. *D. Johnson Collection.*

Right, 4 3/8" Straight Back with signs of resharpening. Manitowoc County Wisconsin. *T. Betka Collection.*

Left, 4 3/8" Straight Back from Ontario, Canada. *Private Collection.* Below, 5" example from Oneida County Wisconsin. *D. Johnson Collection.*

Above, 5 1/2" knife with unusual form, Mackinac County Michigan. Courtesy of the *D. Johnson Collection.*

Left, 5 1/4" Straight Back from Mackinac County Michigan. *D. Johnson Collection.*

Above and below, both sides of a 6" Straight Back Knife that was found in Columbia County Wisconsin. Both sides are punch marked with the marks running in two distinct lines parallel with each other. The redish color in the middle of the blade, best seen in the lower picture, is the result of the knife being bent when it was found and straightened out afterwords, this is a common situation. *Courtesy of the L. Born Collection.*

Above, 6 1/4" Straight Back knife from Lincoln County Wisconsin. *D. Johnson Collection.*

Above, 7" Straight Back Knife from Marquette County Wisconsin. *Private Collection.*

Below, 9 1/2" Straight Back Knife from Barron County Wisconsin. *Courtesy of the Milwaukee Public Museum.*

Above, 7" Straight Back Knife from Vilas County Wisconsin. *D. Johnson Collection.* Below, another example from Vilas County Wisconsin. The thinner profile may be indicative of use-wear. *D. Johson Collection.*

Above, 7 1/4" Straight Back Knife with bent tang, found in Marathon County Wisconsin. *D. Miller Collection.*

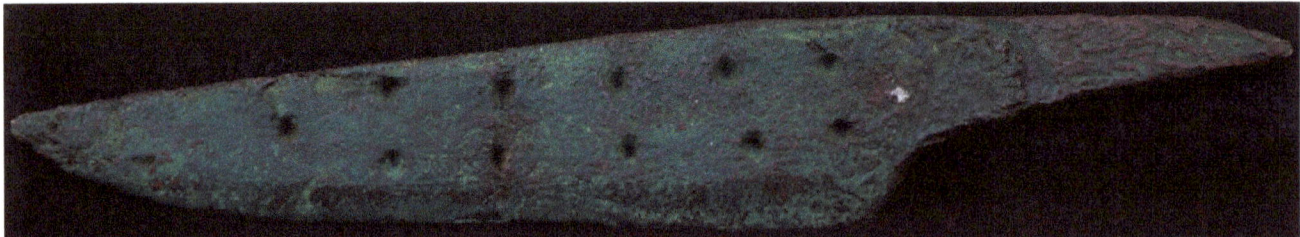

Above, 7 1/4" Straight Back Knife with punch marks, this wonderful example is from the U.P. of Michigan but exact county is unknown. *J. Bussey Collection.*

Left, at just shy of two feet in length this Straight Back Knife is the largest known example and was a surface find along a lake shore in Ontario, Canada. *Private Collection.*

Left, 15 15/16" Straight Back Knife with upturned tang as well as punch marks. This exceptional example was found in Minnesota but the exact county is unknown. The punch marks are interesting because they form lines which are perpendicular to the blade itself which is the opposite of most examples. Inset at the lower left shows a close up of the punch marks. *Courtesy of the Logan Museum of Anthropology.*

Left, large 9" Straight Back Knife from Fond du Lac County Wisconsin. *Courtesy of the Logan Museum of Anthropology.* Right, a large and heavy duty 9" example from Vilas County Wisconsin. *Private Collection.*

Below, 4 3/4" Straight Back Knife with punch marks from Vilas County Wisconsin. *D. Miller Collection.*

Above, 5 7/8" Straight Back with an upward turned tang end to act as a slip stop for the handle. Keweenaw County Michigan. *D. Miller Collection*. Below, 6 1/2" example from Vilas County Wisconsin. *Courtesy of the D. Miller Colection.*

Above and below, both faces of a punch marked Straight Back Knife from Vilas County Wisconsin. *Courtesy of the D. Miller Collection.*

II,A-2
Curved Back Knives

Discussion Curved Back Knives appear to be closely related to Straight Back Knives and in terms of function at least, they overlap. It is unclear if the Curved Backs, in their most extreme form, represent a specialized tool or a stylistic expression that represents the intial or terminal aspect of a particular lineage. The most extreme examples can closely resemble the Banana Knives and therefore the latter might be included in the same lineage. Examples range from those which have nothing more than a slightly upturned distal end to those which demonstrate a deep curvature from the distal to proxial ends. The majority are composed of examples with little curvature and therefore very similar to the Straight Backs. In examples that are nearly straight the slight curvature could be the result of use-wear, specifically, pressure applied to the forward half of the knife while cutting. That type of bending assoicated with use-wear would be more prevelant with thinner, resharpened examples.

Common Names Curved backs, Tanged Knives

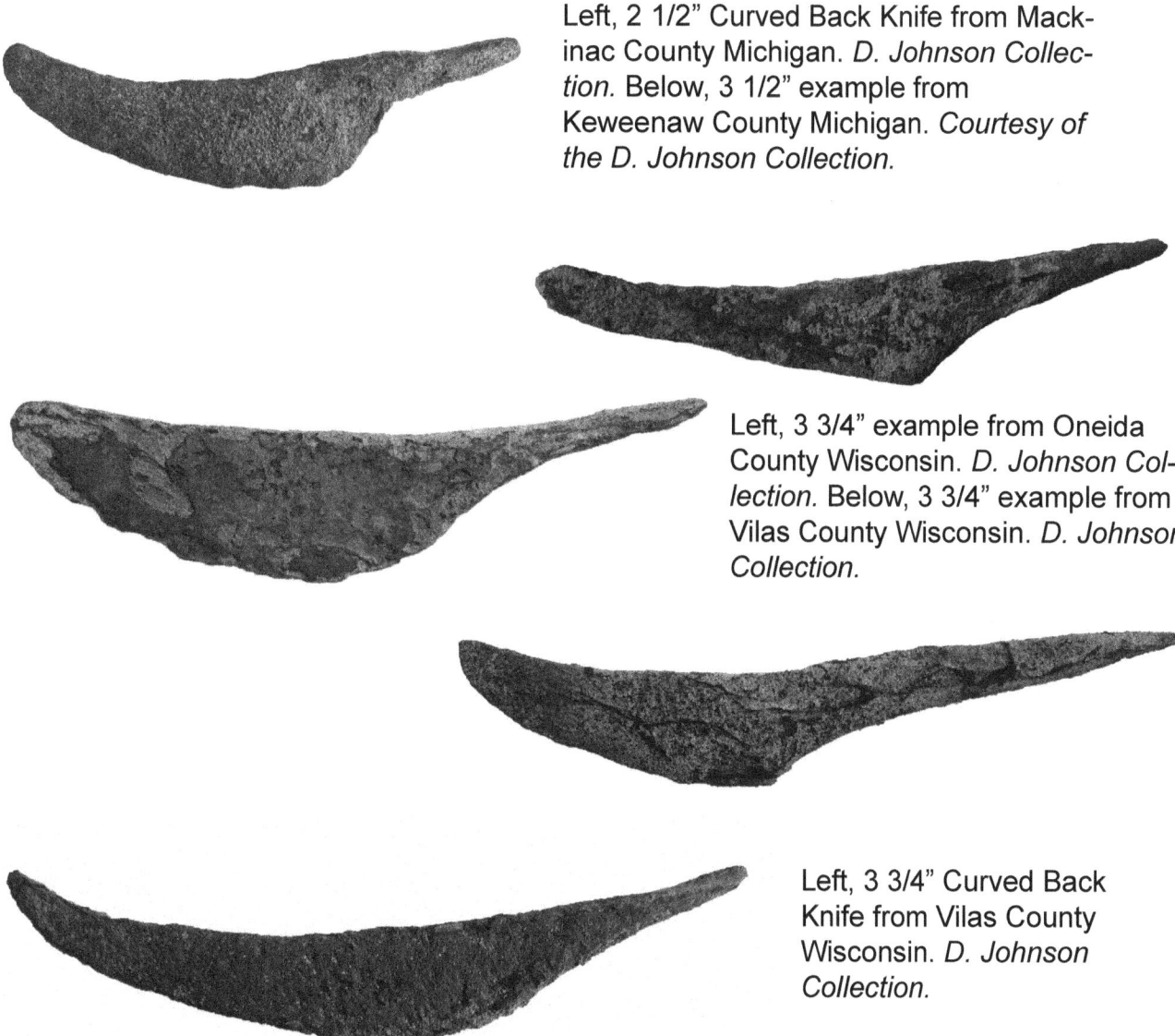

Left, 2 1/2" Curved Back Knife from Mackinac County Michigan. *D. Johnson Collection.* Below, 3 1/2" example from Keweenaw County Michigan. *Courtesy of the D. Johnson Collection.*

Left, 3 3/4" example from Oneida County Wisconsin. *D. Johnson Collection.* Below, 3 3/4" example from Vilas County Wisconsin. *D. Johnson Collection.*

Left, 3 3/4" Curved Back Knife from Vilas County Wisconsin. *D. Johnson Collection.*

Left, 3 15/16" Curved Back from Winnebago County Wisconsin. *G. Weimer Collection.*

Left, 4" Curved Back Knife from Lincoln County Wisconsin. *D. Johnson Collection.* Below, 4" example from Mackinac County Michigan. *D. Johnson Collection.*

Left, 4 1/2" Curved Back from Mackinac County Michigan. *D. Johnson Collection.* Below, 4 1/8" example from Manitowoc County Wisconsin. *T. Betka Collection.*

Left, 4 3/4" Curved Back Knife from Marathon County Wisconsin. *D. Miller Collection.* Below, 4 5/8" example also from Marathon County, piece was folded several times when found. *D. Miller Collection.*

Left, 3 3/4" example from Winnebago County Wisconsin. *G. Weimer Collection.*

Left, 5" Curved Back Knife from Florence County Wisconsin. *D. Johnson Collection.* Below, 5" example from Marathon County Wisconsin. *D. Miller Collection.*

Left, 5" Curved Back Knife fom Oneida County Wisconsin. *D. Johnson Collection.* Below, 5" example from Ontario, Canada. *D. Johnson Collection.*

Left, 5 1/2" Curved Back Knife from Houghton County Michigan. *D. Johnson Collection.*

Right, 5 1/2" example from Vilas County Wisconsin. *D. Johnson Collection.*

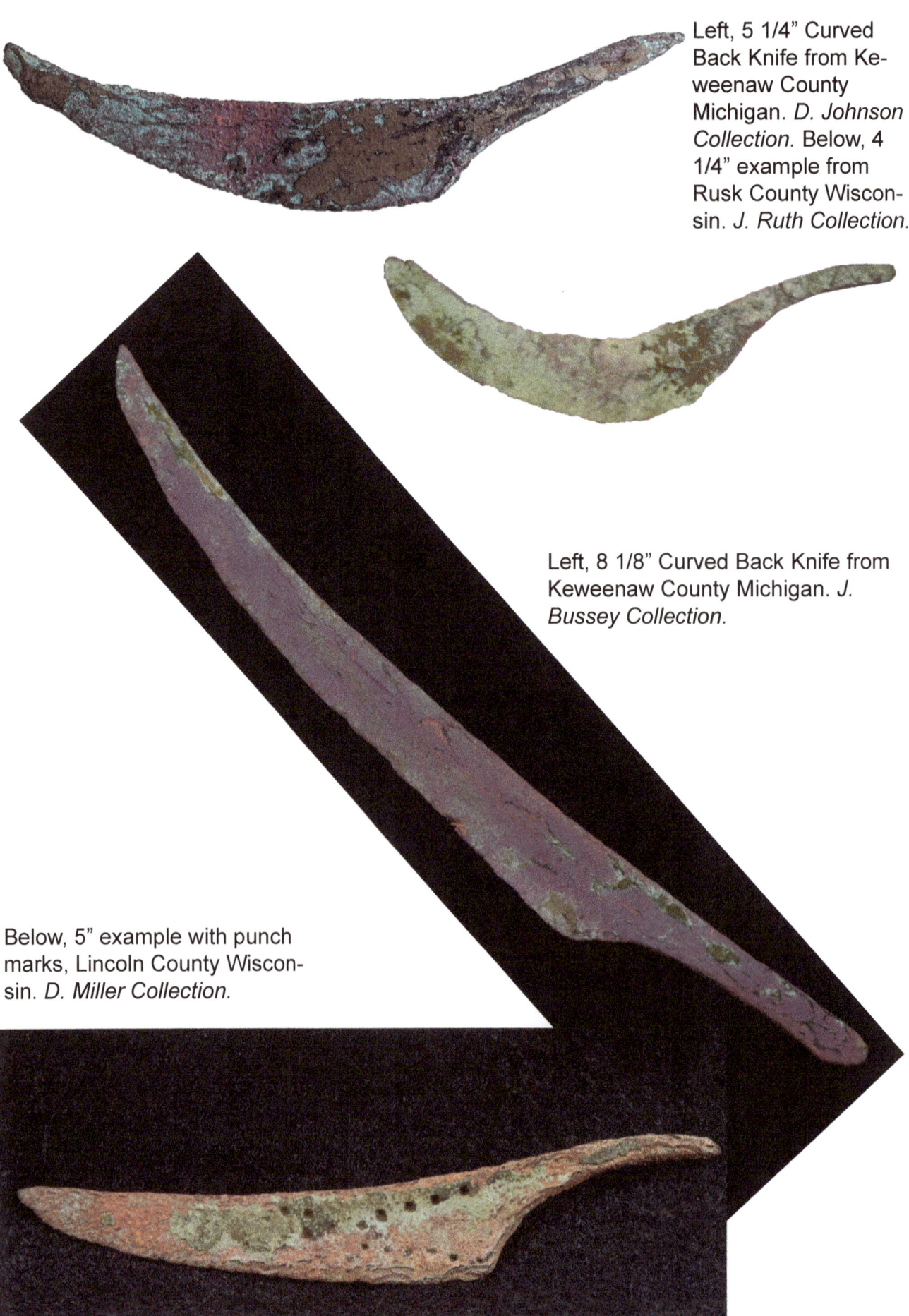

Left, 5 1/4" Curved Back Knife from Keweenaw County Michigan. *D. Johnson Collection.* Below, 4 1/4" example from Rusk County Wisconsin. *J. Ruth Collection.*

Left, 8 1/8" Curved Back Knife from Keweenaw County Michigan. *J. Bussey Collection.*

Below, 5" example with punch marks, Lincoln County Wisconsin. *D. Miller Collection.*

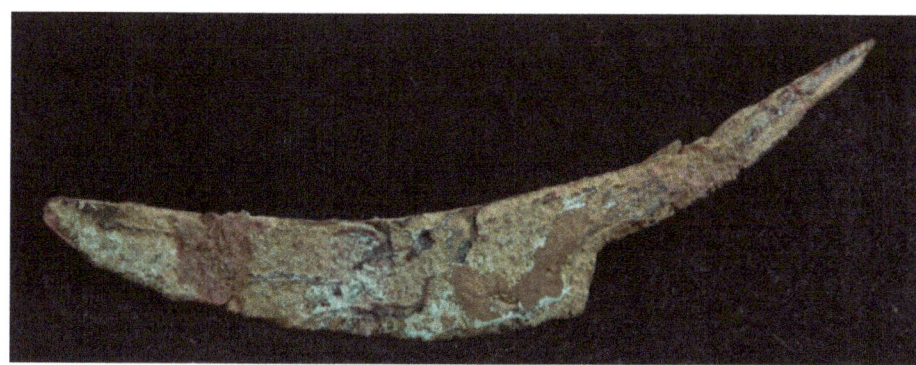

Left, 5" Curved Back Knife from Marathon County Wisconsin. *D. Miller Collection.*

Right, 5 1/2" Curved Back Knife from Vilas County Wisconsin. *D. Miller Collection.*

Left, large 9" example from Winnebago County Wisconsin, one of the better known examples out there. *Courtesy of the G. Weimer collection.*

Left, 2 11/16" Curved Back Knife from Jefferson County Wisconsin. *S. Wasion Collection.* Right, 3" example from Vilas County. *R. H. Mueller Collection*

Left, large 9" example from Jefferson County Wisconsin. *S. Wasion Collection.*

II,B
Banana Knives

Discussion Banana knives are far less common than most other types of knives. There may be some possible overlap between these and curved back knifes. In addition to the back curvature associated with Curved Back Knives, Banana Knives have typically blunt tips and well defined median ridges along the blade face(s). Craftsmanship of this type often looks rough and less refined compared to others.

Common Names Banana knives, Bananas, Ridged Curved Backs, Hocky Sticks

Left, 4 3/8" Banana Knife from Ontario, Canada. *Private Collection.*

Above, 6 7/8" example from Winnebago County Wisconsin. *G. Weimer Collection.* Below, 7 1/2" Banana Knife from Ontario, Canada. *Private Collection.*

Above, 7 1/2" Banana Knife from Jefferson County Wisconsin. *Courtesy of the Logan Museum of Anthropology.*

Left, 4 3/4" example from Chippewa County Michigan. *D. Johnson Collection.*

Above, 10" Banana knife with classic form, unknown provenience. *J. Bussey Collection.*

Above, 7 1/2" Banana Knife from Washington County Wisconsin. *Courtesy of the Logan Museum of Anthropology.* Below, a 9" Banana Knife from Shawano County Wisconsin. *Courtesy of the Milwaukee Public Museum.*

Left, 5 3/8" Banana Knife from Dodge County Wisconsin. *Courtesy of the Milwaukee Public Museum.*

Left, 8 1/4" long example from Dodge County Wisconsin. Right, 8 3/4" example from Shawano County Wisconsin. *Both examples are Courtesy of the Milwaukee Public Museum.*

Above, 4 1/2" example from the U.P. of Michigan. This example, like many, is sharp on both the top and the bottom of the blade. *D. Miller Collection.*

Above, Banana Knife lacking distinct median ridge. Also has a small bend at tip of tang that may have been for a lanyard attachment. Found in Ontario, Canada. *Courtesy of the O. Anttila Collection.*

Below, fine example from Ontario, Canada. *Courtesy of the T. Wilson Collection.*

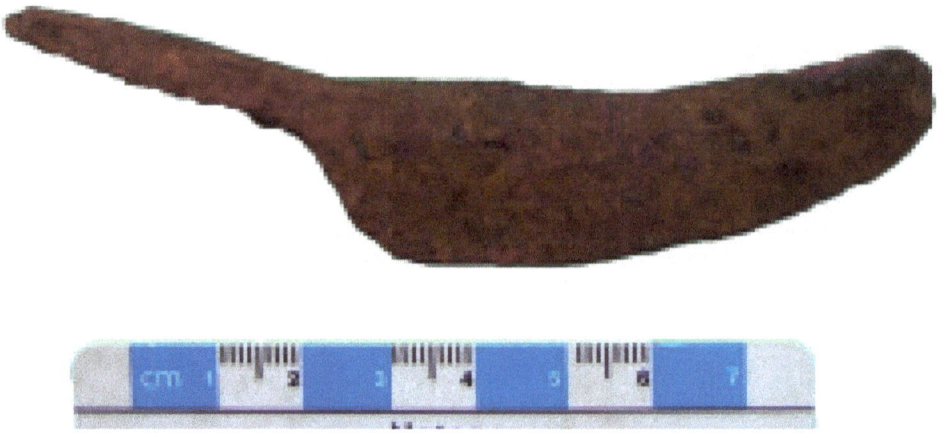

II,C
Socketed Knives

Discussion Socketed Knives are frequently quite large and of sturdy construction. They share a lot of attributes with ovate type projectiles including similar manufacturing techniques, holed sockets, etc, in fact, normally the only real difference between Common Ovates and Socketed Knives is that the latter has a blade that is usually offset to one side giving them a lopsided appearance. Blades are most often uni-edged and sometimes beveled. Socket construction of these are normally more robust than their projectile counterparts.

Common Names Socketed knives

Above, a 7" Socketed Knife from Waukesha County Wisconsin with punch marks. *Courtesy of the Milwaukee Public Museum.*

Above, very nice 6" example of a Socketed Knife from Mackinac County Michigan. Rivet hole in the socket is ruptured. *D. Johnson Collection.*

Above, 5 1/8" Socketed Knife from Racine County Wisconsin with a ruptured rivet hole. *Courtesy of the Logan Museum of Anthropology.*

Below, 8" Socketed Knife from Sheboygan County Wisconsin. *Courtesy of the Milwaukee Public Museum.*

Left 2 3/4" Socketed Knife from Vilas County Wisconsin. Hole in blade face was most likely the result of a flaw in the material. *D. Johnson Collection.*

Left, 4 1/2" Socketed Knife with six notches in the top of the blade. Found in Oneida County Wisconsin. *D. Johnson Collection.*

Below, 5 3/8" example from Milwaukee County Wisconsin. *Courtesy of the Logan Museum of Anthropology.*

Above, 6" example from Keweenaw County Michigan. *D. Johnson Collection.*

Above, 6 1/4" Socketed Knife from Jefferson County Wisconsin. *D. Johnson Collection.*

Above, 6 3/4" Socketed Knife from Shawano County Wisconsin that was found in 1916. *Courtesy of the J. Bussey Collection.*

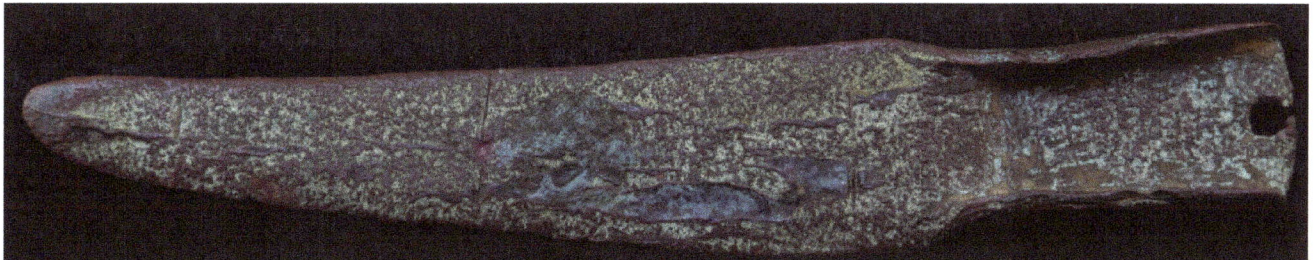

Above, 6 3/4" example from Waupaca County Wisconsin, J. Bussey Collection.

Below, 6 7/8" Socketed Knife with curved back and beveled blade edge. Oconto County Wisconsin. *L. Born Collection.*

Above, 7 1/2" Socketed Knife from Shawano County Wisconsin. *J. Bussey Collection.*

Above, excellent 7 3/4" Socketed Knife from Roseau County Minnesota. Note that this example appears to have been bent in at least one area when originally found, this is common with old, large pieces. *D. Johnsonn Collection.*

Above, Odd 7 3/4" example. Odd because only the top edge in the picture is sharp. Unknown provenience. *J. Bussey Collection.*

Left, 5 5/8" example from Vilas County Wisconsin. *N. Schanen Collection.*

Above, 7 5/8" Socketed Knife made with a heavy duty socket. Found in Door County Wisconsin. *J. Bussey Collection.* Below, large 8 1/4" Socketed Knife with classic form. Shawano County Wisconsin. *D. Johnson Collection.*

Below, 8 15/16" nice large example from Jefferson County Wisconsin. *L. Born Collection.*

Left, 5 1/2" Socketed Knife from Gogebic County Michigan. *D. Miller Collection.*

Left, 9 1/2" example from Forest County Wisconsin. *J. Bussey Collection.* Right, huge 12 3/4" Socketed Knife from Keweenaw County Michigan. Though it is among the largest known examples of a Socketed Knife, it has an exceptionally narrow socket. Some type of organic matter was likely inserted in the narrow socket, perhaps wood, antler, or bone, and then it and the socket itself, was wrapped with cordage or leather to form a solid handle. Courtesy of the *J. Bussey Collection.*

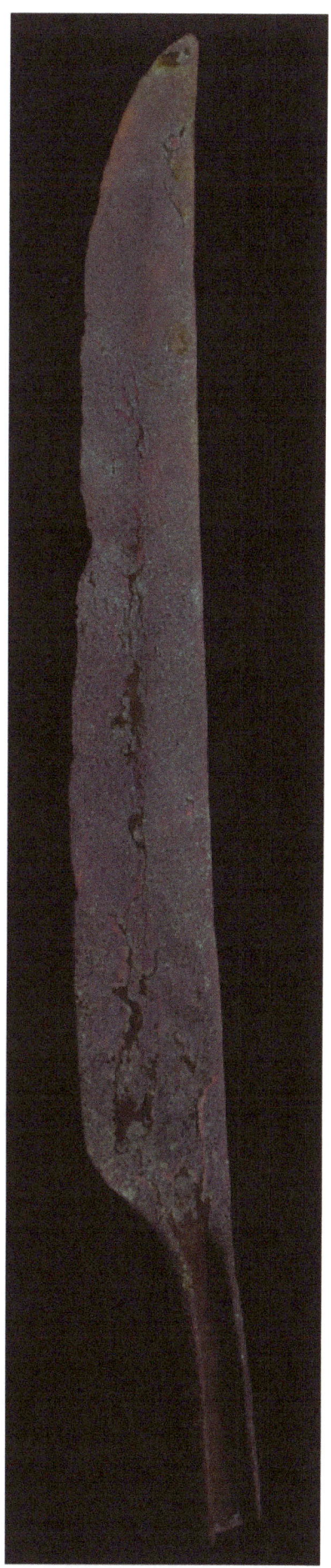

Above, dorsal view of a 5 5/8" Socketed Knife from Vilas County Wisconsin. *D. Miller Collection.* Below, 6 1/2" example from Lincoln County Wisconsin. *D. Miller Collection.*

Below, 6 1/4" Socketed Knife with the nail or rivet still protruding from the hole in the socket. This interesting piece was found in Iron County Wisconsin. *D. Miller Collection.*

Below, 5 3/4" Socketed Knife from Vilas County Wisconsin. *Private Collection.*

II,D
Footed Knives

Discussion Footed Knives resemble straight back knives in most respects but are quite rare by comparison. This type is often fairly large with a relatively narrow blade. The tangs terminate with a small projection that sometimes resembles a doe's hoof. The bend at the end of the tang may curve up or down with different levels of exageration. This tang extention most likely served as a hafting aid, helping to keep the handle from slipping from the knife itself.

Common Names Footed Knives, Doe's Foot

Above, 8 3/4" Footed Knife from Keweenaw County Michigan. *J. Bussey Collection.* Below, 9 1/2" example also from Keweenaw County Michigan. *Courtesy of the J. Bussey Collection.*

Right, a whopping 11" long Footed Knife from Washinton County Wisconsin. *Courtesy of the Milwaukee Public Museum.*

Above, 8" Footed Knife from Langlade County Wisconsin. *Courtesy of the Eugene and Cathy Schug Collection.* Below, 10 1/8" example from Gogebic County Michigan. *D. Miller Collection.*

Below, 9 1/2" example from Gogebic County Michigan. *D. Miller Collection.*

II,E
Stick Knives

Discussion Most Stick Knives appear to be salvaged from other larger types, crescents in particular. None the less, a handfull of examples do appear to be made intentionally as such. They probably represent highly specialized tools in some instances and simply thriftyness in others.

Common Names Stick knives, Hockey sticks

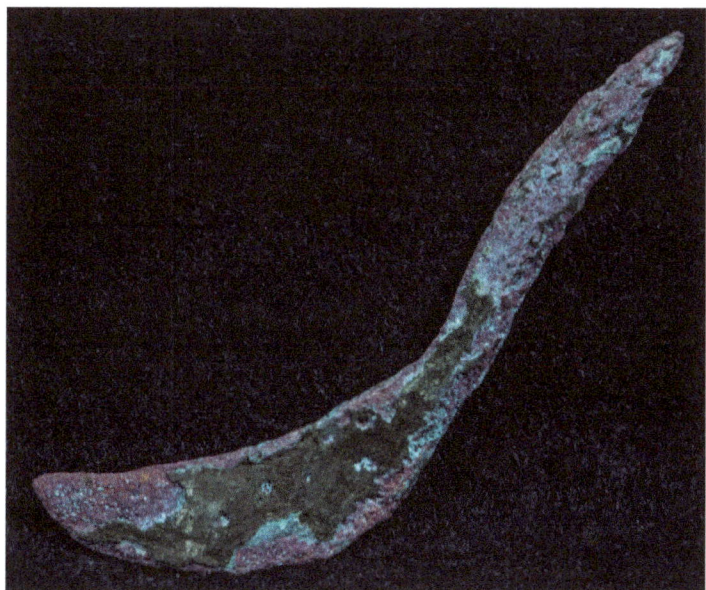

Left, 3 1/2" Stick Knife from Vilas County Wisconsin. This example may also have had it's origins with a failed or exhaused Crescent Knife. *Private Collection.*

Below, 3 1/2" Stick Knife which has clearly been made from a failed or exhausted Tanged Curved Back Crescent. Mackinac County Michigan. *D. Johnson Collection.*

Below, 2 1/4" Stick Knife from Vilas County Wisconsin. *D. Miller Collection.*

Below, 4" Stick Knife from Keweenaw County Michigan. It may be a piece salvaged from another project (chisel cut at left?) or it could've been purposefully made as such. *D. Johnson Collection.*

All six of these Stick Knives were found in Ontario, Canada. *O. Anttila Collection.* Notice that the two middle examples appear to be from broken and salvaged crescents while the other four look like they were intentionally made as such from the beginning.

II,F
Whiptails

Discussion Whiptails have apparently been included with all other Straight Back or tanged knife forms up until now. They have been given their own category here because their individual attributes are so consistentantly different from other tanged knife forms. The unique tang bend found on these was used to hold the handle and hafting materials in place and acted as a slip stop. Blades are usually long, narrow, and steeply beveled. Tangs terminate with a point that bends around back towards the blade.

Common Names Curved Tang Knives, Whiptails, Hook Tangs

Above, a classic formed 2 7/8" Whiptail from Winnebago County Wisconsin. *G. Weimer Collection.*

Above, 3 1/4" example from Gogebic County Michigan. *D. Miller collection.*

Below, 4 1/2" Whiptail from Lincoln County Wisconsin. *Private Collection.*

Above, 4 1/2" example from Ontario, Canada. *Private Collection.*

Below, 5 3/4" Whiptail that shows the strong beveling typical of these knives. Ontario, Canada. *Private Collection.*

Below, 5 3/8" example from Winnebago County Wisconsin. *G. Weimer Collection.*

Below, 6 3/4" Whiptail from Keweenaw County Michigan. *D. Johnson Collection.*

Below, a huge 9 1/2" Whiptail that was found in Waupaca County Wisconsin in 1889. *Courtesy of the Logan Museum of Anthropology.*

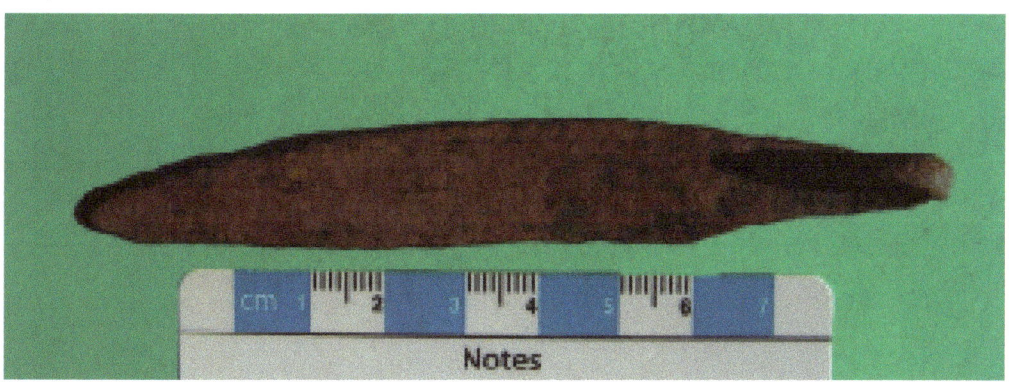

Above, Whiptail from Ontario, Canada. Below, close up of the bent tang on a different example. *Both courtesy of the T. Wilson Collection.*

Below, lot of four examples all found in Ontario, Canada. *Courtesy of the T. Wilson Collection.*

III
Crescent Forms

III,A-1 Tangless Curved Back
III,A-2 Tanged Curved Back
III,D-1 Back Tanged
III,D-2 Box Tanged
III,D-3 Bridge Tanged
III,D-4 Twisted Tang
III,G-1 Tangless Straight Back (both holed and non-holed)
III,G-2 Tanged Straight Back
III,H Spatula Forms

III,A-1
Tangless Curved Back Crescents

Discussion Tangless Curved Back Crescents are likely a compilation of several varieties, deeply curved v shaped examples being one example. There is so much overlap however that it is difficult at best to put defining attributes on all of the individual varieties. For conversation's sake the crescents have here been divided by those which have curved or straight backs and those which have, or do not have, tangs. Some Tangless Curved Back Crescents were likely set into bone or antler handles and used as knives while others may have been used in a decorative fashion like a gorget. The vast majority appear to be utilitarian in nature.

Common Names Tangless Crescents, Banana Crescents, Boomerrangs, Canoe Crescents

Left, 4 3/8" Tangless Curved Back Crescent from Sheboygan County Wisconsin. *Courtesy of the Logan Museum of Anthropology.*

Above, 9 1/8" Tangless Curved Back Crescent. *Courtesy of the L. Born Collection, ex Bussey.*

Left, 3 1/4" Tangless Curved Back Crescent, this example has some damage to one end, found in Marathon County Wisconsin. *D. Miller Collection.*

Left, 3 3/4" example from Mackinac County Michigan. *D. Johnson Collection.*

Right, 4 1/2" Tangless Curved Back Crescent from Vilas County Wisconsin. This example has what may be a lanyard hole at left. It could've also been used to tighten or improve the hafting of the piece in a handle. *D. Johnson Collection.*

Below, 4 1/2" example from Vilas County Wisconsin. *D. Johnson Collection.*

Left, 5" example from Vilas County Wisconsin. *D. Johnson Collection.*

Left, 5 1/4" Tangless Curved Back Crescent from Oneida County Wisconsin. *Courtesy of the D. Johnson Collection.*

Above, 5 5/8" Tangless Curved Back Crescent from Ottertail County Minnesota. *Courtesy of the L. Born Collection.*

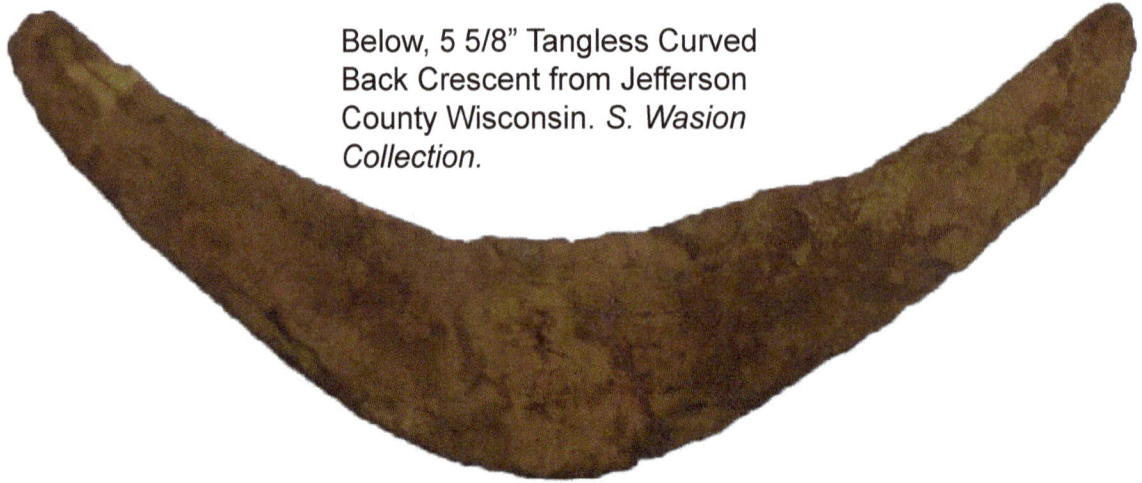

Below, 5 5/8" Tangless Curved Back Crescent from Jefferson County Wisconsin. *S. Wasion Collection.*

Below, 8 1/4" Tangless Curved Back Crescent, Unknown provenience. *J. Bussey Collection.*

III,A-2
Tanged Curved Back Crescents

Discussion Tanged Curved Back Crescents are one of the most common types of crescents. This group has been categorized and pigeon holed in every concievable way, typically based upon the tang shape and length. The crescents group as a whole is not as neatly sorted as it might be but they are instead organized upon the crescent's most basic obvious attributes, that is if they have tangs or not and if the back is straight or curved. Because the curvature of the back is not always very well defined there may be overlap between these and Tanged Straight Back Crescents. Besides the obvious overlap in form, there is almost certainly overlap in use and time between these and some other crescent forms. Like other copper types, the larger heavier examples are believed to be earlier in most cases while the smaller and decorative versions are thought to be newer.

Common Names Tanged Crescents, Curved back Crescents

Left, 5" across, this Tanged Curved Back Crescent has been repaired by pushing a broken tang through the blade face on the lower left. Found in Gogebic County Michigan. *D. Miller Collection.* Above, a close up of the repair work.

Left, a tiny 1 1/4" example from Lincoln County Wisconsin, might represent a "miniature" example. *Private Collection.*

Right, a small 2" Tanged Curved Back Crescent from Mackinac County Michigan. *D. Johnson Collection.*

Left, 2 1/4" example from Vilas County Wisconsin. *D. Miller Collection.*

Right, 2 1/4" wide, 4 3/4" tall, this unusually proportioned Tanged Curved Back Crescent was found in Vilas County Wisconsin. *D. Johnson Collection.*

Left, 2 5/8" Tanged Curved Back Crescent from Vilas County Wisconsin. *D. Miller Collection.*

Right, 2 7/8" example from Ontario, Canada. *Private Collection.*

Below, 2 9/16" Tanged Curved Back Crescent from Vilas County Wisconsin. *Private Collection.*

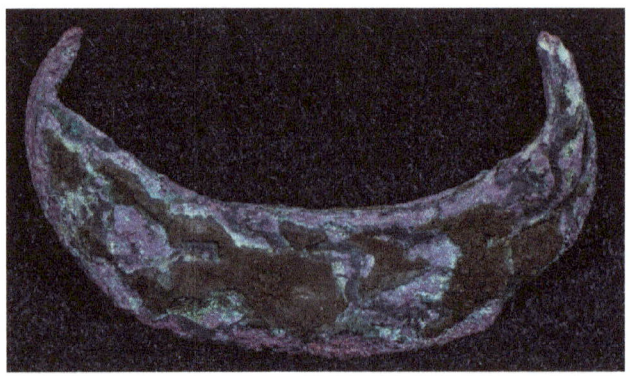

Left, a delicate 3" example from Mackinac County Michigan. *D. Johnson Collection.* Below, 3" Curved Back Tanged Crescent with a curled tang on one side, examples with curled tangs, either one, or both, are exceptionally rare. Vilas County Wisconsin. *Private Collection.*

Below, 3 1/2" example that shows how difficult it can be to call a particular piece either Curved Back or Straight Back. The similarities in all respects (age, use, culture) likely outnumber the differences between this and other types of crescents. Mackinac County Michigan. *D. Johnson Collection.*

Above, 3 1/2" Tanged Curved Back Crescent from Oneida County Wisconsin. *D. Johnson Collection.*

Left, 3 1/2" Tanged Curved Back Crescent from Ontario, Canada. It's difficult to point a finger at what might be called a classic example in a group that is as diversified as the crescent tang family but this example might certainly be in the running. *Private Collection.*

Right, 3 1/4" example from Oneida County Wisconsin. Many collectors refer to this as a "Canoe" style crescent. *D. Miller Collection.*

Left, 3 3/4" Tanged Curved Back Crescent from Mackinac County Michigan. *Courtesy of the D. Johnson Collection.*

Right, 3 3/4" Tanged Curved Back Crescent from Vilas County Wisconsin. *D. Johnson Collection.*

Below, 4 1/2" Tanged Curved Back Crescent found in Vilas County Wisconsin. *Private Collection.*

Left and below, both are 4 1/4" wide crescents with very similar traits, curved backs, and tanged, the only difference being the length of the tang. Both are from Mackinac County Michigan. *D. Johnson Collection.*

Below, 5" across and 3" tall, this example was found in Mackinac County Michigan. *D. Johnson Collection.*

Above, 5 5/8" Tanged Curved Back Crescent from Oneida County Wisconsin. *L. Born Collection.*

6" Tanged Curved Back Crescent from Menominee County Michigan. This unique piece has 32 hash marks indented into it's back or spine. *Courtesy of the L. Born Collection.*

Left, bottom example is 4 1/2" in length, all three examples are from Oneida County Wisconsin. *Courtesy of the D. Johnson Collection.*

Left, 5 1/2" Tanged Curved Back Crescent from Brown County Wisconsin. *Courtesy of the Logan Museum of Anthropology.*

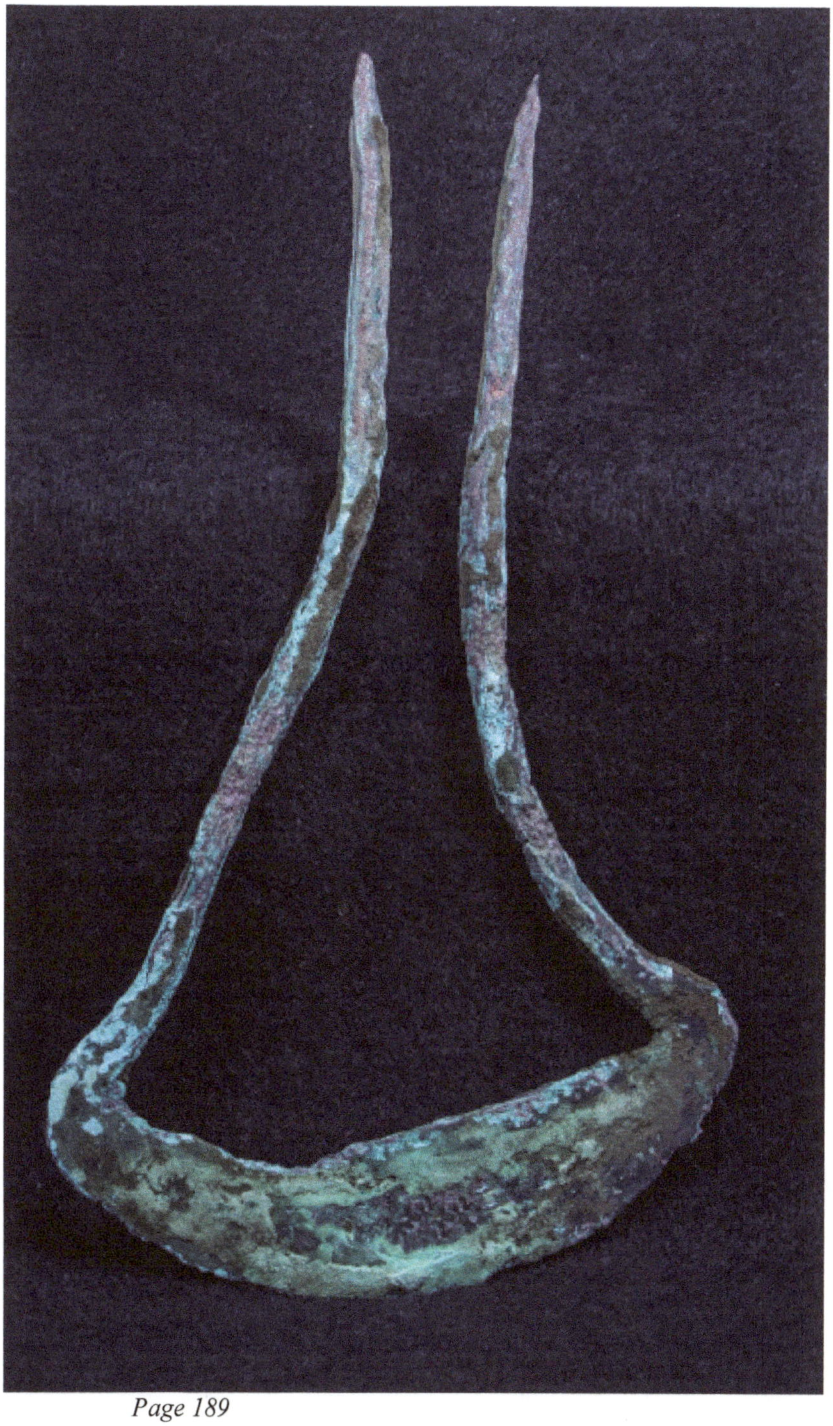

Right, 7 3/8" Tanged Curved Back Crescent from Vilas County Wisconsin. *Private Collection.*

Above, a large 7 1/4" wide example. *Courtesy of the L. Born Collection.*

Right, 4 1/4" Tanged Curved Back Crescent from Iron County Wisconsin. *D. Miller Collection.*

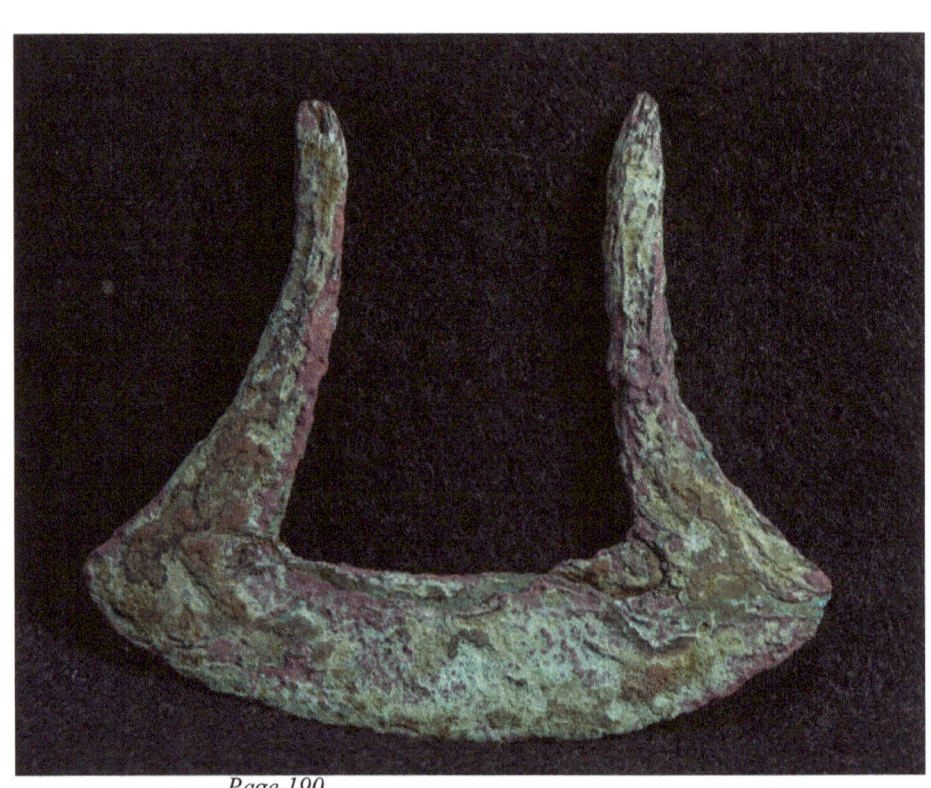

III,D-1
Back Tanged Crescent

Discussion Back Tanged Crescents are rare and there is strong suspicion with the author that the examples with two tangs protruding from the back are frequently, if not always, actually Box Tanged Crescents which have been broken, damaged, coroded, or modified due to material flaws while being made. Even if they were made intentionally without the corss brace between tangs, the hafting and use would've likely been identical to the Box Tanged versions. Likewise, Back Tanged Crescents with only a single tang would've also been hafted and used in similar fashion.

Common Names Back Tanged

Below, 4 5/8" wide X 6 7/8" tall. This large example was found in St. Croix County Wisconsin. *Courtesy of the Milwaukee Public Museum.*

Above, 2 1/2" Back Tanged crescent that may have started it's life as a box tang. Mackinac County Michigan. *D. Johnson Collection.*

Below, 3 1/4" example of this rare type from Vilas County Wisconsin. *D. Miller Collection.*

Below, large 7 1/4" wide Back Tanged Crescent from Sheboygan County Wisconsin. The marks in the patina strongly suggest that the piece was found folded up to some extent and straightened out again. Like most back tanged knives, it looks as though this was originally a Box Tanged Crescent. *Courtesy of the Logan Museum of Anthropology.*

Left, 6 3/4" Back Tanged Crescent from Vilas County Wisconsin, there appears to possibly be a small amount of organic material under the one bent tang. *Private Collection.*

Left, 3 1/2" Back Tanged Crescent, Below, 4 7/8" example from Vilas County Wisconsin. This single tanged variety is quite rare, even when compared to Box Tanged Crescents. *Courtesy of the L. Born Collection.*

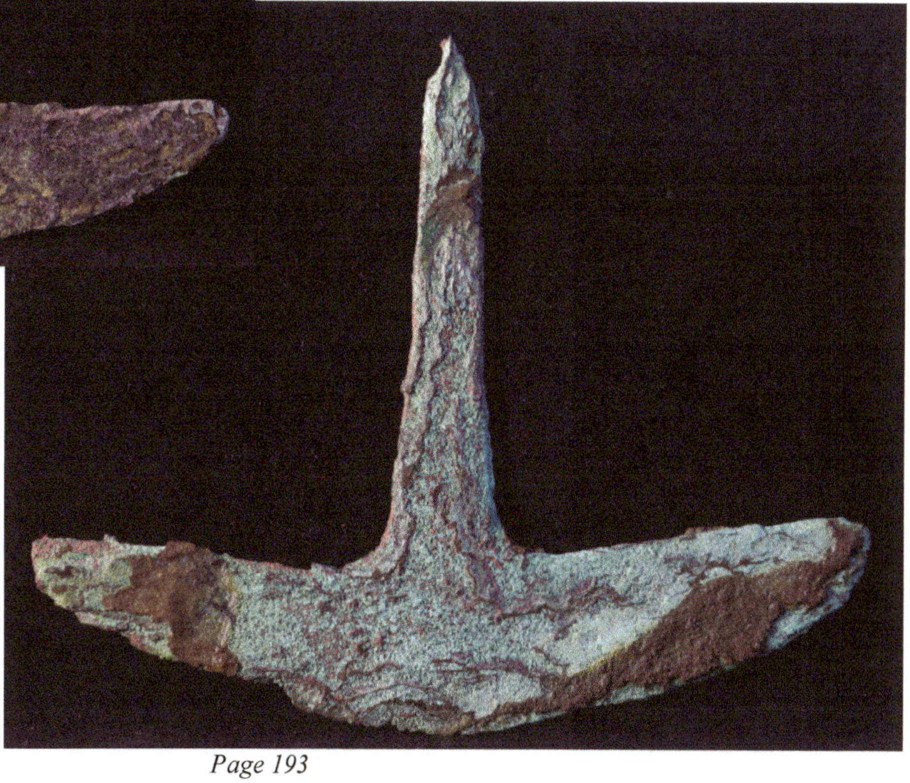

Left, 4 5/8" wide Back Tanged Crescent from Vilas County Wisconsin. Below, 5 1/2" example that might have been salvaged and used in similar fashion to a Tangless Straight Back Crescent. Found in Vilas County Wisconsin. *Both artifacts are courtesy of the D. Miller Collection.*

III,D-2
Box Tanged

Discussion Box Tanged Crescents are exceptionally rare when compared to most other crescent forms besides perhaps the Back Tanged (and single tanged variant). There is frequently discussion concerning the use of chisel cutting to form these long and well executed handles but there is no evidence to support it. The tangs were instead carefully formed, one as a female and end and one as a male end, then hammered carefully together, with a couple of thousand years of time and corosion this joint is not always immediately obvious. These represent the work of some truly skilled craftsmen.

Common Names Box tanged

Above, A classic 6 1/2" wide and 5 3/8" tall, this fine example was found in Oconto County Wisconsin. *L. Born Collection.*

Left, 4" tall and 3 1/2" wide, this Box Tanged Crescent was found in Lincoln County Wisconsin. *J. Bussey Collection.*

Right, this lanky 4" wide example was broken and repaired where the left side tang attached to the blade. The fact that prehistoric man took the time to repair a broken tang in this fashion certainly must speak in part to their value. Oneida County Wisconsin. *D. Johnson Collection.*

Left, 4 3/4" wide and 6 3/4" tall, this fine Box Tang was found in Vilas County Wisconsin. *L. Born collection.*

Right, Box Tang that is 5 1/2" wide. This example is particularly well-executed. Waukesha County Wisconsin. *J. Bussey Collection.*

Above, Box Tang Crescent that is 6 1/2" wide, 5 1/4" tall, and found in Oneida County Wisconsin. This piece has also been repaired by punching a hole in the blade and pulling the tang through. *J. Bussey Collection.*

Left, 5" wide and 5 1/4" tall Box Tanged Crescent from Iron County Wisconsin. *Private Collection.*

Left, 4 1/2" wide example from Vilas County Wisconsin. *D. Miller Collection.*

Right, 5" Box Tanged Crescent from Vilas County Wisconsin. *D. Miller Collection.*

III,D-3
Bridge Tanged

Discussion Bridge Tanged Crescents are the single rarest type of crescent known. They appear to be a sub-variety of box tanged crescents as they employ the same tang union attributes. Future revisions to the system might include this exceptionally rare type as a sub-variety of the Box Tang or perhaps the Tanged Curved Back Crescent.

Common Names Bridge Backs

Above, one of the very few known examples of the Bridge Tang Crescent. 5 9/16" wide, Mackinac County Michigan. *L. Born Collection.*

III,D-4
Twisted Tangs

Discussion The real differences between Twisted Tangs, Tanged Straight Backs, and Tanged Curved Backs is likely minimal. Slight differences in hafting perhaps but they were probably used for similar, if not identical work tasks. Some of them could've been contemperaneous with one another while others might represent a linear progression over time. The form versus distribution has not been looked at so I can't comment on regional differences in forms or types. Most twisted tangs were twisted and then had the twisted portion of the tangs hammered down to some degree, often times flat.

Common Names Twisted Tangs

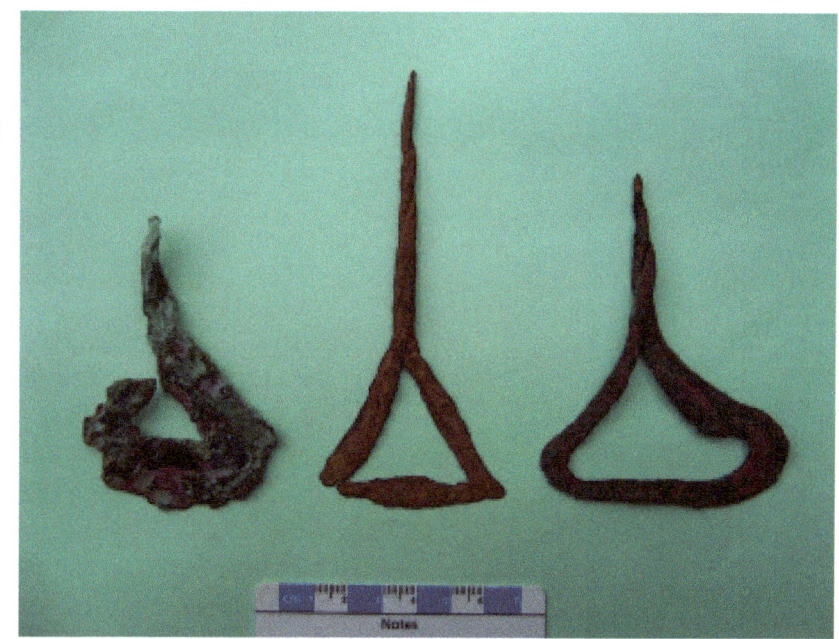

Right, 3 well used examples from Ontario, Canada. *T. Wilson Collection.* Examples with very thin blades likely represent last stage artifacts, artifacts that were mostly "used up" and perhaps even discarded in some cases in much the same way that spent stone knives were discarded.

Left, 4 1/4" Twisted Tang from Vilas County Wisconsin. *Private Collection.* A portion of the twisted tang appears to have broken away in ancient times. Damaged pieces were frequently adjusted or manipulated in some form so that they could be continued to be used.

Page 201

Left, 6 1/8" tall and 5 5/16" wide, this classic example comes from Vilas County Wisconsin. *Courtesy of the Private Collection.*

Above, 1 5/16" example from Vilas County Wisconsin, this piece looks like the tangs might have originally been longer but broke off for one reason or another. *Private Collection.*

Above, 2 5/8" Twisted Tang Crescent from Vilas County Wisconsin. *D. Miller Collection.*

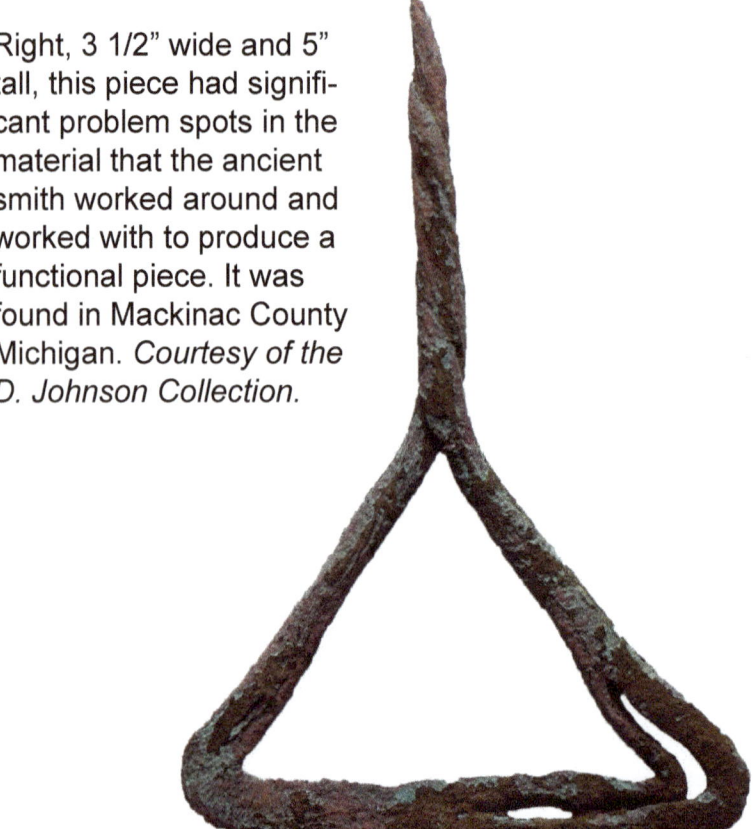

Right, 3 1/2" wide and 5" tall, this piece had significant problem spots in the material that the ancient smith worked around and worked with to produce a functional piece. It was found in Mackinac County Michigan. *Courtesy of the D. Johnson Collection.*

Left, 3 3/4" Twisted Tang Crescent from Vilas County Wisconsin. *Private Collection.*

Below, 3, 3/4" wide Twisted Tang Crescent, unknown provenience. *J. Bussey Collection.*

Left, 3 15/16" Twisted Tang Crescent with many small silver inclusions in it. Vilas County Wisconsin. *Private Collection.*

Left, 5" tall example, unknown provenience. *J. Bussey Collection.*

Right, 5" wide and 5 3/4" tall, this fine example has stout tangs compared to a relatively thin blade, indicative of long term use and many resharpenings. Found in Kent County Michigan. *J. Bussey Collection.*

Left, 4 1/4" Twisted Tang Crescent from Vilas County Wisconsin. *D. Miller Collection.*

Below, 5 3/4" Twisted Tang from Vilas County Wisconsin. This example has only minimal tang-twisting and the twisted portion does not appear to have been hammered flat like most examples. *D. Miller Collection.*

III,G-1
Tangless Straight Backs

Discussion Tangless Straight Backs are similar in function to other crescents but were most likely set into bone or wood handles. Historic accounts of similar formed metal knives were found on the great plains which had been set into green bone, when the bone was dried it shrank slightly and helped to hold the blade in. Prehistoric copper examples may have very well been made and hafted preciesly the same way. Rarely they are holed, presumably this was some additional feature used for securing the piece in a handle, in other cases it might be indicitive of a piece which was worn like a gorget around the neck. Wittry originally categorized holed and un-holed versions of these as completely different types but I see no reason not to group them together here. Most appear to be utilitarian, having sharp lower edges, but some of the holed examples in particular look as thought they may have been decorative.

Common Names Crescents, Straight Back Crescents, Tangless Straight Backs, Holed Crescents, Tangless Crescents

Below, 5" Tangless Straight Back Crescent with a hole. Vilas County Wisconsin. *D. Miller Collection.*

Left, 3 1/4" wide Tangless Straight Back Crescent from Vilas County Wisconsin. *Private Collection.*

Right, 3 1/4" example from Vilas County Wisconsin. *D. Miller Collection.*

Left, 3 1/8" Tangless Straight Back Crescent that is badly corroded. This is a common problem with these often thinly made knives. Vilas County Wisconsin. *Private Collection.*

Right, 3 3/4" wide example that has holes which likely aided in hafting the piece to it's handle. Known to have come from northern Wisconsin. *J. Bussey Collection.*

Left, Tangless Straight Backed Crescent from Ontario, Canada. The owner has catalogued this artifact as a "gorget", which is also a reasonable explanation on examples lacking a sharp bottom edge and other utilitarian like features. It's also worth noting that the holes appear to have worn through as thought it had been suspended. *T. Wilson Collection.*

Left, 3 5/16" wide Tangless Straight Back Crescent from Vilas County Wisconsin. *Private Collection.*

Right, 4 1/2" example from Ontario, Canada. *D. Johnson Collection.*

Left, interesting 4 1/2" Straight Back Crescent that is much wider than most and likely indicitive of an early stage piece. Ontario, Canada. *Private Collection.*

Right, 4 1/2" example from Vilas County Wisconsin. *D. Johnson Collection.*

Left, 5" example from Mackinac County Michigan. *Courtesy of the D. Johnson Collection.*

Above, 5 1/2" Straight Back Crescent from Koochiching County Minnesota. *D. Johnson Collection.*

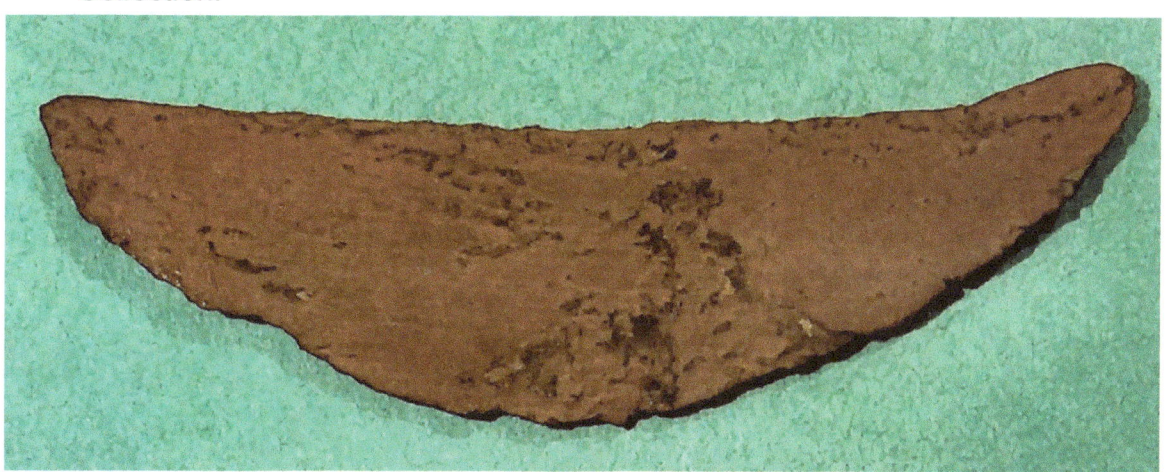

Above, Straight Back Crescent from Ontario, Canada. *O. Anttila Collection.*

Right, 5 1/8" holed example from Ontario, Canada. *Private Collection.*

Above, 5 1/16" wide Straight Back Crescent from Vilas County Wisconsin. *Private Collection.*

Above, 5 7/8" holed example from Vilas County Wisconsin. *Private Collection.*

Above, 6" wide Straight Back Crescent from Houghton County Michigan. *D. Johnson Collection.*

Above, huge 7 7/8" wide Straight Back Crescent from Menominee County Michigan. This remarkable crescent has well developed worm tracks but is still in an excellent state of preservation. *L. Born Collection.*

Left, 4 1/2" example from Vilas County Wisconsin. Slight back curvature may be result of corrosion. *N. Schanen Collection.*

Below, 7 3/8" Tangless Straight Back found by Robert Hrouska in Oconto County Wisconsin. *Courtesy of the L. Born Collection.*

III,G-2
Tanged Straight Backs

Discussion The differences between this type and other crescents is likely minimal but separating them by different characteristics like this should hopefully aid in our ability to describe them. These were probably contemperaneous with many other crescent types and were likely hafted the same. Use was likely something similar to that of an Ulu. Tanged Straight Back Crescents have tangs of differing lengths from short pseudo-tangs to long, thin, tendril-like tangs.

Common Names Tanged Crescents, Tanged Straight Back Crescents

Right, excellent example from Ontario, Canada. *Courtesy of the T. Wilson Collection.*

Left, 4 9/16" wide Tanged Straight Back Crescent from Shawano County Wisconsin. This particular example has the tips of the tangs folded over, presumably for some sort of hafting modification. *Courtesy of the Milwaukee Public Museum*

3 1/2" wide Tanged Straight Back Crescent found in St. Louis County Minnesota, notice the many bits of silver mixed in with the copper. *Private Collection.*

Below, a nicely formed example of a Tanged Straight Back from Ontario, Canada. *Courtesy of the O. Anttila Collection.*

III,H
Spatulates

Discussion Spatula forms were originally given their own group level status by Wittry and Steinbring, why they did this I'm not sure. In terms of function and form they are not all that different from other crescent knives. The best preserved examples that I have been able to examine had very sharp lower edges, on round bladed examples the sharpened areas reach around slightly on both sides to cover essentially the lower half of the "ball". As examples were used and resharpened they may have become more triangular in shape. Examples used beyond this point may have been heated and re-hammered back into a first stage piece, each time a little bit of length would be lost from the tang. Securely hafted into a bone, antler, or wood handle, these would've been effective knives or even scrapers. Many also believe that they could've been used as an effective tool for spreading sap while building bark canoes.

Common Names Spatulas, Spatula knives, Ping Pong Paddles, Paddle knives, Spatulates

Left, 3 1/2" Spatulate from Vilas County Wisconsin. *Private Collection.* Right, Canadian example that was originally recorded as an axe. *O. Anttila Collection.*

Left, 3 1/2" Spatulate knife from Vilas County Wisconsin. *D. Johnson Collection.* Below, 5 1/2" example from Houghton County Michigan. *Courtesy of the Chicago Field Museum.*

Left, 4 7/8" wide Spatulate knife from Oneida County Wisconsin. *J. Bussey Collection.*

Above, 5" Spatulate from Vilas County Wisconsin. *D. Johnson Collection.*

Above, 5 3/4" Spatulate from Lincoln County Wisconsin. *D. Johnson Collection.*

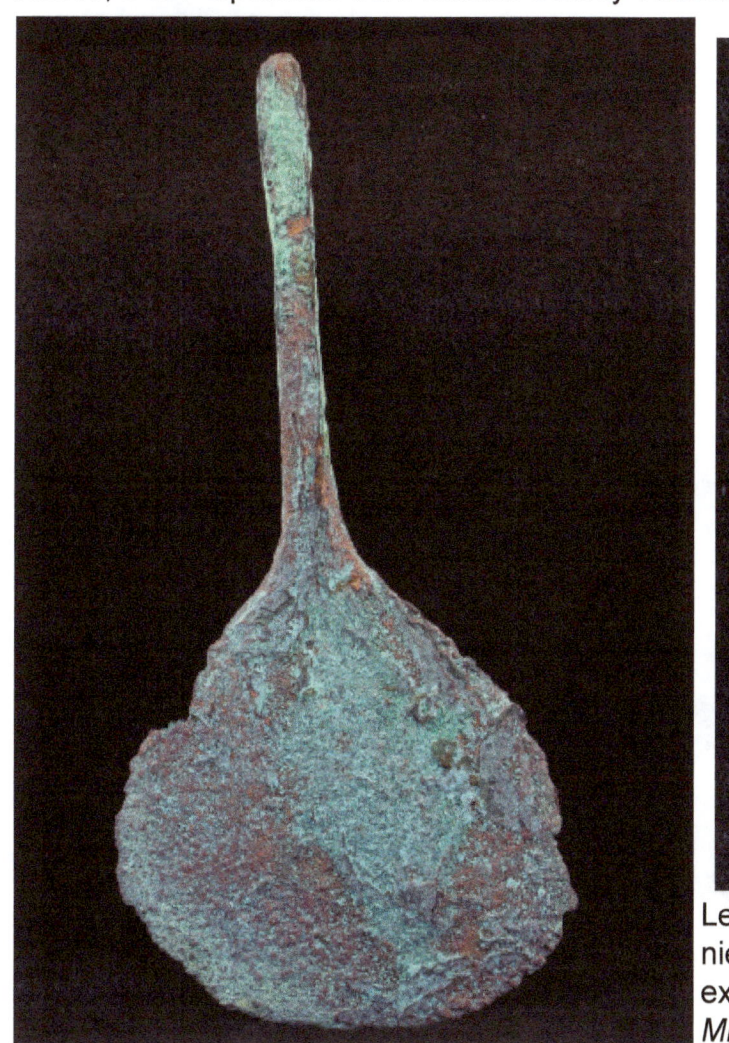

Left, 5 7/8" tall Spatulate, unknown provenience. *J. Bussey Collection.* Above, 3 1/4" example from Vilas County Wisconsin. *D. Miller Collection.*

Right, 4" example from Vilas County Wisconsin. *Courtesy of the D. Miller Collection.*

Above, large 7 1/4" Spatulate from Oneida County Wisconsin. *Courtesy of the K. Leszcynski Collection.*

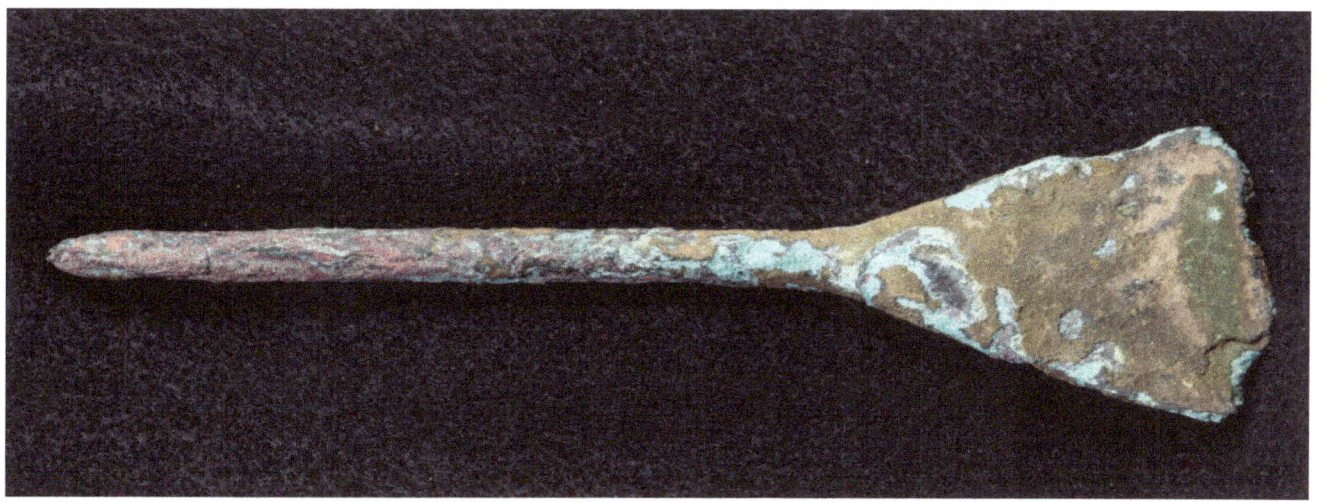

Above, 7" Spatulate from Vilas County Wisconsin. *D. Miller Collection.*

Right, 6 1/14" Spatulate from Vilas County Wisconsin. *Private Collection.*

Below, 4 7/8" Spatulate from Vilas County Wisconsin. Exceptional example. *N. Schanen Collection.*

IV
Awls, Punches, Needles, Pikes, Mandrels

IV,A-1 Square Awls
IV,A-2 Round Awls
IV,B Punches
IV,D Needles
IV,E-1 Square Pikes
IV,E-2 Round Pikes
IV,F Mandrels

IV,A-1 and IV,A-2
Square Awls and Round Awls

Discussion Form and function of both square and round awls was likely the same. Square versus round might represent personal preference, regional preferences, cultural preferences, or temporal differences. Some of the larger, thicker, round awls appear to have a thicker patina than smaller square types which has lead to speculation that the round variety is older. As is the case with so many other details here, more work is needed on the subject. Regardless of age or function, they are without question, one of the most common of all copper artifacts, in fact, they are likely *the* most common. Some examples could be gorges or leister components as well.

Common Names Awls

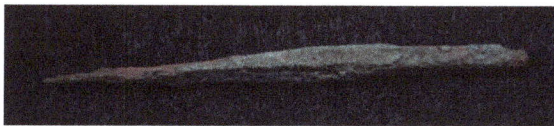
Left, 2 1/2" Awl from Lincoln County Wisconsin. *Private Collection.*

Right, 3 1/2" Awl from Houghton County Michigan. *D. Johnson Collection.*

Left, 3 1/2" example from Manitowoc County Wisconsin. *T. Betka Collection.*

Right, 3 3/8" Awl from Koochiching County Minnesota. *D. Johnson Collection.*

Left, 3 1/4" flat Awl from Vilas County Wisconsin. *Private Collection.*

Right, 3 1/8" Awl from Winnebago County Wisconsin. *Private Collection.*

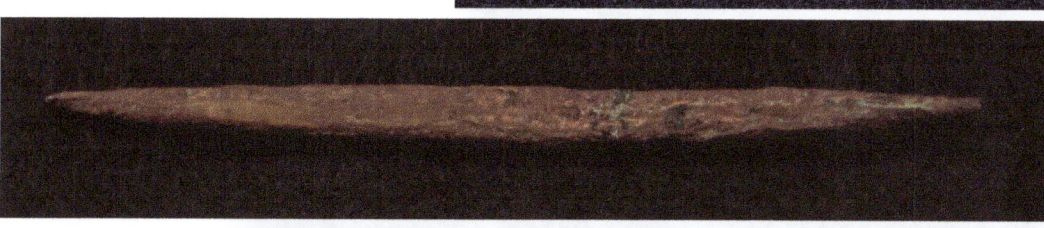
Left, 4 1/16 Awl from Manitowoc County Wisconsin. *T. Betka Collection.*

Right, 4 1/16" example from Vilas County Wisconsin. *Private Collection.*
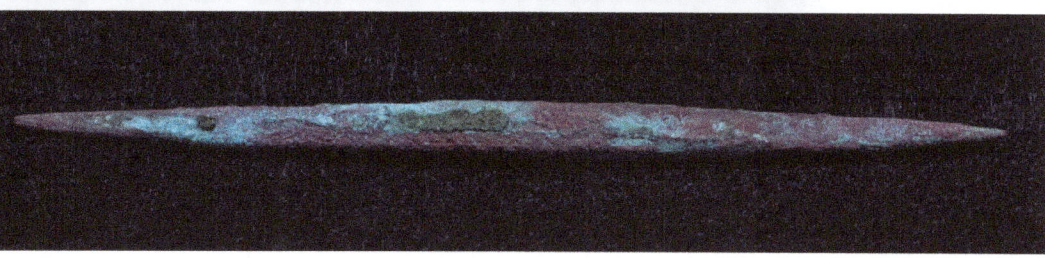

Left, 5 and 5 1/2" Awls from Mackinac County Michigan. *D. Johnson Collection.*

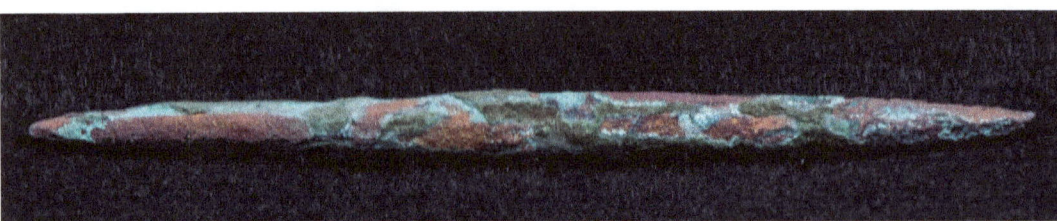

Left, 5 1/2" Round Awl from Vilas County Wisconsin. *Private Collection.*

Above, 5 7/8" example from Vilas County Wisconsin. *Private Collection.*

Above, 6" Awl from Koochiching County Minnesota. *D. Johnson Collection.*

Above, 6 1/4" example from Clayton County Iowa. *D. Johnson Collection.*

Above, 7" Awl from McHenry County Illinois. *D. Johnson Collection.*

Above, 7 1/2" Awl from Sawyer County Wisconsin. *D. Johnson Collection.*

Above, 7 3/4" example from Oconto County Wisconsin. *T. Betka Collection.*

Above, 8" Awl from Oneida County Wisconsin. *Private Collection.*
Below, 7" Square Awl from Lincoln County Wisconsin. *N. Schanen Collection.*

Below, 8" Square Awl from Whiteside County Illinois. *D. Miller Collection.*

IV,B
Punches

Discussion Punches are easy to identify by their close resemblance to modern day nails, they typically have a wider mushroomed head that files down to something of a point. Sometimes that point or distal end is also mushroomed, though often to a minor degree by comparison. It is presumed that these punches were used on a variety of materials including hides and even copper. In at least once instance, a copper punch and a copper bracelet with punch marks were found together offering proof that at least some punches were used to decorate copper. Though rare, punches like these were almost certainly used to mark Ovates as well.

Left, 2 3/8" Punch mushroomed on both ends from use, Lincoln County Wisconsin. *D. Miller Collection.*

Above, 1 3/4" Punch from Vilas County Wisconsin. *D. Johnson Collection.*

Right, 2" Punch, Koochiching County Minnesota. *D. Johnson Collection.*

Left, 2 1/8" example from Winnebago County Wisconsin. *G. Weimer Collection.* Above, 3 5/16" example from Winnebago County Wisconsin. *G. Weimer Collection.*

Right, 2 1/8" Punch, Winnebago County Wisconsin. *G. Weimer Collection.*

Left, 3 5/8" example from Winnebago County Wisconsin, such tools could have been used in multiple ways. *G. Weimer Collection.*

Left, 2 3/4" example from Mackinac County Michigan. *D. Johnson Collection.*

IV,D
Needles

Discussion
Needles are an easy and straightforward class of copper artifact that would not at all be out of place in the modern tool assemblage. The delicate nature of these needles however, combined with their antiquity, means that many have severly corroded eyes. In some cases the eyes are only just barely descirnable. We must therefore assume that some copper tools currently classified as awls may have once been needles that simply had the eye-end corrode away. Needles, in comparison to awls are rare, well preserved examples are even more rare and may come from later Woodland sites in some instances. We also know that awls and needles were still valued much later and at great distances such as those found in Spiro Mounds in Arkansas (Hamilton H, Hamilton J., Chapman E. 1974)

Above, a very nice 3 7/8" example from Winnebago County Wisconsin. *G. Weimer Collection.*

Right, well preserved 3 1/16" example with in tact eye. Unknown provenience. *B. Wasemiller Collection.*

Above, a remarkably well presrved needle from Manitowoc County Wisconsin. It measures 3 3/4" in length. *T. Betka Collection.*

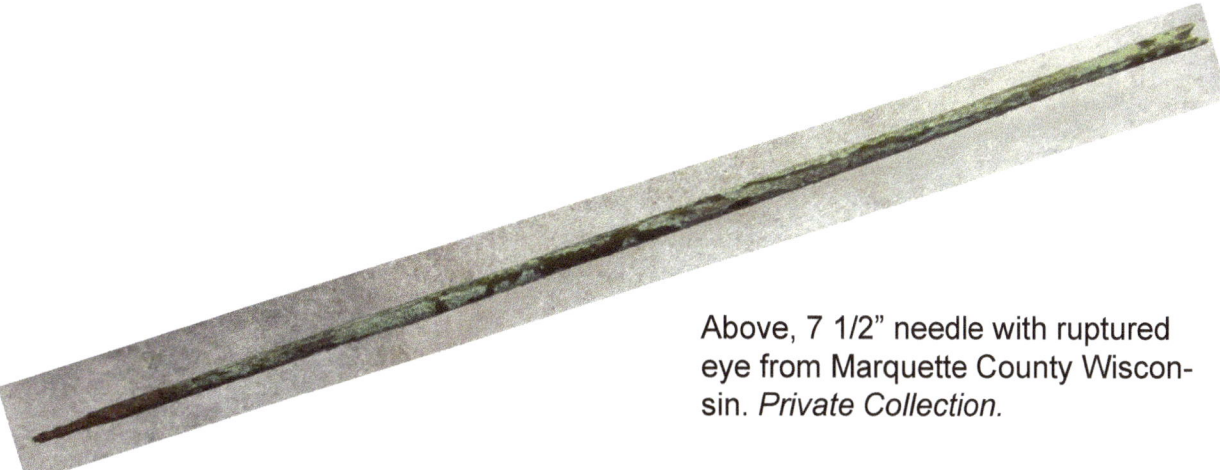

Above, 7 1/2" needle with ruptured eye from Marquette County Wisconsin. *Private Collection.*

IV,E-1 and IV,E-2
Round Pikes and Square Pikes

Discussion

Both round and square pikes are rare. Both are large, often exceeding a foot or more in length, and both are very heavy duty. The use for these large and heavy pieces is unknown. Some theoretical uses include ice picks, lance or spear heads, and mining tools. The round types are presumed to be older and are on average of a slightly larger construction in both length and girth. Lines between large awl and small pike are blurred and probably insignificant.

Some of the smaller examples of what we deem to be pikes may have been used for weaving, mat fabrication, or even bark canoe construction. Round and square type pikes are differentiated between primarily because of an assumed temporal speration or perhaps linear progression from thick round tyles to more recent squared styles.

Left, while still a large and heavy artifact, this 8" pike is on the small end as far as pikes are concerned. This example was found in Houghton County Michigan. *D. Johnson Collection.*

Right, 8 1/2" Square Pike from Winnebago County Wisconsin. *G. Weimer Collection.*

Left, 9 1/2" Pike from Koochiching County Minnesota. *D. Johnson Collection.*

Left, a nice 10 1/2" Pike from Mackinac County Michigan. *D. Johnson Collection.*

Right, large 14 1/2" Round Pike with native silver plainly visible. Thought to have been found in the Upper Peninsula of Michigan, unknown what county. *J. Bussey Collection.*

Left, large 10 1/4" example from Houghton County Michigan. *D. Johnson Collection.*

Right, 9 1/8" Square Pike from Oneida County Wisconsin. Heavy duty construction. *Private Collection.*

Right, Round Pike with well developed worm tracks and oxidation. It measures a little over 18" in length! Found in Green Lake County Wisconsin. Please note that the artifact is whole and undamaged, white string that attatches an information tag to the piece made it look this way against the white background. *Courtesy of the Logan Museum of Anthropology.*

IV,F
Mandrels

Discussion

Mandrels were most likely missed by Wittry, Steinbring, and others because of their close resemblance to bars or other early phase copper poundings. They in fact were not readily recognized as tools until they started to turn up in large numbers at workshop sites in northern Wisconsin and the Upper Peninsula of Michigan, in some cases they were found with artifacts who's sockets matched the corresponding mandrel "like a glove". (Personal conversation with S. Livernash 2013; Schanen,Hunzicker 2013) The biggest distinguishing attribute of mandrels, when trying to differenciate between them and the more numerous bars or ingots, is they are not rectangular like bars or ingots, at least not in their entirety. Usually one end is somewhat blunted or rounded to aid socket formation. Organic materials like anter or bone could've also been used but copper certainly would've been the most durable.

Left, 3 5/8" Mandrel from a Vilas County Wisconsin manufacturing site. *N. Schanen Collection.*

Below, 7 1/4" possible Mandrel that fits perfectly inside this conical, both of which were found in the same general area. It may have been used to make this very conical. Lincoln County Wiscosin. *N. Schanen Collection.*

Above, 5" Mandrel from Oneida County Wisconsin. *Courtesy D. Miller Collection.*

Above, 5" overall, here is a Mandrel that fits a conical found at the same site "like a glove". Marathon County Wisconsin. *D. Miller Collection.*

Left and below, two possible Mandrels from Ontario, Canada. *Courtesy of the T. Wilson Collection.*

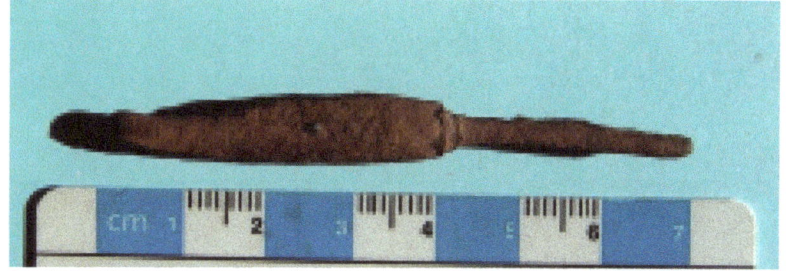

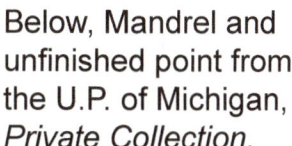
Below, Mandrel and unfinished point from the U.P. of Michigan, *Private Collection.*

V
Spuds

V,A Triangulate (Narrow and Wide)
V,B Pinched
V,C Ovate (Narrow and Wide)
V,D Pointed

V,A
Narrow and Wide Triangulate Spuds

Discussion Different classification systems have handled the group of spuds in as many different ways as there are systems. Wittry had broken the Triangulate Spuds into two different types, essentially a Narrow Triangulate Spud and a Wide Triangulate Spud. Here they are lumped together because they appear to have far more in common than not. All have median ridges, angular sockets, and tabs just like their Triangulate projectile counterparts. A difference in age or distribution between Wide and Narrow Triangulate Spuds might warrant future revision but for now the similarities seem to outweight the differences. Both types could also be contemporaneous with each other and simply made for slightly different functions or even by two different groups around the same time. These spuds may have been hafted with wood, bone, or antler handles and wielded in similar fashion to an adze (likely with similar function as well). It's interesting that so many of the early copper tools were large, heavy-duty wood working tools. We all picture them making dug-out canoes of course, but I suspect their carpentry skills didn't end with canoes.

Common Names Spuds, Traingulate spuds

Below, 6 7/8" example from Oneida County Wisconsin, piece has strong median ridge, well formed tab, and strong, angular socket. *Courtesy of the Milwaukee Public Museum.*

Left, 3 1/4" Triangulate Spud showing both the ventral and dorsal surfaces. Note that it has all of the same features associated with Triangulate projectiles including a median ridge (dorsal surface), a well defined tab, and angular construction. Found in Vilas County Wisconsin. *D. Miller Collection.*

Left, small but classic 2 1/2" example from Mackinac County Michigan. *D. Johnson Collection.*

Below, 5 1/8" Triangulate Spud, Vilas County Wisconsin. *D. Miller Collection.*

Above, nice 3 3/4" example from Lincoln County Wisconsin. *J. Bussey Collection.*

Left, both surfaces of a 3 1/2" Triangulate Spud from Waupaca County Wisconsin. *Courtesy of the Logan Museum of Anthropology.*

Left, incredible 6 3/8" Triangulate Spud from Portage County Wisconsin. The exceptionally long bit may look out of place when compared to most examples but it is important to remember that many artifacts that are found, including copper, represent late stage pieces. This example, with it's excpetionally long bit, simply represents an early stage piece which has not suffered bit loss from extended use-wear. In other words, it was likely lost rather than discarded. *Courtesy of the J. Bussey Collection.*

Below, 3 1/8" example from Vilas County Wisconsin. This example has had the bit worn down to the bit-socket wall junction and is more typical of what we find in cases. *Courtesy of the D. Miller Collection.*

This 7 1/2" Triangulate Spud is arguably one of the most interesting ever found. The craftsman who made it had taken copper smithing to a new level by adding a raised shaft stop near the bit-socket junction. Pieces like this are exceptionally rare and might represent the terminal classic period of copper manufacturing. The long bit suggests it was lost at an early to mid stage. Most examples have been used so much that their bits have worn down or been sharpened enoguh times that they are close to the socket. This piece was found in Lincoln County Wisconsin. *J. Bussey Collection.*

Above, classic form Triangulate Spud with strong median ridge, tab, and angular socket. Measures 5 5/8" in length and was found in Dodge County Wisconsin. Notice the stress fracture in the middle, this sort of damage is common in many spuds, testiment to their hard use and the inherent weakness of the material. *Courtesy of the Milwaukee Public Museum.*

Below, interesting salvaged example which started off as a typical Triangulate Spud, but then had the socket walls removed and smoothed over. This was most likely the result of a stress fracture. The owner presumably decided to salvage it, figure out a new hafting method, and continued using it, perhaps in celt like fashion. Measures 5 7/8" in length and was found in Sheboygan County Wisconsin. *Courtesy of the Milwaukee Public Museum.*

Left, both ventral and dorsal surface views of a long Narrow Triangulate Spud that was found in Vilas County Wisconsin, measures 5 1/2" in length. *Private Collection.*

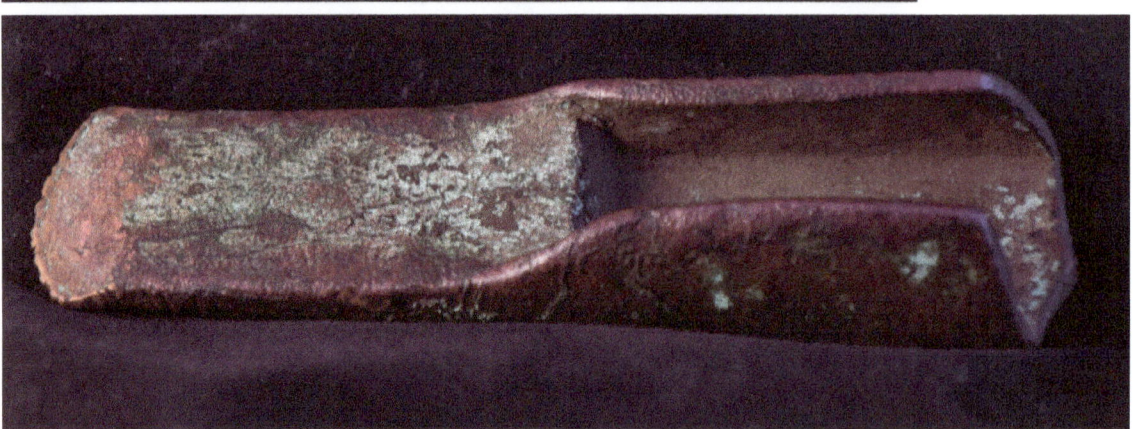

Above, exceptional 5 5/8" example from Winnebago County Wisconsin. *L. Born Collection.* Note the well formed step, triangular socket and tab. The long bit is indicitive of a piece lost at an early stage.

Left, 4 1/2" Triangulate Spud with a flared bit. Vilas County Wisconsin. *D. Miller Collection.*

V,B
Pinched Spuds

Discussion Pinched type spuds are interesting in the fact that might well be the only true "spud" of the group. Their form matches very closely with eighteenth and nineteenth century logging spuds which were mounted in line with the handle and used to strip bark off logs. The close resemblence begs the question, were these used in the same fashion? Other types of spuds appear to have been hafted perpendicular to the shaft and swung/used like an adze to shape wood. These Pinched type spuds may have been used differently however. Some people have theorized that they were in fact ice spuds, used to break through ice in the winter to fish or gather water. They are rare compared to Triangulate and Ovate types of spuds.

Common Names Spuds, Pinched Spuds

Left, 6" Pinched Spud from Racine County Wisconsin. *Courtesy of the Milwaukee Public Museum.*

Below, 6 1/4" example from Marquette County Wisconsin. *Courtesy of the Milwaukee Public Museum.*

Above, 4 3/4" Pinched Spud from Winnebago County Wisconsin. *L. Born Collection.*

V,C
Ovate Spuds

Discussion Ovate Spuds come in a wide range of sizes and forms. Some people have suggested that this type be further broken down into other sub types, especially when one views some of the large, wide, and flat examples. As with the Triangulates however, I feel that similarities between these different examples far outweight the differences. If chronological or distributional differences are found and noted between the different "subtypes" revisions might need to be made. I'm assuming for now that the classic Ovate Spuds like the one pictures below and the very wide flat examples were contemperaneous with one another.

Common Names Ovates, Ovate Spuds, Spuds

Left, one of the finer Ovate Spuds ever found. The piece is very well preserved and nearly flawless. Found in Ontario, Canada. *Courtesy of the O. Anttila Collection.*

Left, a small 1 1/2" Ovate Spud with no obvious signs of use-wear. Very well preserved. Unknown provenience. Might be considered a "miniature" or votive. *J. Bussey Collection.*

Below, 1 1/4" example with an exhausted bit. Small spuds like these would have been useful for woodworking tasks. Found in Oneida County Wisconsin. *D. Johnson Collection.*

Left, 1 5/8" Ovate Spud with a well formed step in the socket. Notice the bit on this is example is very nearly exhausted as well. Oneida County Wisconsin. *D. Miller Collection.*

Below left, 2 1/2" example from Keweenaw County Michigan, it was part of a copper tool cache. Below right, 2 1/8" spud from the same cache as the one at left. *D. Miller Collecton.*

Above, both dorsal and ventral views of a 4 1/4" Ovate Spud recovered in Ozaukee County Wisconsin. Bit shows considerable wear and the socket, as most, has a strong step. Dorsal side shows slight bulging that may have been part of a custom fit to the handle. *Courtesy of the Logan Museum of Anthropology.*

Left, 2 3/4" narrow bit spud. The over all shape and quality of this piece suggests that it could have been made from a salvaged piece. It was found in Whiteside County Illinois. *D. Miller Collection.*

Left, 2 5/8" example from Fond du Lac County Wisconsin. *J. Bussey Collection.*

Right, 2 5/8" example from Jefferson County Wisconsin. *J. Bussey Collection.*

Below, very well preserved 3" Ovate Spud with early stage bit from Keweenaw County Michigan. *D. Johnson Collection.*

Left, very well formed 3" example from Keweenaw County Michigan. *D. Johnson Collecton.*

Right, 3" Ovate Spud from Vilas County Wisconsin. *D. Miller Collection.*

Below, 3 1/2" narrow example from Keweenaw County Michigan. Example has a step in socket like most, Narrow example may have been used in identical fashion to the more typical wide-bit examples but used to accomplish more detailed work perhaps. *D. Johnson Collection.*

Above, 3 3/8" example from Vilas County Wisconsin. *D. Miller Collection.*

Right, 3 1/4" Common Ovate from Vilas County Wisconsin. The close proximety of the bit end to the socket walls suggests a long-lived and well worn piece. *Private Collection.*

Left, 3 1/4" Ovate Spud with well formed worm tracks and step in socket. Found in Washington County Wisconsin. *J. Bussey Collection.*

Left, 3 3/4" Ovate Spud from Sauk County Wisconsin. *J. Bussey Collection.*

Right, 3 3/16" well-used example from Keweenaw County Michigan. *J. Bussey Collection.*

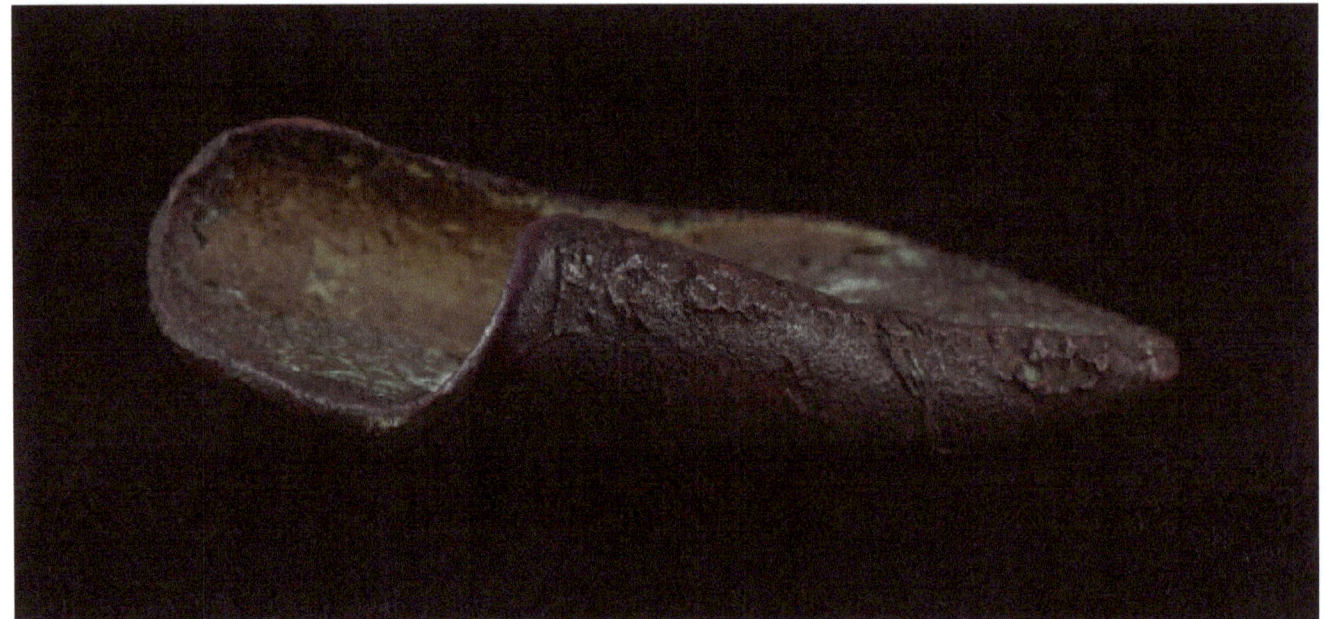

Above, close up on the socket end of an Ovate Spud that shows the classic rolled socket shape. 3 7/8" in length, it was found in Outagamie County Wisconsin. *J. Bussey Collection.*

Below, a 4" Ovate Spud from Ionia County Michigan. *J. Bussey Collection.*

Left, the ventral surface of the spud pictured above. Pieces this well made and preserved are rare. Again, 4" in length, from Ionia County Michigan. *J. Bussey Collection.*

Left, 4" Ovate Spud with steep, angular step in socket. Short bit suggests a later stage artifact. Notice the many hammerstone marks that are visible all over the surface. Marquette County Wisconsin. *Private Collection*.

Below, 4 1/8" Ovate Spud with fairly flat profile. Found in Langlade County Wisconsin. *Courtesy of the J. Bussey Collection*.

Left, 5" example from Keweenaw County Michigan. Notice the stress fracture at the bit-socket junction on the right side. This failure was likely the result of impurities or other issues that the ancient smith tried to work around. This stress crack might explain why the piece still has a long bit compared to most (representing an early stage example). It is somewhat surprising that it was not recycled into other useful tools. *N. Schanen Collection*

Right, another outstanding 5" example of an Ovate Spud. This one is from Mackinac County Michigan and has very well developed worm tracks over portions of the artifact. Note that this piece also has a lot of bit life left. *D. Johnson Collection.*

Right, beautiful 5 1/4" Ovate Spud with well defined step, medium bit life, and rounded socket. This fine example was found in Milwaukee County Wisconsin. *J. Bussey Collection.*

Left, 6 3/4" long, 5 1/4" wide spud from Shawano County Wisconsin. Very few spuds were made this large. Below, a profile picture of the same artifact. Some might argue that these wide flat examples could represent a different type or sub-type of Ovate Spud but the similarities outweigh the differences. *J. Bussey Collection.*

Above, 5 7/8" example found in Dubuque County Iowa. Again, these large and very flat types of spuds may represent an independant type. The unique shape of these may be due to nothing more than hafting material preference, or, on the other hand, may represent a step in the evolutionary ladder of copper. More of these rare types need to be studied and compared. *J. Bussey Collection.*

Left, an enlarged picture of a 2 1/2" spud from Dane County Wisconsin which is completely exhausted. The bit has been worn back to the socket itself and in some cases these can be mistaken for Pinched Spuds. Likewise, completely exhausted Pinched Spuds may look to be worn Ovate Spuds. *This example is courtesy of the Logan Museum of Anthropology.*

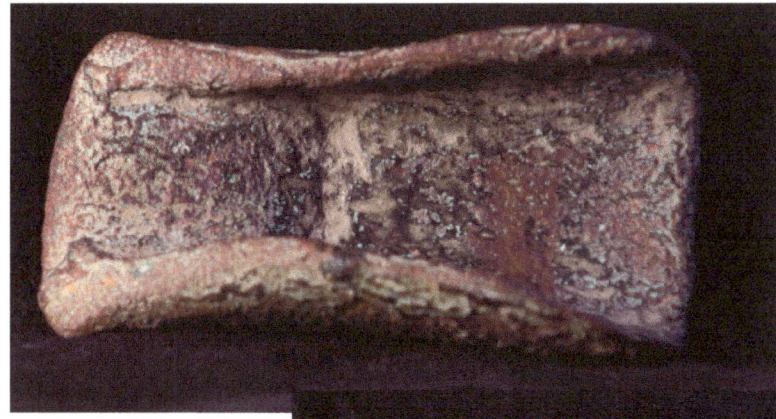

Left, 2 3/4" Ovate Spud from Oconto County Wisconsin. *L. Born Collection.*

Right, 5 example from Houghton County Michigan, found in 1905. *L. Born Collection.*

Right, a super 4" spud from Sheboygan County Wisconsin. Note the medium length bit, well formed worm tracks, strong step, and remarkable state of preservation. *Courtesy of the Logan Museum of Anthropology.*

Left, 5 3/4" Ovate Spud with early stage bit. Gogebic County Michigan. *D. Miller Collection.*

V,D
Pointed Spuds

Discussion Pointed Spuds are a new type in this classification systems which haven't been previously described by many people. They most closely resemble Ovate Spuds in their socket construction but their bit ends are not bits at all, but rather thickened, blunt points. It's difficult to surmise their function. The most popular theory currently is that they were used as either digging sticks or as ice spuds for breaking through the ice in winter. I personally tend to follow the latter only because it's important to measure usefullness against the time and material required to make a tool. Access to lakes and streams frozen over with ice in the winter time would be considered a huge advantage for a person or group of people who were required to live off the land. A copper ice spud might be more durable than a stone counterpart as well. In the end the time and effort required to make a tool like this seems to make more sense to me for use as an ice spud than a digging stick. They appear to have been hafted inline with their handles, probably like a Pinch Type Spud.

Common Names Digging Clads, Pointed Spuds

Below, 5 5/8" Pointed Spud found as part of a small cache found in Menominee County Michigan. *S. Wasion Collection*.

Below, 4 5/16" Pointed Spud from Langlade County Wisconsin. *Private Collection.*

Below, rare 3 1/4" Pointed Spud. These are typically very stout with thick pick-like bit and heavy wall construction. This example is from Vilas County Wisconsnin. *D. Miller Collection.*

Below, another very rare Pointed Spud. At a glance it might look better suited to the projectile category but make no mistake about it, it is made exactly like any other Oovate Spud except that instead of having a wide bit, it has a pointed bit. These are rare by any standards and this is one of the finest examples I have seen to date. It is just short of 7" in over-all length and very heavy duty. Note that the pointed end is not thin or sharpened, but thick and durable. Found in Vilas County Wisconsin. *Private Collection.*

VI
Celts, Adzes, Wedges, Chisels, Gouges, Axes

VI,A Tapering Celts
VI, B Pointed Celts
VI,C Straight Celts
VI,D Adzes
VI,G Wedges and Chisels
VI,H Gouges
VI,I Axes

VI,A
Tapering Celts

Discussion My choices with the celt group were tough. What most have done is create many different types based upon individual traits such as tapering, thickness, flaring bit ends, size, or any number of other attributes. Because we have very little understanding of the chronological ordering of these tools from the archaeological record, and because their function was essentially all the same regardless of form, they have been put together here. It goes without saying that some of these examples are much older than others and some may be attributable to the later Hopewell or Mississippian people, but without knowing how much the forms overlap or how to discern one from another (particularly in the case of Hopewell versus Mississippian) there seems to be no point in naming everything. When more solid evidence can be gleaned from the archaeological record to better define Middle Archaic celt forms from later Woodland forms, and Hopewell from Mississippian, they can best be discussed as simply Straight and Tapering celts. Future generations, with better archaeological data will almost certainly need to break these down into different types with stylistic attributes that are more readily identifiable.

Above, 6 1/2" Tapering Celt from Vilas County Wisconsin. The well developed worm tracks might suggest an older cultural assignment while there are others who might argue that oxidation and patination are not a reliable method of determining antiquity. *D. Miller Collection*

Right, close up of a small Tapering Celt with silver in the poll end. 2 1/4" in length. *Private Collection.*

Left, a 2" Tapering Celt from Winnebago County Wisconsin. *G. Weimer Collection.*

Right, 2 3/4" Tapering Celt from Marquette County Wisconsin. *Private Collection.*

Left, 2 3/8" example from Fond du Lac County Wisconsin. *Private Collection.*

Right, 2 5/8" example from Oconto County Wisconsin with heavy worm track development. *L. Born Collection.* Below, 4 1/4" Tapering Celt from Ashland County Wisconsin. *Courtesy of the Chicago Field Museum.*

Left, 3" Tapering Celt from Mackinac County Michigan. *D. Johnson Collection.*

Above, example from Mackinac County Michigan. It actually measures 3 1/4" in length but was purposely enlarged here to show detail. It's most remarkable because it was made from a salvaged spud. The socket walls of the spud have been removed but there are two small projections left from where the socket walls joined the ventral face. The dorsal side of the piece is flat and so it would have been an Ovate Spud. While we occasionally find copper pieces made from salvaged pieces it is quite rare to see a celt made from a spud. How many times this sort of thing was done may have had an enormous impact on the numbers of copper artifacts we find today. Copper's very nature means that tools that broke or were exhausted did not necessarily have to be discarded, they could be reworked into other pieces. If this was as common of a practice as I suspect it was it would mean that there wrere many times more copper tools than what we find today and help explain all the "missing" copper. *D. Johnson Collection.*

Left, 3 1/4" Tapering Celt from Ontario, Canada. *Private Collection.*

Right, 3 1/4" example from Shawano County Wisconsin. *D. Johnson Collection.*

Below, 3 3/4" example from Iron County Wisconsin. *D. Johnson Collection.*

Above, 3 3/4" example that has been enlarged to show the surface better, surface shows traces of woven fabric which were preserved by the copper salts. Found in Washington County Wisconsin. Probably Hopewell. *D. Johnson Collection.*

Below, 4" example from Mackinac County Michigan. *D. Johnson Collection.*

Below, 4" example from Oneida County Wisconsin. *D. Johnson Collection.*

Below, 4 1/2" example from Mackinac County Michigan. *D. Johnson Collection.*

Below, 4 3/4" example that was found in Racine County Wisconsin in 1897. *J. Bussey Collection.*

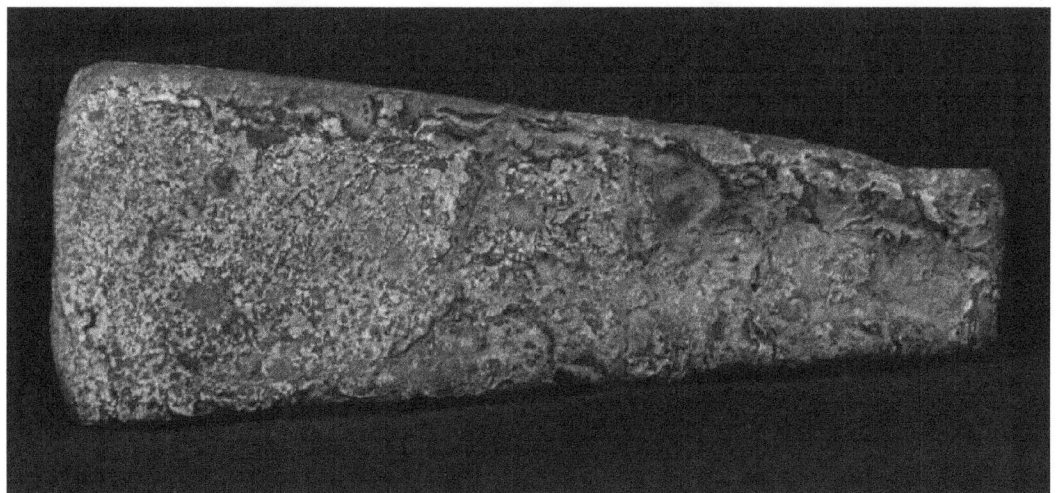

Above, 4 3/4" example from Madison County Illinois. *J. Bussey Collection.*

Above, 4 3/8" Tapering Celt from Ontario, Canada. *Private Collection.*

Above, 4 5/8" example with evindence of use-wear on the poll end, from Manitowoc County Wisconsin. It's interesting to note that it is also common to find damage on the poll end of stone axes. *T. Betka Collection.*

Above, 7 1/4" Tapering Celt from Fond du Lac County Wisconsin. *Courtesy of the Milwaukee Public Museum.*

Above, 6" Tapering Celt from Adams County Wisconsin. Probably Hopewell. *Private Collection.*

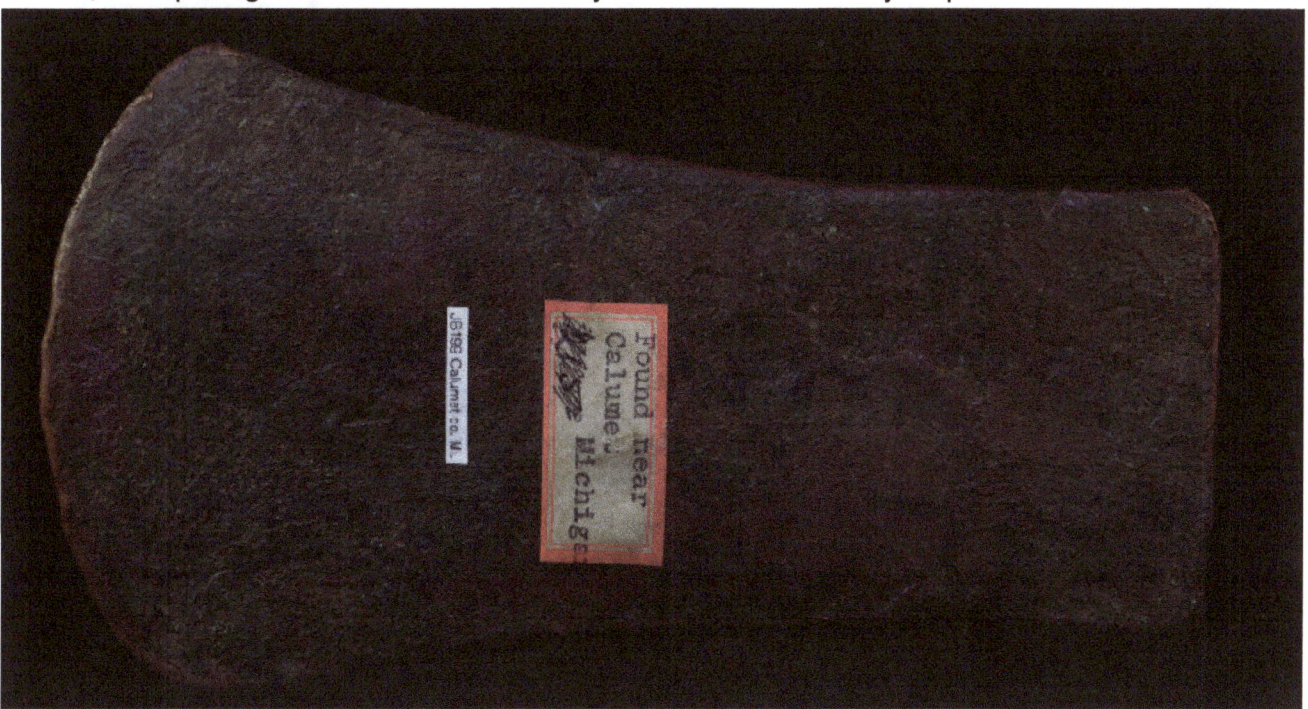

Above, 6 7/8" example from Calumet County Wisconsin. This particular example might have been considered the bell type by Wittry in 1950. *J. Bussey Collection.*

Below, 3 1/2" example from Portage County Wisconsin, note slight mushrooming of poll end. *Courtesy of the Logan Museum of Anthropology.*

Left, 7 1/2" Tapering Celt from Calumet County Wisconsin. Probably Hopewell. *Courtesy of the James R. Beer Collection.*

Right, 4 7/8" example from Columbia County Wisconsin. *Logan Museum of Anthropology.*

Below, a typical 5" Tapering Celt from Ozaukee County Wisconsin. *Courtesy of the Milwaukee Public Museum*

VI,B
Pointed Celts

Discussion I try to be weary of my own cultural bias' but still, these small pointed celts would seem to be at it's surface, the ultimate tool for warfare. It's easy to picture larger and older celts being used to fell trees, build canoes, or other tiresome tasks, it's also easy to picture these small, light, well-made, pointed celts being weilded with deadly efficeincy. If the notion is wrong and they were like their larger siblings and used for wood working purposes it must have been for some detailed or more delicate task than most.

Common Names Celts, Pointed Celts, Woodland Celts

Above, 5 1/4" Pointed Celt from Winnebago County Wisconsin. *G. Weimer Collection.*

Below, 6 5/8" Pointed Celt from Winnebago County Wisconsin. *G. Weimer Collection.*

Above, 4 1/4" Pointed Celt from Vilas County Wisconsin. *N. Schanen Collection.*

Below, 4 3/4" Pointed Celt from Ontario, Canada. *D. Johnson Collection.*

Below, 4 3/4" Pointed Celt from Vilas County Wisconsin. *D. Miller Collection.*

Below, 5 7/8" Pointed Celt from Vilas County Wisconsin. *D. Miller Collection.*

VI,C
Straight Celts

Discussion Straight Celts are just that, straight, generally thinner than Tapering Celts and generally longer. They sometimes exhibit very slight tapering but more often than not, they don't. In most cases they lack well developed worm tracks or any other indication of great age, in fact, many of this type might represent Mississippian use of the metal. Examples found in mounds with good preservation showed that at least some were mounted perpendicular to the shaft like a modern day axe. Because of this, use is assumed to have been the same. Most Straight Celts however seem to come from either caches or burials which makes one wonder if they had a utilitarian function at all or if they had more of a ceremonial or status role in Mississippian society. To see how they were likely hafted look at pg 184-185 in Spiro Mound Copper, Memoir Missouri Archaeological Society, No. 11 December 1974.

Above, cache of Straight Celts from Eagle Harbor Michigan. All were found stacked, one upon the other. Longest piece is slightly over 14" in length. *Courtesy of the D. Miller Collection.*

Above, 4 3/4" Straight Celt example from Oneida County Wisconsin. *D. Johnson Collection.* Below, 8" Straight Celt from Houghton County Michigan. *Courtesy of the Chicago Filed Museum.*

Below, 6 3/4" example from Lincoln Count Wisconsin. *D. Miller Collection.*

Below, 7" Straight Celt from Keweenaw County Michigan, interesting because it appears to have possibly been double bitted. It is the only such example that I have seen and has a well developed patina suggesting the potential for greater age than most Straight Celts. *D. Johnson Collection.*

VI,D
Adzes

Discussion Adzes sometimes have similar outlines to celts but most will have median ridges along their dorsal surface and a slight curvature to their overall form when viewed in profile. These were hafted perpendicular to the handle and swung like a modern hoe or adze, presumably to shape wood. Preserved wooden fragments at a few coppr mining sites (Martin, 2004) had chop marks indicitive of having been formed with a tool like an adze or axe. These tools, set into a sturdy wooden or antler handle would've been efficient at shaping large pieces of wood in quick fashion. The fact that many flaked and ground stone examples are also found at copper related sites is testimony to their utilitarian nature as well as their usefulness to ancient man.

Above, an Adze with an expanding bit, Ontario, Canada. *Courtesy of the O. Anttila Collection.* Below, 5" example from Gogebic County Michigan, at a glance it may look like a celt, but the faint median ridge and slight curvature of the piece make it's intent clear. *D. Miller Collection.*

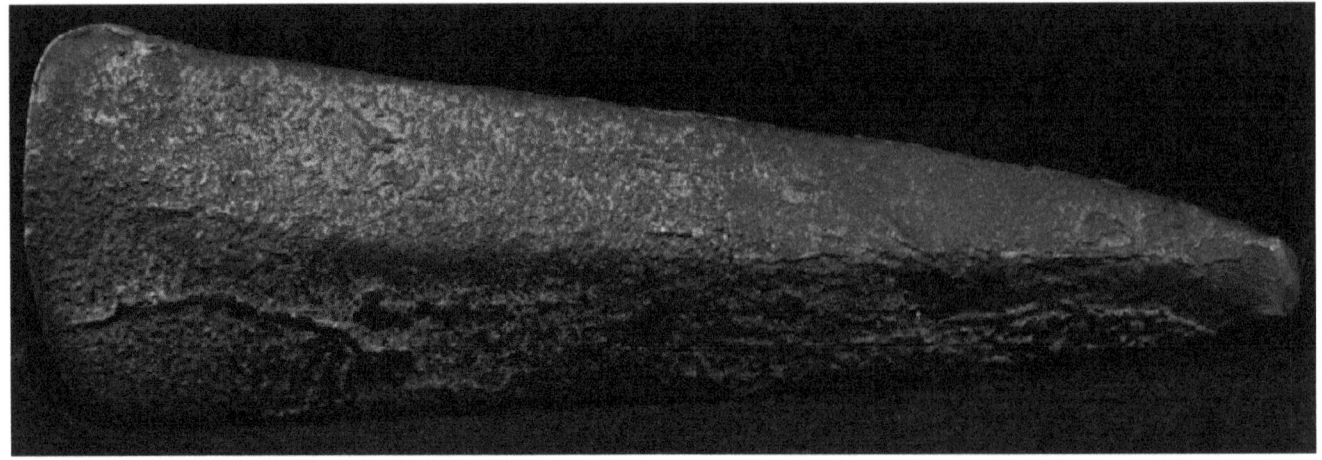

Above, 5 3/4" Adze. Strong median ridge and lightly abused poll. Columbia County Wisconsin. *J. Bussey Collection.*

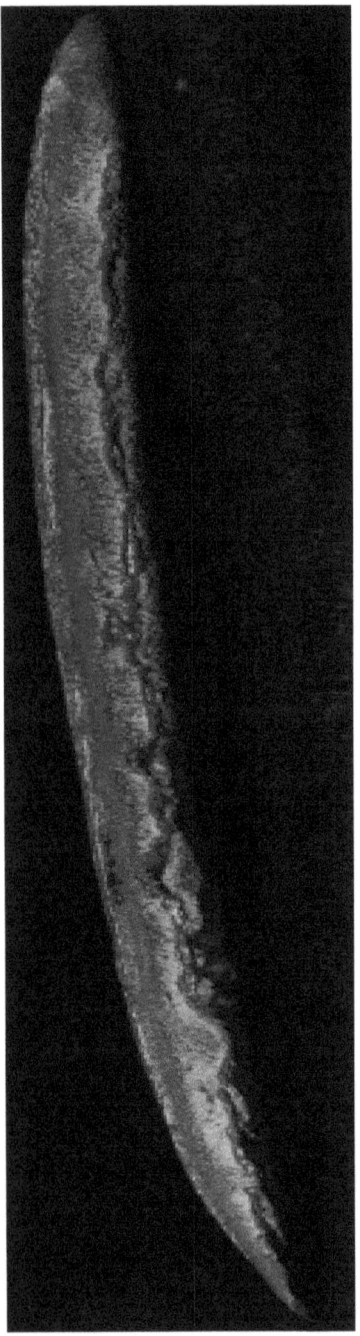

Pictured both left and right, a classic 10" Adze with median ridge and slight curvature. Well-defined worm tracks and large heavy pieces like this are both indicitive of great age. Unknown provenience. *J. Bussey Collection.*

Left, 10 1/2" Adze from Columbia County Wisconsin. *J. Bussey Collection.* Right, 10 1/4" example with strong curvature, unknown provenience. *J. Bussey Collection.*

Left, 9 1/2" Adze from Calumet County Wisconsin, Center, 13" examle from Waupaca County, Right, 10 1/4" example from Waupaca County Wisconsin. *All three artifacts are Courtesy of the Milwaukee Public Museum.*

Left, beautiful 11" Adze from Shawano County Wisconsin. *James R. Beer Collection.* Below center, unusual form that has 7 faint facents to it, some have compared it to the fluting sometimes found on Wisconsin fluted axes (Highsmith). Owner and label call this and others gouges but overall form suggests use as an Adze with a handle hafted perpendicular to the bit. Regardless, gouges and adzes most likely served very simialar wood working functions. This rare example is from Houghton County Michigan. *Courtesy of the James R. Beer Collection.*

Right, ridged Adze from Green Lake County Wisconsin, little over 8" in length. *James R. Beer Collection.*

Both top and bottom side of an exceptionally rare socketed adze with near flawless crafsmanship. This incredible copper tool was found in Ontario, Canada. *Courtesy of the T. Wilson Collection.*

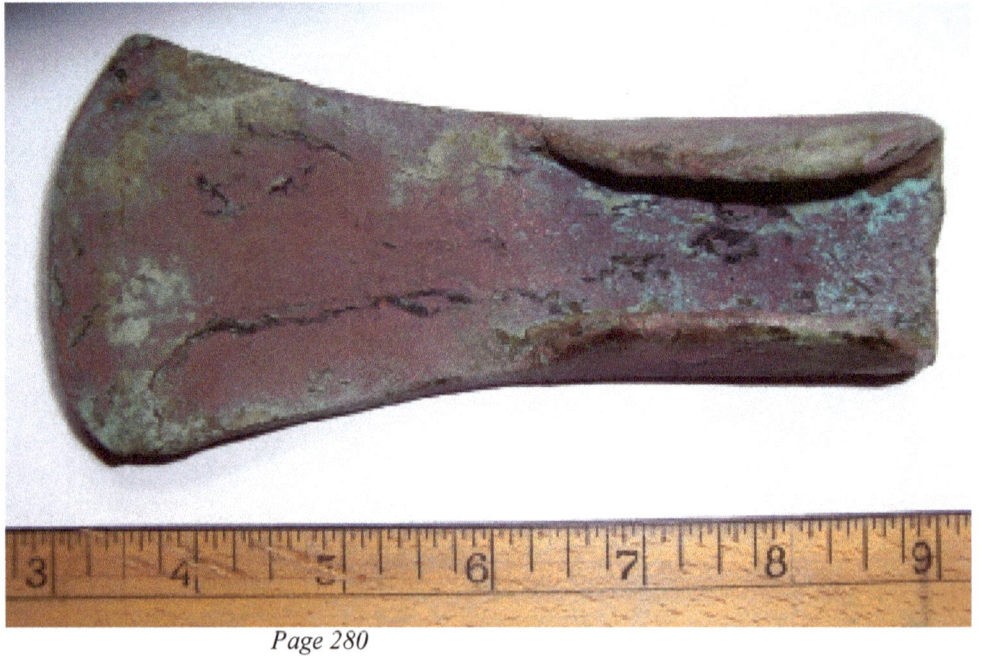

VI,G
Wedges and Chisels

Discussion Wedges and Chisels are included in nearly everyone's previous attempts at classification but what defines one from the other isn't normally the topic of much discussion. Personal communication with many collectors and researchers has lead me to the belief that most of the examples that are long, narrow, and have a small bit are generally thought of as being chisels while larger, heavier, and poll-mushroomed examples are thought of as Wedges. Further complicating things, what differentiates a Wedge from an un-used celt is not defined either. If a celt shows up with heavy poll battering it's likely to be called a Wedge, if a Wedge shows up with no evidence of poll deformation it will most likely be called a celt. Some of the largest examples come from the copper mining areas and it has been suggested that they may have been used in mining raw material. There are less theories explaining the use of long, but thick and heavy made "chisels".

Below, long narrow chisel form from Ontario, Canada.
Courtesy of the T. Wilson Collection.

Above, 3 5/8" Wedge from Keweenaw County Michigan. *J. Bussey Collection*. Below, 5" heavy Wedge also from Keweenaw County Michigan. *D. Johnson Collection.*

Below, 5" Wedge from Keweenaw County Michigan (profile of above piece). *D. Johnson Collection.*

Above, 5 1/4" Wedge from Keweenaw County Michigan. *J. Bussey Collection.* The fact that the vast majority of wedges encountered come from the mining areas of the U.P. supports the idea that such pieces were put to use in the mining operations located there.

Left, a socketed piece with chisel-like bit. Certainly not the typical chisel by any means but likely used in the same wood working capacity of true chisel and thus placement here. Lincoln County Wisconsin. *J. Bussey Collection.*

Above, 6" Chisel from Roseau County Minnesota. *D. Johnson Collection.*

Right, 7 1/4" heavy duty Chisel from Oneida County Wisconsin. Very large heavy examples like this could've also been used in mining raw material like some of the wedges. *J. Bussey Collection.*

Right, whopping 15" Chisel with sharp bit end at lower left. Slight bend at poll end seems to suggest that perhaps it was used as a pry bar of sorts as well. Thick, heavy piece of copper, combined with extreme worm track formation, all point to a copper artifact of considerable age. U.P. of Michigan, precise county is unknown. *James R. Beer Collection.*

Above, a heavy duty 7 1/4" example from Rock County Wisconsin. *Courtesy of the Milwaukee Public Museum.*

Left, 11 1/2" heavy duty Chisel type tool. *Private Collection.*

VI,H
Gouges

Discussion Gouges are one of the very few copper tools which are identical to their stone counterparts. These cupped tools were undoubtedly used for shaping, or "gouging" out wood. They vary in size but all have a cup shaped bit. Most of the time the entire tool is cup shaped. It's interesting to note that such a large percentage of early copper tools were being used for wood working purposes, one can only guess what they might have been making.

Below, 8" Gouge from Calumet County Wisconsin. *Courtesy of the Milwaukee Public Museum.*

Below, 7 1/4" Gouge from Dodge County Wisconsin. *Courtesy of the Milwaukee Public Museum.*

Above, top to bottom, 4 1/4", 5", and 5 1/2" Gouges that were all found together in a cache in Vilas County Wisconsin. These are all classic forms and useful wood working tools. *Private Collection.*

VI,I
Axes

Discussion Three years, thousands of miles, and dozens of large collections both public and private netted only one *potential* example from the Western Great Lakes Region. It is not the ideal specimen that Wittry might have drawn in 1950, nor does it closely match it's stone counterparts. Instead it fills the type as the only thing I could find which was close. Wittry did not detail the type, Steinbring failed to find any examples and also questioned it as a type in general. Here it remains again because it seems like there should be more examples. There are a couple of very nice examples pictured in *The Redskin* Volume XIII, No. 4 1978, Specialized Copper Issue pg 26-27 but I was not able to locate any of these examples for personal examination with the exception of one very odd example which was from much farther south. I suspect that the total number of true copper axes as pictured by Wittry numbers less than a half dozen total. Surprisingly, even with the use of modern detectors, no new examples of this type have been found to my knowledge in the last thirty or more years.

Left, the bit end of a 5" "Axe" head from Berrien County Michigan. Note that it's flat on one side and curved on the other suggesting at least the possibility that it was more of an adze than an axe. *Courtesy of the Chicago Field Museum.*

The bit is the most obvious thing about this artifact. It's impossible to be sure, but after examing this piece at length it seems to me that it may have been a convient piece of float copper that was manipulated just enough to make it useful. Wether that means as an adze or as an axe I don't know.

Below, while not ideal, it does have some pseudo grooves around the central portion that would potentially allow for hafting.

Bit end

Above, the poll end does not show obvious signs of use-wear.

Bit end

VII
Hooks, Gorges, Leisters, Gigs

VII,A Hooks
VII,B Gorges
VII,C Leisters & Gigs

VII,A
Hooks

Discussion Hooks, some large, some small, some with obvious ways of attaching line, some without. Undoubtedly most were likely used for fishing in a manner not too different than we do today. Other examples however may have been used for other purposes, like to suspend pots for cooking around a fire or perhaps to latch a door flap shut. Of the hooks with a means to attach a line there appears to be three different primary ways. A traditonal eye was made in some by chisel cutting a hole. In other instances the end of the hook looks like it was simply bent over itself to provide a place to tie the line off at. Lastly, some examples have a small notch cut into the shaft of the hook to facilitate line attachment.

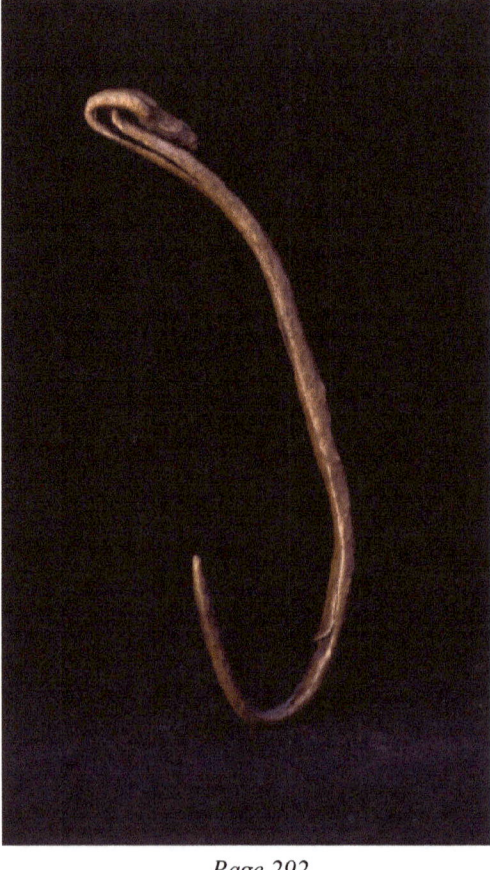

Left, 1 5/8" hook form from Vilas County Wisconsin. *N. Schanen Collection.*

Below, 1 9/16" example from Lincoln County Wisconsin. *N. Schanen Collection.*

Right, 2 1/2" hook from Vilas County Wisconsin. *N. Schanen Collection.*

Left, 1 1/4" hook with grooved shank for line attachment. Marquette County Wisconsin. *Private Collection.*

Right, 1 3/4" hook with folded shank for line attachment. Marinette County Wisconsin. *D. Johnson Collection.*

Right, 1 5/8" hook from Lincoln County Wisconsin. *N. Schanen Collection.*

Left, 1 1/2" cluster of hooks fused together by countless generations of lying undisturbed in the soil. Found in Manitowoc County Wisconsin. This incredible and unique cluster suggests at least the possibility that they were part of a stored trot line. *G. Weimer Collection.*

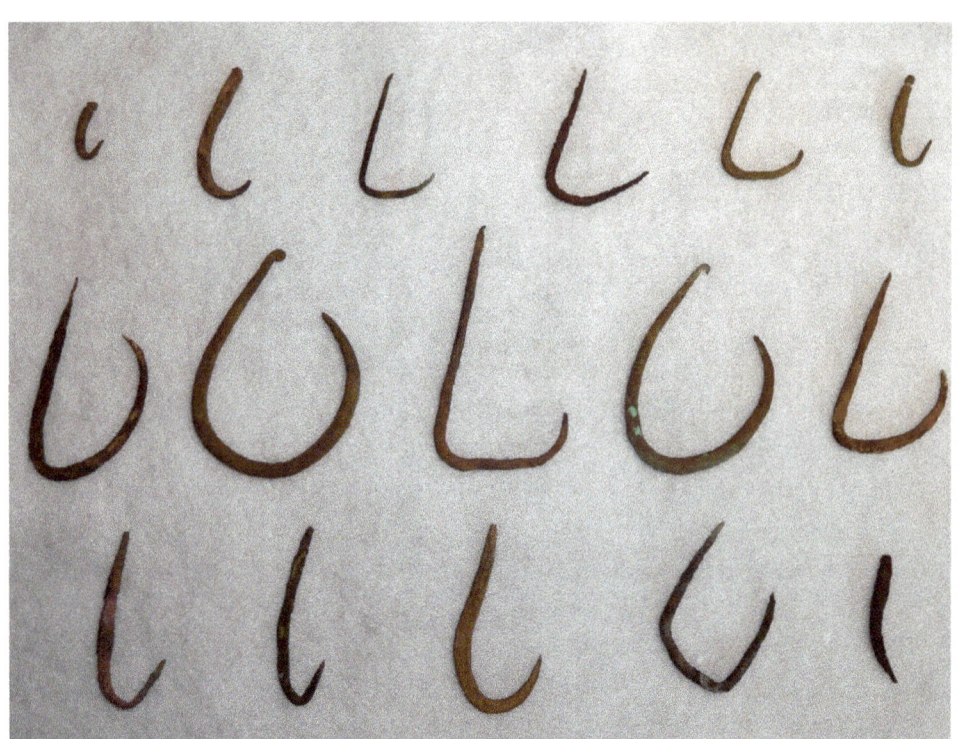

Left, a fine collection of hooks showing more than one line attachment method and more than one style of hook. These hooks are from Wisconsin and the majority are from Jefferson County Wisconsin. *S. Wasion Collection.*

VII,B
Gorges

Discussion There's still considerable discussion concerning these artifacts. Some believe they are awls with a slip stop feature that prevented the awl from slipping back into the handle or the user's hand for that matter. Others contend that the hump in the middle allowed for a line attachment so that it could be used as a gorge. Neither argument is overly convincing and unless the archaeological record shines a light upon it we may never know for sure.

Common Names Gorges, Slip stop awls, Straight line hooks

Left, 2 7/16" Gorge from Marathon County Wisconsin. *D. Miller Collection.*

Right, 3 5/8" example from Vilas County Wisconsin. *D. Miller Collection.*

Below, 5" Gorge from Vilas County Wisconsin. *Private Collection.*

Above, 3 1/4" longest, all from Oneida County Wisconsin. *D. Johnson Collection.*

Page 295

Above and below, several nice examples that the original owner labeled as awls. I don't believe that the awl-gorge arguement will be settled anytime soon. Perhaps both parties are correct and some were used as slip-stop awls while others were used as gorges. These wonderful examples were found in Ontario, Canada. *Courtesy of the O. Anttila Collection.*

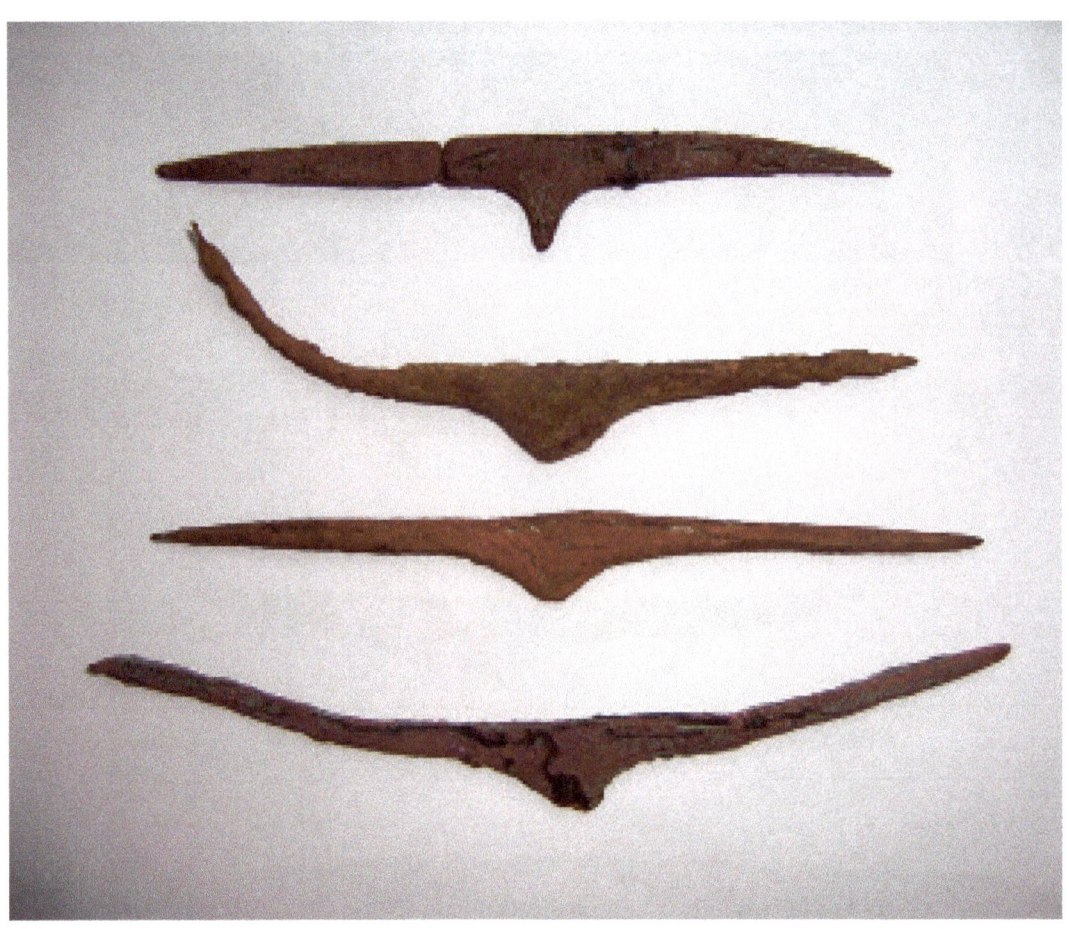

VII,C
Leisters and Gigs

Discussion It's tempting to picture large fishing spears harvesting migrating salmon along the Northwest coast when we think of leisters and gigs but it's important to remember that these could've been equally effective in the taking of smaller fish species, frogs, snakes, amphibians, and any other number of small game animals.

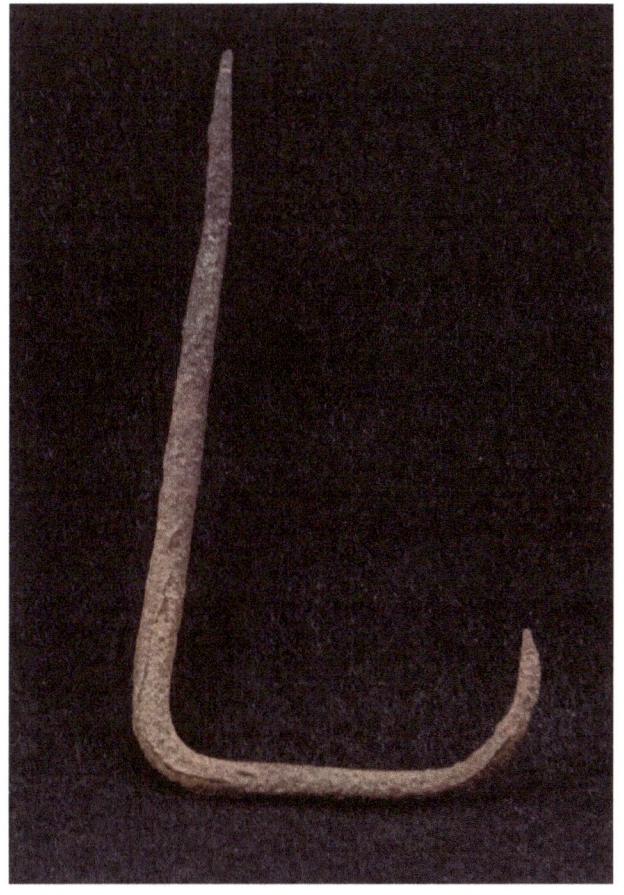

Left, 3 1/4" Leister from Lincoln County Wisconsin. Leisters and gigs differ from traditional fishing hooks by size, angular construction, and by the fact that they never have an eye or other method of line attachment visible at the end of the shank. This is because the end of the shank was inside the hafting element next to the shaft. *D. Miller Collection.*

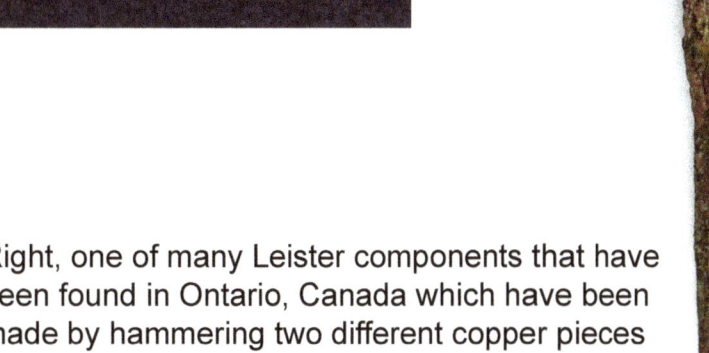

Right, one of many Leister components that have been found in Ontario, Canada which have been made by hammering two different copper pieces together with a "wrap". *O. Anttila Collection.*

Right, 2 1/8" Leister or Gig from Winnebago County Wisconsin. *G. Weimer Collection.*

Below, 4" example from Oneida County Wisconsin. *D. Johnson Collection.* Left, 3 7/8" piece from Vilas County Wisconsin. *D. Miller Collection.*

Left, a huge 12" "gaff" hook. Pieces like this were quite possibly used as modern gaff hooks to help with the retrival of fish from the water or even through the ice. Keweenaw County Michigan. *D. Johnson Collection.*

Left, picture showing potential Leister configuration, all of these pieces are from Ontario, Canada. *Courtesy of the O. Anttila Collection.*

Below, another Canadian Leister example showing the multi-piece construction. *O. Antilla Collection.*

Left, Leister component from Ontario, Canada which has been made from a single piece of copper. *O. Antilla Collection.*

VIII
Decorative Items

VIII,A Beads
VIII,B Bracelets
VIII,C Rings
VIII,D Pendants
VIII,F Spirals

VIII,A
Beads

Discussion There are essentially two things to point out about beads. They come in basically two forms, round and tube, or "rolled" beads. Technically all beads were made by rolling but the term seems to refer more so to the long cylindrical forms versus the rounder forms. The second important thing to know is that beads were not strictly a later period phenomonon, decorative items, including beads, were in fact manufactured during the Middle Archaic as well based upon the number of beads found by metal detectorists at sites which appear to be Archaic. The earlier bead forms seem to be round types and larger than average. The tubular forms seem to be from later Woodland times.

Common Names Round Beads, Tubular Beads

Left, two 1/2" beads made by coiling flat copper. Lincoln County Wisconsin. *D. Miller Collection.*

Left, close up of a round bead found in Ontario, Canada. *Courtesy of the O. Anttila Collection.*

Left, 1" wide bead from Mackinac County Michigan. *D. Johnson Collection.*

Below, 1 1/4" long rolled tubular bead and a small 3/8" example from Washara County Wisconsin. *G. Weimer Collection.*

Left, 1/4" round bead from Oneida County Wisconsin. *Private Collection.*

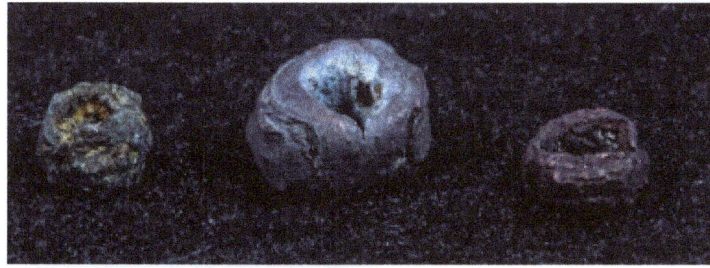

Left, largest example is 3/4" across. Winnebago County Wisconsin. *Private Collection.*

Left, 5/8" bead from Winnebago County Wisconsin. *G. Weimer Collection.*

Above, 3/4" bead from Mackinac County Michigan. *D. Johnson Collection.*

Left, 1/2" example from Marathon County Wisconsin. *D. Miller Collection.* Below, small strand of beads from Oconto County Wisconsin. *Private Collection.*

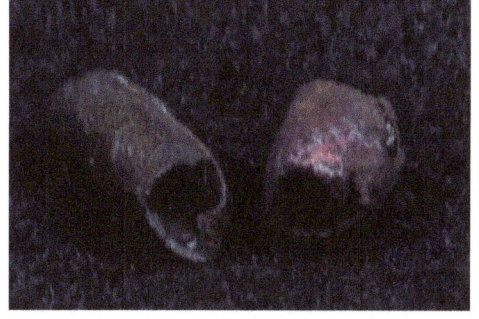

Above, two 3/4" beads from Winnebago County Wisconsin. *Private Collection.*

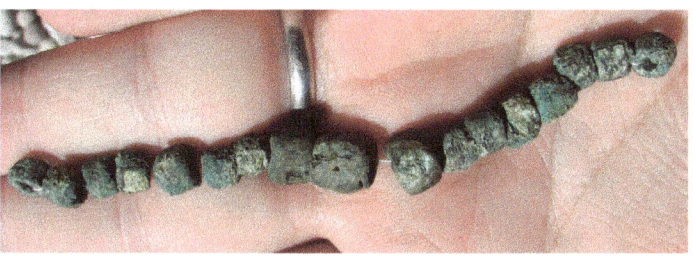

Above, bead set that includes a 1 1/4" wide wooden bead covered in copper. This rare set was excavated from a Crawford County Wisconsin mound in 1884. This is the only complete wooden covered bead encountered while researching the book. *Courtesy of the Logan Museum of Anthropology.*

Left, grouping of beads from Koochiching County Minnesota, longest is just under 1". *Courtesy the D. Johnson Collection.*

Right, tube bead found in Ontario, Canada. *Courtesy of the O. Anttila Collection.*

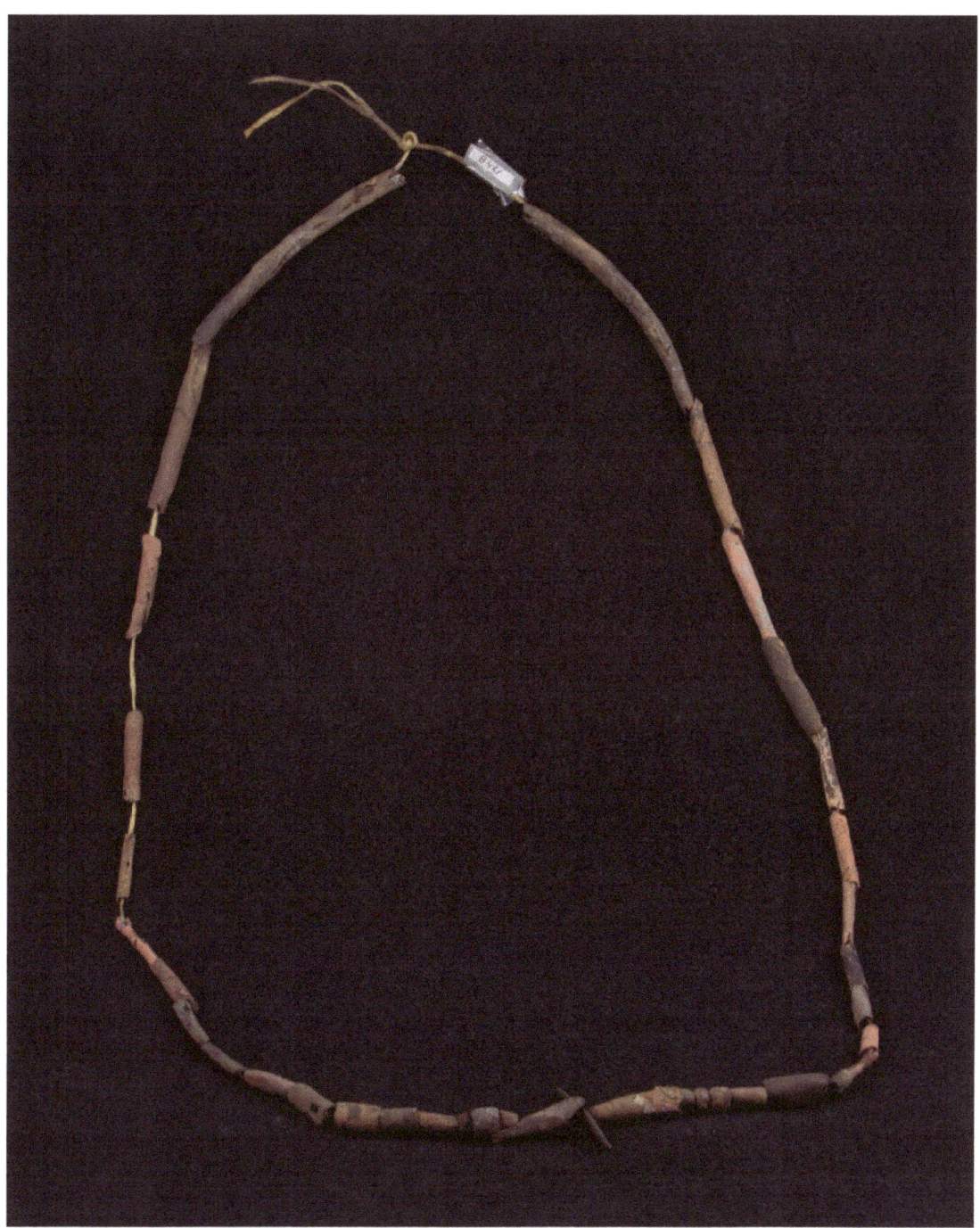

Above, a full strand of beads found in Lincoln County Wisconsin. *D. Miller Collection.*

VIII,B
Bracelets

Discussion There's little to be said about bracelets, their form and function probably didn't vary much from today's use for the same thing. These ancient examples may have been status symbols however and represented an investment of time and materials to make. Wide, thick, heavy examples like the one below were likely Archaic. Smaller more delicate examples are most often assoiciated with later period sites.

Above, 3 1/8" punch marked bracelet from Oconto County Wisconsin, one of the finest examples known. Heavy construction and large size suggest an early date for this piece. It's excellent preservation is equally impressive given it's potential age. *L. Born Collection.*

Left, 1 3/4" bracelet from Vilas County Wisconsin. This example's exceptionally small diameter suggests at least the possibility that it may have been manufactured for a child. *Courtesy of the D. Miller Collection.*

Right, well made 2" bracelet from Keewenaw County Michigan. *D. Johnson Collection.* Below, 2 1/2" bracelet with a much narrower construction. It was found in Vilas County Wisconsin. *Courtesy of the D. Miller Collection.*

Below, another narrow band example that measures 2 1/2" wide and was found in Winnebago County Wisconsin. It's narrow construction combined with it's excellent level of preservation would seem to suggest a relatively newer assignment in terms of age but it's hard to be sure. *Private Collection.*

Right, 2 1/8" wide punch marked bracelet from Vilas County Wisconsin. Most examples are not this decorative. *Private Collection.*

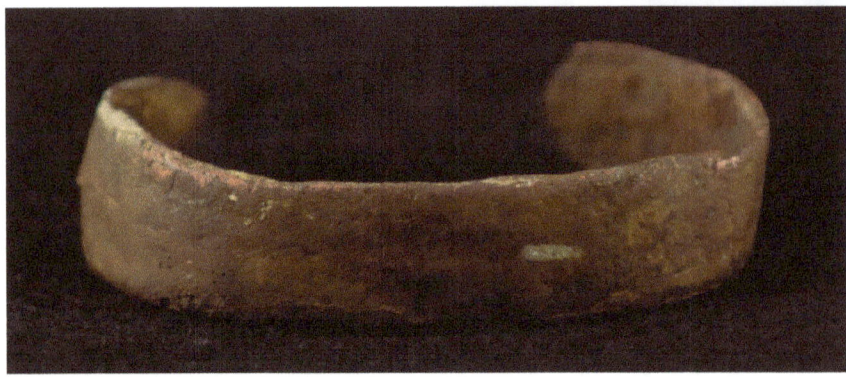

Left, 2 1/8" example from Winnebago County Wisconsin. *G. Weimer Collection.*

Right, 2 3/4" narrow style bracelet from Lincoln County Wisconsin shown in profile. *Courtesy the D. Miller Collection.*

Left, 2 3/8" bracelet from Gogebic County Michigan. *D. Miller Collection.*

Left, top, center, and bottom, two bracelets which were found as is, one inside the other. This highly unusual find was found in Oneida County Wisconsin. It measures approximately 2 3/4" wide. *Courtesy of the D. Miller Collection.*

Left and below, a 2 1/2" and 2 3/8" bracelt from Keweenaw County Michigan, both were found together. Both are heavy, robust examples for their size. *Private Collection*.

Below, a punch marked, and straightened out, bracelet from Ontario, Canada. *Courtesy of the T. Wilson Collection.*

VIII,C
Rings

Discussion The simple title "rings" might be somewhat deceptive. This type represents all types of rings, not only rings as we think of them today, that is, worn on a finger, but also flat rings which could've been worn in the nose or on clothing. The flat style thought to be nose rings in fact outnumber the traditonal type of finger ring.

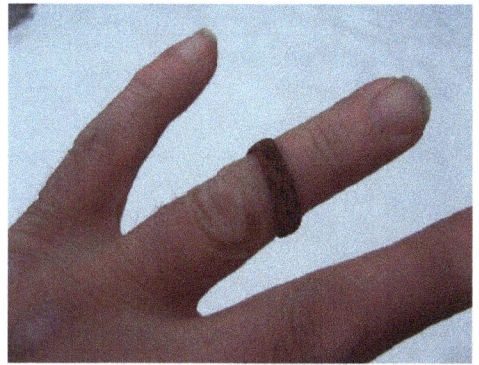

Left, old ring on a modern finger! Found in Ontario, Canada. *Courtesy of the T. Wilson Collection.*

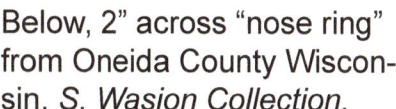

Below, 2" across "nose ring" from Oneida County Wisconsin. *S. Wasion Collection.*

Left, three nose rings from Lincoln County Wisconsin. *D. Miller Collection.*

Left, group of 4 Wisconsin rings, average size is 3/4" across. *N. Schanen Collection.*

Above, a fine assortment of nose or ear rings. Most of these range in the 1 1/2" to 2" in width. These are from a number of locations, mostly in Wisconsin and some without provenience. *Courtesy of the J. Bussey Collection.*

Below, the rings one either side were found in Menominee County Michigan, the center piece, at around 3" across might have been an arm band and was found in Oneida County Wisconsin. *S. Wasion Collection.*

Left, 1" across ring from Koochiching County Minnesota. *D. Johnson Collection.* Right, 1 1/2" punch marked ring from Vilas County Wisconsin. Very few of these decorations were punch marked. *D. Miller Collection.*

Left, 1 1/8" nose or earring from Lincoln County Wisconsin. *D. Miller Collection.* Below right, 1 3/8" example from Vilas County Wisconsin. Courtesy of the *D. Miller Collection.*

Below, 2" example from Winnebago County Wisconsin. *G. Weimer Collection.*

Below, 1" across, this example was found in Marquette County Wisconsin. *Courtesy of the Milwaukke Public Museum.*

Page 313

VIII,D
Pendants

Discussion Pendants have seldom, if ever, been discussed independantly other than to be pointed out, as all decorative items, as being from some later manifestation. Research conducted during the course of this book strongly suggests however that decorative items were also an intrinsic part of what is generally thought of as the "Old Copper Culture". They appear not only in the grave goods of the Riverside site and others, but also at OCC copper manufacturing sites all over the upper Great Lakes Region. While there was certainly a general shift from utilitarian to decorative use of copper over time I must stress that decorative items were also manufactured and valued early on.

Right, 1 3/4" Pendant from Oneida County Wisconsin. *Private Collection.*

Below, 2 1/2" Pendant from Houghton County Michigan. *Courtesy of the Milwaukee Public Museum*

Below, 1 3/8" punch marked Pendant from Vilas County Wisconsin. *D. Miller Collection.*

Below, 2 1/2" punch marked Pendant from Vilas County Wisconsin. *D. Miller Collection.*

Left, 2 1/2" tooth or claw pendant from Marathon County Wisconsin. *D. Miller Collection.*

Below, 2 1/2" horn Pendant from Vilas County Wisconsin. *D. Miller Collection.*

Left, 2 3/4" forked Pendant from Vilas County Wisconsin. *D. Miller Collection.*

Below, 3" horn Pendant from Lincoln County Wisconsin. *D. Miller Collection.*

Above, 3/4" across, this Pendant is reminiscent of the "four winds" motif commonly found on decorative items from historic times. *D. Miller Collection.*

Right, 3 3/8" horn Pendant from Vilas County Wisconsin. *D. Miller Collection.*

Below, 2" round Pendant from Lincoln County Wisconsin. *N. Schanen Collection.*

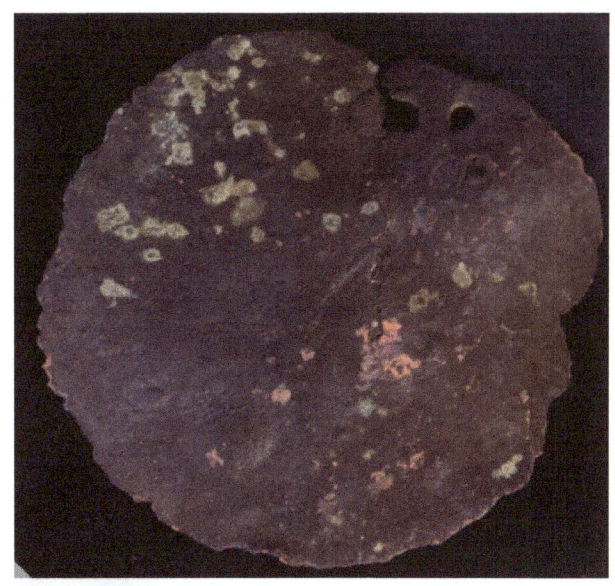

Above, 1 1/2" Pendant, unknown provenance but notice the chisel cut marks at the bottom. Below, 2 1/4" pendant with ruptured suspension hole. *Both are courtesy of the N. Schanen Collection*

Left, small two holed Pendant from the *J. Marz Collection..*

Right, 5 1/2" Snake effigy from Marinette County Wisconsin. *S. Wasion Collection.*

Left, 1 1/2" Oneota related Pendant from Winnebago County Wisconsin. *G. Weimer Collection.*

Above, a 6" wide piece of flat copper that has been placed here in the pendant section but might just as easily be called a gorget. Note the two holes on the upper portion, presumably for suspension. This is an exceptionally rare artifact for Wisconsin. It's likely Hopewell or Mississippian related. Found in Marathon County Wisconsn. *Courtesy of the D. Miller Collection.*

Left, Top Kenosha County Wisconsin, Left middle, Wisconsin River, Right middle, Jefferson County Wisconsin, and the "turtle effigy" bottom center was found in Oneida County Wisconisn. *Courtesy of the S. Wasion Collection.*

Below, interesting Pendant from Ontario, Canada. *T. Wilson Collection.*

Page 318

VIII,E
Spirals

Discussion Spirals are a rare form of decoration that was presumably used as a hair wrap or attached in some other way to a person or their clothes. Most examples thus far seem to be from Northern Wisconsin.

Left, 1 1/4" Spiral from Winniebago County Wisconsin. *D. Miller Collection.*

Below, 1" example from Oneida County Wisconsin. *Private Collection.*

Below, the largest spiral I have come across thus far, at nearly four inches in length it's more than double the average example. *Courtesy of the G. Weimer Collection.*

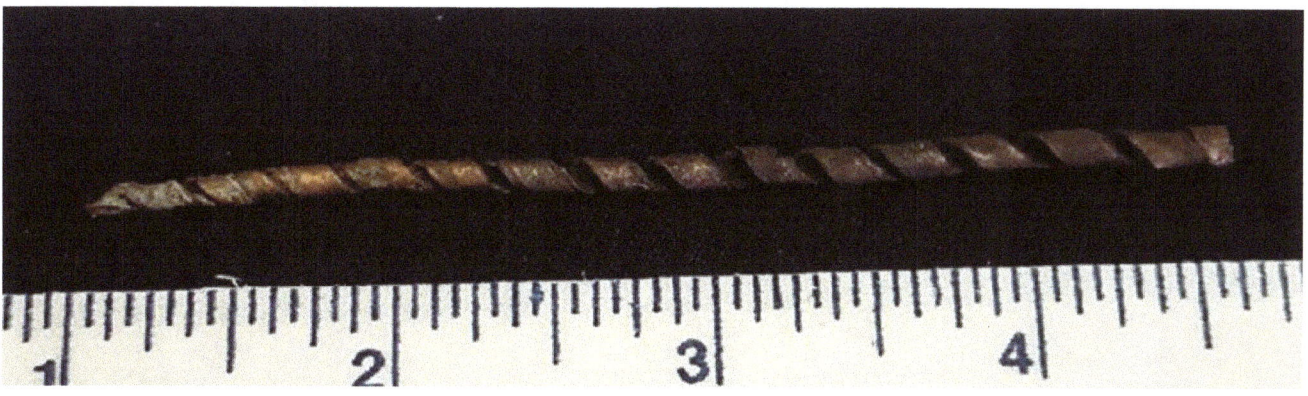

Interesting Specimens

Above, 4 7/8" tall winged bannerstone found by a road crew in Fond du Lac County Wisconsin, it's an unique specimen. Modern copper smiths (Neubauer), using only ancient techniques, have been able to replicate this piece including the hole through the central portion but it is something that only a master copper smith would attempt. *Courtesy of the Milwaukee Public Museum.* Below, Triangulate Spud as found with a tanged knife inside the socket, held in place by oxidation and careful excavation. The spud measures roughly 3 1/4" in length and appears to be end-stage as the bit is worn back to the start of the socket walls.

Above, 4 3/8" mated "digging sticks" as they were found in Pine County Minnesota. The larger one I would place in the Pointed Spud type while the smaller one is a bit more puzzeling. *Private Collection.*

Right, 2 5/8" exceptional snake effigy found in Vilas County Wisconsin. Rare, and most likely from a later time period, perhaps Hopewell or Mississippian related. *D. Miller Collection.*

Below, an interesting copper "hammerstone" covered with a thick mineral patina. The outside edges are flattened, pot-marked, and appear to have wear patterns that would be consistent with use as a hammerstone. Found in Vilas County Wisconsin. *Private Collection.*

Above, a fantastic cache of artifacts that were all found in Vilas County Wisconsin. It contained not only 3 completed spuds, but also the mandrels which were used to manufacture them! Largest spud is approximately 3" in length. *D. Miller Collection.*

Left, 4 7/8" projectile preform. This particular example was most likely going to be made into an Ovate, both sides were flat. If it was going to be a Triangulate the dorsal plain would've already had the median ridge formed. The maker still needed to pound the blade edges out to a sharp edge and the socket needed further expanding before being wrapped around to form the socket. Unknown provenience. *Courtesy of the M. Sainz Collection and the Little Eagle Arts Foundation of Wisconsin Dells.*

Below, another unfinished piece, here we have a Tanged Crescent knife that was abandoned for one reason or another prior to the tangs being bent upward, pulled out, and the blade being expanded. Mid-stage pieces like this are rare, the material flaw on the left side may have played a role in the owner discarding it or planning on coming back to it later. Vilas County Wisconsin. 7" wide. *D. Miller Collection.*

Five punch marked Ovates that were all found together as a cache, almost certainly all made by one craftsman. Winnebago County Wisconsin. *D. Miller Collection.*

Left, and below left, a number of examples of potential flintknapping tools. There is still considerable debate on the use of these tools, but out of many supposed examples these examples from Ontario appear to be the most likely candidates. *Courtesy of the T. Wilson Collection.*

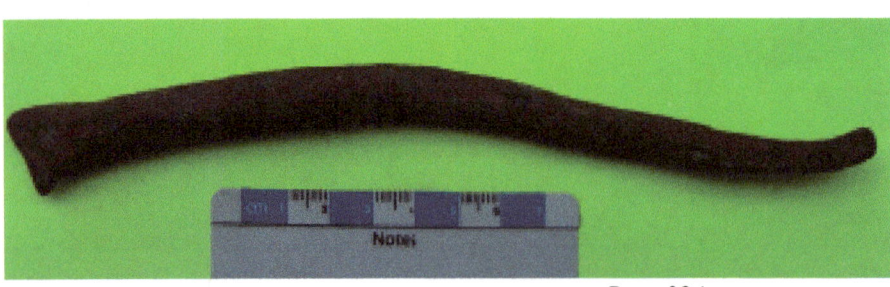

Left, 13" "Silver Sword" from the U.P. of Michigan. Of the thousands of artifacts looked at over the making of this book this is most likely the single most unique item I've come across. It appears to be mostly composed of native silver, this, combined with the enormous size and unique form make it an interesting piece to say the least. *Courtesy of the D. Miller Collection.*

Left, 7 1/2" copper artifact recovered in Winnebago County Wisconsin. There's considerable speculation on what it may have been used for but the owner lovingly refers to it as his "tent stake". *Courtesy of the G. Weimer collection.*

Below, possible bannerstone. Oneida County Wisconsin. I managed to lose the measurements on this interesting piece but believe it was roughly 2 1/2" to 3" in width. *Courtesy of the J. Bussey collection.*

Page 325

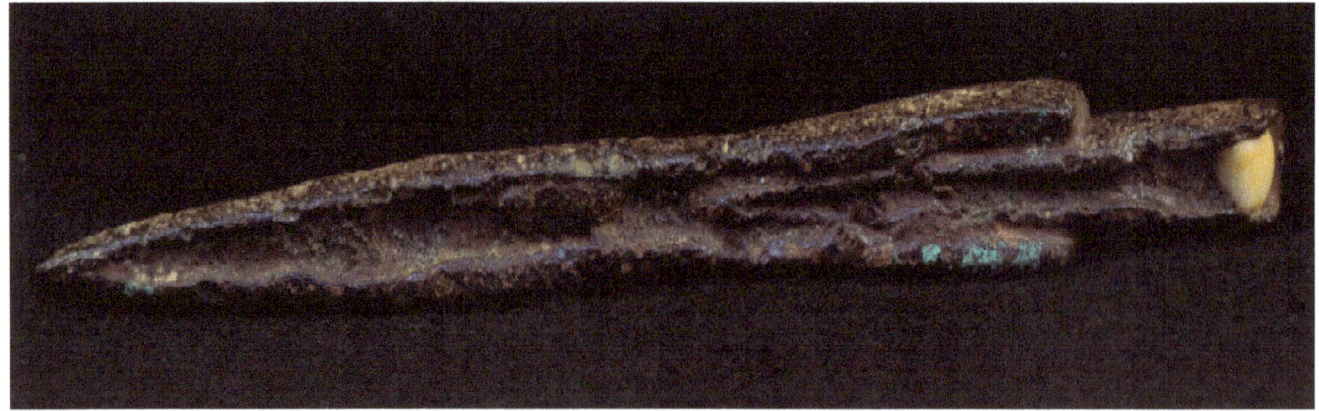

Above, 6 1/4" overall and recovered in Dane County, these two points were found as is, one stuck inside the other. *J. Bussey Collection.*

Left, copper plummet, unknown provience, as far as I know this is the only known example. *J. Bussey Collection.*

Below, 3 1/16" point and hook were found together in this position in Vilas County Wisconsin. *Private Collection.*

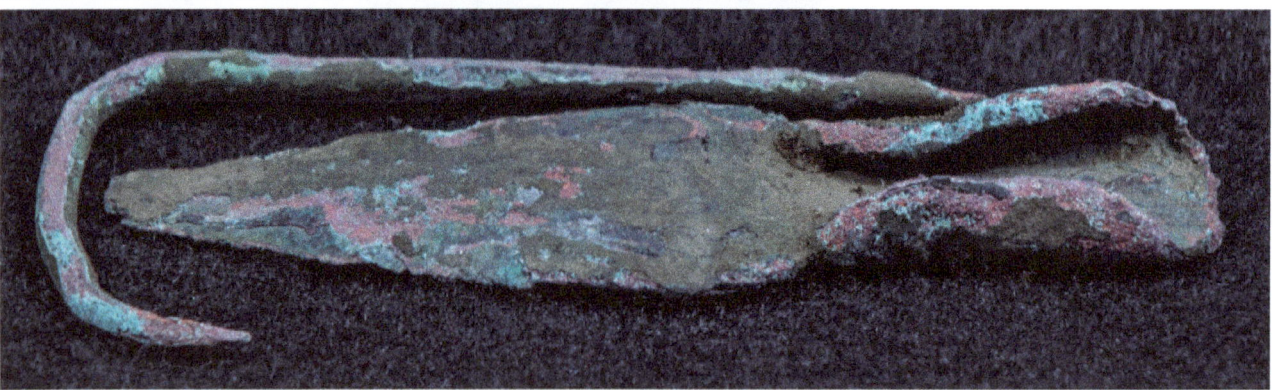

Below, conical form with punch marks, highly unusual. Ontario, Canada. *Courtesy of the T. Wilson Collection.*

Left, 8 7/8" copper tool found in Minnesota, unknown county. Unknown purpose. Very stout, heavy construction. Minor tip blunting that may have been ancient or dropped on a hard surface in modern times. *J. Bussey Collection.*

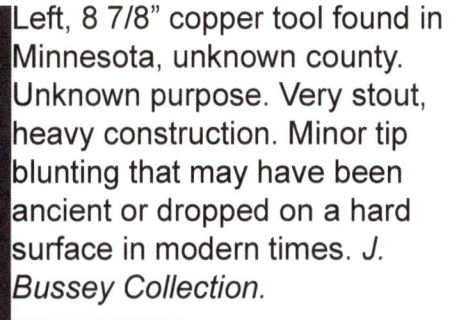

Left, 4" copper tool from Oneida County Wisconsin. *J. Bussey Collection.* Right, another roughly 4" example of the same type of unknown tool, this one is from Sheboygan County Wisconsin. *J. Bussey Collection.* Below, two more examples. The most popular theory currently is that they were used as ice picks. *Courtesy of the James R. Beer Collection*

Left, historic period rib with metal blade set into it for use as a knife or scraper, found in South Dakota, but still offers a look at how some ancient copper could've potentially been hafted as well. *Courtesy of the Logan Museum of Anthropology.*

15 1/2" Triangulate from Monroe County Wisconsin. This incredible artifact is not only the largest Triangulate known, but one of the largest of all copper artifacts period. *Courtesy of the James R. Beer Collection.*

Above, small cache found in Vilas County Wisconsin. Longest piece in the center is 7" long. *Courtesy of the S. Wasion Collection.*

Left, three piece copper cache found in Vilas County Wisconsin, longest piece is 9 3/4" in length. *Courtesy of the James R. Beer Collection.*

Left, 8 1/8" weaving tool or extra large needle, above, close up of folded over end to form the eye. Found in Rusk County Wisconsin. A piece like this might have been used for weaving together bark on a canoe or other heavy duty tasks. *Courtesy of the J. Ruth Collection.*

Left, Two "golf tees" about 2" in length. It's hypothesized by some that these rare tools may have been set into a handle and used as a miniature anvil head for fine copper edge work. These two were both found in Iron County Wisconsin. *Private Collection*. Below, another nearly identical example that was found in Oneida County Wisconsin. *Courtesy of the R. H. Mueller Collection.*

Left, unfinished conical point from Vilas County Wisconsin. *R. H. Mueller Collection.*

Above, odd Triangulate type point which has suffered a lot of damage to the end of the socket. It's difficult to even hypothesize what may have happened in this instance. *Private Collection.*

Left, right, and above. A Swallowtail point which has had the tip rolled back to form a loop, presumably for suspension. It measures 2 7/16" in length. The owner suspects that it may have been a lucky talisman of sorts. Unfortunately we will likely never know. *Private Collection.*

References and Suggested Readings

Anttila, Oliver N. 2009. "Ancient Copper Crosses Borders: The Old Copper Culture Migrates out of Minnesota into Northwestern Ontario," *The Minnesota Archaeologist,* Vol. 68

Bell, Robert E. 1972. "A Copper Spearhead from Wisconsin in Oklahoma," *Plains Anthropologist,* Vol .17, No. 55

Beukens, R. P., Pavlish, L. A., Hancock, R. G. V., Farquhar, R. M., Wilson, G. C., Julig, P. J., and Ross, William 1992. "Radiocarbon Dating of Copper-Preserved Organics," *Radiocarbon,* Vol. 34, No. 3, pg. 890-897

Binford, Lewis R. 1962. "Radiometric Analysis of Bone Material from the Oconto Site," *The Wisconsin Archaeologist,* 43 (2):31-34
Bleed, Peter 1969. "The Archaeology of Petega Point: The Preceramic Component," *Minnesota Historical Society,* St. Paul

Brown, Charles E. 1904 . "The Native Copper Implements of Wisconsin," *The Wisconsin Archaeologist,* Vol. 3, No. 2
Brown, Charles E. 1904. "The Native Copper Ornaments of Wisconsin," *The Wisconsin Archaeologist,* Vol. 3, No. 3
Brown, Charles E. 1924. "Indian Gravel Pit Burials in Wisconsin," *The Wisconsin Archeologist,* 3(3):65-82

Crook, Sara 2016. "Experimental Archaeology and Native Copper: Metallographic Analysis of Cold Forging Versus Hot Forging," *The Wisconsin in Archaeologist,* 97(2): 9-27

Cushing, Frank H. 1894. "Primitive Copper Working: An Experimental Study," *American Anthropologist,* 7:93-117

Drier & DuTemple. 1961; 1965. "Prehistoric Copper Mining In The Lake Superior Region. A Collection of Reference Articles," Published Privately

Emerson, McElrath, Fortier. 2000. "Late Woodland Societies; Traditions and Transformation across the Midcontinent," University of Nebraska Press

Emerson, McElrath, Fortier. 2009. "Archaic Societies; Diversity and Complexity across the Midcontinent," *State University of New York Press,* Albany, New York

Farnsworth, Kenneth B., Emerson, Thomas E. 1986. "Early Woodland Archeology," *Center for American Archeology Press,* Kampsville Illinois

Fitting, James E. 1975. "The Archaeology of Michigan; A Guide to the Prehistory of the Great Lakes Region," Cransbrook Institute of Science, Bloomfield Hills, Michigan

Flaskerd, G. 1940. "A Schedule of Classification, Comparison, and Nomenclature for Copper Artifacts in Minnesota," *The Minnesota Archaeologist,* 6(2):35-50

Fogel, Ira L. 1963 "The Dispersal of Copper Artifacts in the Late Archaic Period of Prehistoric North America," *Wisconsin Archaeologist,* Vol 44, No. 3

Fregni, Giovanna. 2009. "A Study of the Manufacture of Copper Spearheads in the Old Copper Complex," *The Minnesota Archaeologist,* Vol. 68

Fundaburk, Emma Lila, and M.D.F. Foreman. 1957, "Sun Circles and Human Hands," Luverne, Ala.: Fundaburk

Gibbon, Guy 2012 "Archaeology of Minnesota; The Prehistory of the Upper Mississippi River Region," *University of Minnesota Press*

Goodman, Claire Garber. 1984. "Copper Artifacts in Late Eastern Woodlands Prehistory," Center for American Archaeology

Griffin, James B. 1952. "Archeology of Eastern United States," *The University of Chicago Press*
Griffin, James B. 1954. "The Calumet Ancient Pit," *The Michigan Archaeologist,* 12(30:130-133)
Griffin, James B. 1961. "Lake Superior Copper and the Indians Miscellaneous Studies of Great Lakes Prehistory," Anthropological Papers 17. Ann Arbor: Museum of Anthropology, University of Michigan

Hamilton, Henry W., Hamilton, Jean Tyree, Chapman, Eleanor F. 1974. "Spiro Mound Copper," Memoir Missouri Archaeological Society, No. 11, December

Highsmith, Gale V. 1985. "The Fluted Axe," Palmer Publications, Inc.

Holmes, William H. 1901. "Aboriginal Copper Mines of Isle Royal, Lake Superior," *American Anthropologist,* New Series, Vol. 3

Hruska, Robert. 1967. "The Riverside Site: a Late Archaic Manifestation in Michigan," *The Wisconsin Archaeologist,* 48(3):145-260

Martin, Susan R. 1999. "Wonderful Power: The Story of Ancient Copper Working in the Lake Superior Basin," Wayne State University Press Detroit

Martin, Susan R. & Pleger, Thomas C. 2002. "The Complex Formerly Known as a Culture: T*he Taxonomic Puzzle of 'Old Copper'*, pg. 61-70. In Taming the Taxonomy: Toward a New Understanding of Great Lakes Archaeology, edited by Ronald F. Williamson and Christopher M. Watts, Eastend Books and the Ontario Archaeological Society, Toronto Canada

Mason, Ronald J. 1981. "Great Lakes Archaeology," Department of Anthropology, Lawerence University, Appleton, Wisconsin

Miles, Suzanne W. 1951. "A Revaluation of the Old Copper Industry," *American Antiquity,* Vol. 16, No. 3

Moorehead, Warren K. 1910. "The Stone Age in Norther America," Houghton Mifflin Company, Boston and New York

Muro, Paloma Carcedo. 1998. "Cobre Del Antiguo Peru," *Integra AFP,* Lima, Peru

Ostberg, Neil J. 1956. "Additional Material from the Reigh Site," *The Wisconsin Archaeologist,* 42(4):143-155

Overstreet, David F. 1988. "Osceola Revisited: Archaeological Investigations on the Potosi Terrace, Grant County, Wisconsin," The Wisconsin Archaeologist, 69 (1-2):1-61

Peterson, David H. 2003. "Red Metal Poundings and the 'Neubauer Process': Copper Culture Metallurgical Technology," *Central States Archaeological Journal,* 50 (2):102-107

Peterson, David H. 2004. "The Neubauer Process: 1999-2003 Observations," *Central States Archaeological Journal,* 51(1):56-59

Penman, John T. 1977. "The Old Copper Culture: An Analysis of Old Copper Culture Artifacts," *The Wisconsin Archaeologist,* 58(4):3-23

Pfeiffer, Susan. 1988. "Summary of Osceola Site Skeletal Remains," *The Wisconsin Archaeologist,* 69(1-2), 61-62

Platcek, Eldon P. 1965. "A Preliminary Survey of a Fowl Lake Site," *The Minnesota Archaeologist,* 27(2):51-92

Pleger, Thomas C. 1998. "Social Complexity, Trade, and Subsistence during the Archaic/Woodland Transition in the Western Great Lakes (4000-400 B.C.): A Diachronic Case Study of Copper Using Cultures at the Oconto and Riverside Cemeteries. Ph.D. Dissertation, University of Wisconsin-Madison

Pleger, Thomas C. 1992. "A Functional and Temporal Analysis of Copper Implements from the Chautauqua Grounds Site (47-Mt-71), a Multi-component Site Near the Mouth of the Menominee River. *The Wisconsin Archaeologist,* 73(3):160-176

Pleger, Thomas C. 2000. "Old Copper and Red Ocher Complexity," *Midcontinental Journal of Archaeology,* 25:169-190

Pleger, Thomas C. 2001. "New Dates for the Oconto Old Copper Culture Cemetary." Papers in Honor of Carol I. Mason. Edited by Thomas C. Pleger, Robert A. Birmingham, and Carol I. Mason. *The Wisconsin Archaeologist,* Vol. 82, No. 1 & 2, pg. 87-100

Popham, Robert E. & Emerson, J. N. 1954. "Manifestations of the Old Copper Culture in Ontario," Dept. of Anthropology, University of Toronto, Canada, Pennsylvania Archaeologist, Vol. 4(2)

Pulford, Mary H. 2009. "Copper Types of Northeastern Minnesota," *The Minnesota Archaeologist,* Vol. 68

Quimby, George Irving. 1954. "The Old Copper Assemblage and Extinct Animals," *American Antiquity,* Vol. XX, No. 2
Quimby, George Irving. 1960. "Indian Life In The Upper Great Lakes 11,000B.C. to A.D. 1800," The University of Chicago Press
Quimby, George Irving. 1963. "Late Period Copper Artifacts in the Upper Great Lakes Region," *The Wisconsin Archaeologist,* Vol. 44(4)

Ritzenthaler, Robert E. 1953; 1970. "Prehistoric Indian of Wisconsin" *Milwaukee Public Museum Popular Science Handbook,* Series No. 4
Ritzenthaler, Robert E. 1957. "Reigh Site Report," *The Wisconsin Archaeologist,* Vol. 38, No. 4
Ritzenthaler, Robert E. 1970. "Another Radiocarbon Date for the Oconto Site," *The Wisconsin Archaeologist,* 51(2):77

Ritzenthaler, Robert and Paul Scholz. 1946. "The Osceola Site, An Old Copper Site Near Potosi, Wisconsin," *The Wisconsin Archaeologist,* 27(3):53-70

Ritzenthaler, Robert and Warren L. Wittry. 1952. "The Oconto Site, An Old Copper Manifestation," *The Wisconsin Archaeologist,* 33(4):199-223

Ritzenthaler, Robert E., Neil Ostberg, Kirk Whaley, Martin Greenwald, Penny Foust, Ernest Schug, Warren Wittry, Heinz Meyer, and Edward Lundsted. 1957. "Reigh Site Report - No. 3," *The Wisconsin Archaeologist,* 38(4):278-310

Sampson, Kevin and Duane Esarey. 1993. "A Survey of Elaborate Mississippian Copper Artifacts from Illinois," *Illinois Archaeology: Journal of the Illinois Anthropological Society,* Vol. 5 Nos. 1 & 2

Schanen, Paul F. 2015."Conversation with Bob Hrouska 3-27-14," *Wis Arch News,* Vol. 15 No. 1 Spring

Schanen, Hunzicker. 2013. "Native American Artifacts of Wisconsin," Lauric Press

Steinbring, Jack (John) H. 1966. "Old Copper Culture Artifacts in Manitoba," *American Antiquities,* 31(4):567-573
Steinbring, Jack (John) H. 1 1968. "A Copper Blade of Possible Paleo-Indian Type," Manitoba Archaeological Newsletter 5(1-2):3-12 Spring-Summer

Steinbring, Jack (John) H. 1970. "Evidence of Old Copper in a Northern Transitional Zone," Ten Thousand Years, Archaeology In Manitoba. Manitoba Archaeological Society, Winnipeg 71-75

Steinbring, Jack (John) H. 1975. "Taxonomic and Associational Considerations of Copper Technology During the Archaic Tradition," University of Minnesota, Ph.D Dissertation

Steinbring, Jack (John) H. 1980. "Old Copper On The Winnipeg River," Papers in Manitoba Archaeology, Miscellaneous Paper No. 9, An Introduction To Archaeology On The River. Department of Anthropology, University of Winnipeg, Department of Cultural Affairs & Historical Resources. 178-243

Steinbring, Jack (John) H. 1990. "Early Copper Artifacts In Western Manitoba," *Manitoba Archaeological Journal 1(*1):25-72

Stoltman, James B. 1986. "The Archaic Tradition," *The Wisconsin Archaeologist,* 67(3-4):207-238

Spohn, Don. 2005-2016. "The Prehistoric Copper Artifact Journal," Multiple Volumes Great Lakes Copper Research, Coopersville Michigan

Travelyan, Amelia M. 2004. "Miskwabik, Metal of Ritual; Metallurgy in Precontact Eastern North America," The University Press of Kentucky

Wendt, Dan and Romano, Anthony D. 2009. "Experimental Application of Hammer and Bar Flintknapping to Knife Lake Siltstone from Northern Minnesota," *The Minnesota Archaeologist,* Vol. 68

West, George W. 1933. "The Greater Copper Pike," Milwaukee: T*he Wisconsin Archaeologist,* 12(2):30-33

Wittry, Warren L. 1950. "A Preliminary Study of the Old Copper Complex," B.A. Thesis, University of Wisconsin, Madison
Wittry, Warren L. 1957. "A Preliminary Study of the Old Copper Complex," T*he Wisconsin Archaeologist,* 32(1):1-18

Wright, J.V. 1972. "The Shield Archaic," National Museums of Canada, *Publications in Archaeology,* No. 3, Ottowa

www.ingramcontent.com/pod-product-compliance
Lightning Source LLC
Chambersburg PA
CBHW051353110526
44592CB00024B/2968